QUILL
GORDON

QUILL
GORDON

JOHN McDONALD

 ALFRED A. KNOPF · NEW YORK · 1972

Copyright © 1939, 1972 by John McDonald

All rights reserved under International and Pan-American
Copyright Conventions. Published in the United States by Alfred A. Knopf, Inc.,
New York, and simultaneously in Canada by Random House
of Canada Limited, Toronto.
Distributed by Random House, Inc., New York.

LIBRARY OF CONGRESS CATALOGING IN PUBLICATION DATA

McDonald, John Dennis
  Quill Gordon.

Includes modern version of A treatyse of fysshynge
wyth an angle by J. Berners and edited version of
C. Cotton's contribution to The compleat angler.
Includes bibliographical references.
1. Fly fishing. 2. Flies, Artificial.
3. Fishing—History. I. Berners, Juliana, b. 1388?
A treatyse of fysshynge wyth an angle. II. Cotton,
Charles, 1630–1687. III. Title.
SH456.M164   1972   799.1′2   72–2253
ISBN 0–394–46989–5

The following portions of this work appear through the courtesy of the
respective publishers.

Chapters 2, 11, 12, 13: Adapted and reprinted from *The Origins of Angling*
(Chapters 1, 5, 4, 2, and 3 respectively) by John McDonald assisted by
Sherman Kuhn and Dwight Webster and the editors of *Sports Illustrated*
(Doubleday and Co. Inc.) Illustrations for Chapter 11 by John Langley
Howard for *Sports Illustrated*. Copyright © 1957, 1963 Time Inc.

Chapter 6: Adapted and reprinted from "The Best Vacation Trout Fishing,"
Sports Illustrated, August 16, 1954. Copyright 1954 Time Inc.

Chapter 7: Adapted and reprinted from "Armstrong's Creek," *Sports Illustrated*,
April 7, 1958. Copyright © 1958 Time Inc.

Chapter 3: Illustrations by John Atherton and accompanying text for *Fortune*
Magazine; Copyright 1946 Time Inc. Text copyright 1947 by the Theodore
Gordon Flyfishers.

Chapter 10: Illustrations by John Atherton and accompanying text for *Fortune*
Magazine; Copyright 1948 Time Inc.

Chapter 4: From *American Trout Fishing* edited by Arnold Gingrich. Copyright
© 1965 by the Theodore Gordon Flyfishers. Published by Alfred A. Knopf,
Inc.

Manufactured in the United States of America
First Edition

CONTENTS

CONTENTS

PREFACE

The subject of this book is fly-fishing, an art whose special claim is that it is concerned with the most beautiful objects in nature. The fly is an artifact representing insects bred in water, centrally the incomparable May fly. It may also represent terrestrial insects, a minnow, shellfish, or even the fin of a fish. Fishing has long been divided into three kinds according to the depth of the water at which one fishes: bottom, middle, or top. Fly-fishing characteristically is fishing at the top. It is most spectacular when the fly rides on the surface, though I venture the thesis that the fly is versatile with respect to depth and under certain conditions will outfish bait or lure.

I do not wish to claim too much for fly-fishing. I have been intrigued by fishing of all kinds since I was very young, and have no better memory than of the time at the age of twelve when I fished every morning before school off the pier at Santa Monica. No fishing, I believe, has more charm than that of old men and young boys on ocean piers, black women in colorful dresses reclining on the banks of slow-moving Southern streams, the Sunday troller on lake, lagoon, or bay, and the spinner in the surf. But fly-fishing is my subject.

Like most fishing books, this one runs more to pattern than plan. The pattern here has emerged from the experience of fishing in water and libraries. With so many masters from the past, one could—I'd like to say, drown in them. But one can fish among them in imagination and be saved from that fate by the eternal novelty of the sport. The old and new, the classic and modern, the two sides of the Atlantic, the traditional East and modern West in the United States—these are the patterns of the book. Many contemporaries are here, and as the tradition of angling is genial (except toward polluters), they are here in a pleasant connection. Praise—short, I trust, of fatuity—abounds for meadow streams, wild streams, trout, insects, varieties of artificial flies, and fishermen.

Two pivotal figures from the past whose work is still pervasive in the ideals and practices of the sport enter into the pattern of the book. One is the author of *The Treatise of Fishing with an Angle*, who first codified the sport in the fifteenth century; the other is Theodore Gordon, who at the beginning of the twentieth turned American fly-fishing into its present course. The author of the *Treatise of Fishing* is said to be Juliana Berners, but most of what has been recorded about her is imaginary. It is a fact that she was a hunting writer of the fifteenth century; in legend, she was also a nun, sportswoman, and fishing writer, whom many anglers and most librarians insist upon as the first known writer on fishing as a sport. Although I write about her legend at length and express strong doubt about her authorship of the treatise, I sometimes follow the convention of referring to her as the author.

The title Quill Gordon is the name of a trout fly renowned among anglers for its intrinsic beauty and for its designer. I have put the pieces in this book under the aegis of Gordon's fly because of the meaning of the man's life and of his work in the sport—a meaning which I have attempted to explore here and there throughout.

Fly-fishing is a conservationist's way of fishing. It has long been a convention in angling to speak of "killing" fish, whether or not the fish is actually killed—fishing is indisputably a "blood sport." But the code of fly-fishing is to kill few. The action of the fly makes this possible: The thin wire fly hook usually catches a fish lightly in the hard cartilage of its mouth, leaving the fish free to fight hard and the fisherman free to release it with little or no physical injury done. Fly-fishermen thus set standards not only for the preservation of cold, clear streams and rivers but also for restraint in taking fish from the water. All sport may be defined as the invention of man-made rules in a natural setting. Fly-fishing, with its delicate tackle, makes even small fish a thrilling catch, and the expert knows almost no upper limit on the size of freshwater fish he can connect with. A seven-inch brook trout, a four-pound cutthroat, and a thirty-pound salmon all will rise to a quarter-inch wisp of fur and feather. Although the fish discussed in this book are mainly inland trout, there is something here also about the salmon and that sea-running trout, the steelhead.

Having many aspects of angling to deal with, some of them recurring in different contexts, I have occasionally repeated a point or observation in order to maintain each chapter as a self-contained whole. I have attempted to be consistent in using initial capital letters for artificial flies, lower case for naturals (except for that perennial problem the May fly).

Chapter 13 presents a special modern version of *The Treatise of Fishing with an Angle* which is, I believe, about as definitive as it can be made, and which has not been published before in this form. It contains all that has come down to us in the sole surviving manuscript (c. 1450) of the first angling classic. As for the portions of the manuscript that did not survive, I have filled in from the first printed edition (1496). In Chapter 14, I have brazenly edited Charles Cotton's contribution to *The Compleat Angler*. I have always wanted to see what it would be like if Cotton's imitation of Walton's stylistic devices were removed and one could read the underlying fly-fishing essay for its own sake. Some Waltonians may be horrified by this editing, and I can't blame them. But for what it is worth, here, starkly presented for the first time, I think, is the first specialized essay on the art of the fly. Chapter 15 contains a curiosity which I imagine has seldom been read. It is one of the earliest essays on the fly in the United States. George Washington Bethune hid it in a footnote in his edition of *The Compleat Angler* in 1847.

In the book as a whole, the historical chapters owe much to the collaboration of scholars from several fields. For Chapter 11 Dwight Webster, professor of fishery biology at Cornell University, made the trout-fly analysis and tied the flies for the illustrations of the "Berners" flies. He also collaborated in writing that chapter and has been a generous consultant on many other matters, among them on the trout-fly illustrations which were painted by artist John Atherton. The modernization of *The Treatise of Fishing with an Angle* (Chapter 13) is the work of Sherman Kuhn, editor of the *Middle English Dictionary*. Professor Kuhn also contributed substantially to the historical studies in Chapters 2 and 12. Warner G. Rice, chairman of the English department at the University of Michigan, made valuable detailed comments on a draft of Chapter 2. A. L. Binns of the University, Hull, England, kindly read the material on the authorship of the *Treatise of Fishing* and made helpful notes in letters and in the draft, which I worked into Chapter 12. Jeannette Fellheimer, Walter Magnusson, the late John C. McPherson, and William Whipple also made contributions to the historical chapters. Hence in those chapters, I say "we." Discussions with Christie Vance and Eugene Vance are reflected in various parts, especially in matters concerning pastoral poetry in Chapter 1. The entomologists J. W. and F. A. Leonard (*Mayflies of Michigan Trout Streams*, 1961) kindly read and commented on Chapter 5, Green Drake Eyes. Discussions with Joan and Richard Miller gave evidence of the truth that "all sport is one." Dorothy McDonald read and made valued comments on the entire manuscript.

The Beinecke Rare Book and Manuscript Library of Yale University made available its extraordinary resources in the field of angling, including the sole surviving manuscript of *The Treatise of Fishing with an Angle* and a copy of the first edition of Part II of *The Compleat Angler*. The New York Public Library and the British Museum also kindly put their treasures at my disposal. I wish to thank the Cambridge University Library in England for its courtesy in finding and checking various things; the Bodleian Library, Oxford, for its many willing favors; and Columbia University Library in New York.

The great work on the second *Book of St. Albans* is Joseph Haslewood's facsimile edition in 150 copies (1810). My debt to his notes will be apparent in Chapter 12 on the authorship of the *Treatise of Fishing*. Before Haslewood, there was the pioneering essay on the *Book of St. Albans* by William Oldys, presented in a note to his piece on Caxton in *Biographia Britannica* (1748). The *Treatise of Fishing* acknowledges a debt to the hunting treatise *Master of Game*, a connection which was noticed by writers in the nineteenth century. The first to develop the thesis that *Master of Game* is the probable model of the fishing treatise, however, appears to be John Waller Hills in *A History of Fly Fishing for Trout* (1920). My debt to Hills is evident in Chapter 2 on the origins of angling; in Chapter 11 on trout flies we go sometimes with him, sometimes against, as noted. The late Charles H. Haskins, medievalist of Harvard, made a number of valuable excursions into the field of sports; I have attempted to note my debts to him where they occur.

Portions of this book have appeared in *Fortune Magazine, Sports Illustrated*, publications of the Theodore Gordon Flyfishers, *Town and Country*, and my earlier book, *The Origins of Angling*, published by Doubleday. I wish to thank the publishers and T.G.F. for their permission to reprint that material. John Atherton's paintings of trout and salmon flies were first reproduced in *Fortune* in 1946 and 1948 respectively, along with texts in Chapters 3 and 10. John Langley Howard's paintings of trout flies were first reproduced in *Sports Illustrated* in 1957, along with text in Chapter 11. These paintings are reproduced again here by courtesy of those magazines.

All the chapters in the book owe something tangible or intangible to others. Much of what I have written reflects talks or correspondence with my old friend and fishing companion Dan Bailey, a great teacher of angling by word and example, and my teacher; the fishermen around his Fly Shop in Livingston, Montana, among them John Bailey, Chester Marion, Red Monicle, and Fred Terwilliger; also there or in other places with Maxine and Jack Atherton, Helen Bailey, Joe Brooks, Arnold Gingrich, Theodora Gordon (Theodore's cousin), Ann Hengstenberg of *Fortune*, Virginia Kraft of *Sports Illustrated*, Robert La Hotan, Sid Neff, Sparse Grey Hackle, Roy Steenrod, Lionel Trilling, Lee Wulff, and Ed Zern. I am indebted to scribe-critics Grace Hagen and Barbara Mullen for producing the manuscript with editors' eyes; to William Kienbusch for finding old and scarce fishing books; and to Mary Barnett and Angus Cameron for their editing of this book, to Robert Aulicino for its design, and to Bette Alexander for participation in its design.

J. McD.

QUILL
GORDON

Chapter 1
QUILL GORDON

In the minds of fishermen who know of him, Theodore Gordon is not a simple figure. Though once a real person, he has become our myth. Many miles of good upstream fishing water still survive in the United States, yet his sylvan life is our lost world. Urbanity was his mark, yet he fled the city, the industrial revolution, and the almighty dollar to live alone beside a stream in the Catskills just at the time when country people began to abandon mountain and farm. Now we are no longer a nation of farmers but a city-nation, urbanized in mind, with scarcely an old-fashioned country person left among us. And now, by a peculiar logic of the imagination, we perceive the natural earth as vanishing and for the first time collectively value it; we have suddenly become a nation of environmentalists.

The anglers' vision of their country retreat—a vision that has remained constant over centuries—is a miniature of the nation's newfound vision of the earth, which is to say that the national mood has significance beyond our worry over smarting eyes and mercury-poisoned fish. Alien clouds cover the cities, streams become purling sewers—clearly these are the issues of the moment. Learned and unlearned struggle over the questions whether pollution of the air, water, and land is increasing, and where, and whether it is gathering into an ecological catastrophe. We have known and largely accepted the fact that areas of nature have been progressively deformed over centuries, even before the heavy deterioration caused by the industrial revolution. The 1911 edition of the *Encyclopaedia Britannica* tells us, "The nuisance created by coal smoke seems to have been recognized in London since 1306, when a citizen was tried, condemned, and executed for burning 'sea cole' in the city of London." But as an argument the anecdote is a quibble, its draconic ending notwithstanding. We know the devastation of Lake Erie as a fairly recent event in which no one was even fined until a researching (and typically conservationist) angler, Robert Boyle, together with his Hudson River Fisherman's Association, in 1966 came across the 1899 federal act that forbade such perversions of waterways. The fact is that in recent years the pollution of air and water has not increased as rapidly as the national awareness of it. Complacency about the earth, encouraged by millenniums of limited capability to pollute, has come suddenly to an end. Man is the only polluting animal—the only earthling capable of destroying the earth—and recognition of this potential was enough to arouse widespread fear and the first concerted effort at restraint since the industrial revolution began.

Economists tell us in the lingo of game theory that we shall be negotiating and making new rules of law for some time before we get a satisfactory reallocation of the social costs of industrial production and community sewage. A major force in this line of action will be the ideals embodied in our revaluing of the earth, which some say is a vogue and some a cultural revolution.

Imagine the issues of pollution more or less satisfactorily resolved. Imagine vast urbanization, with the natural earth surviving in patches— the state we have reached in mind and are moving further into in physical fact. What then are the conflicts and the harmonies between city and country? Today pollution and the city both threaten nature, but the former is subject to control, while the latter is accepted as the irreversible condition of present and future society. In this recognition lies the awakening: the nation has been seized with the pastoral myth of the lost world of nature and the sense that its innocence is departing at the same speed with which the natural earth is seen receding. Anglers have long had a sense of this double loss. Together with flower pickers, bird watchers, lepidopterists, certain poets, and many other walkers in nature, they have seen it prefigured in their ideal enclaves, and have explored it in conversation and writing long before it became the national mood.

The pastoral myth entered the recorded history of angling through its first known written work, *The Treatise of Fishing with an Angle* (c. 1420). Not a trace of true angling literature has been found before this volume. In it the pastoral is clearly part of the angling experience; the three other major elements are the rule of rod, line, and hook, the moral of courtesy, and not least, the pleasures of study. In the artifice of angling—like all sport, it is contrived—all four of its elements are essential.

Angling rests upon its setting of stream, trees, sun, and shade; thus the *Treatise of Fishing,* arguing the advantages of angling over heroic sports like hunting, sets down its pastoral logic:

4

And yet, at the very least, he will have his wholesome and merry walk at his own ease, and also many a sweet breath of various plants and flowers that will make him right hungry and put his body in good condition. He will hear the melodies of the harmony of birds. He will also see the young swans or cygnets following their brood swans, the ducks, the coots, the herons, and many other birds with their broods, which seem to me better than all the noise of hounds and blasts of horns. . . . And if the angler catches the fish with difficulty, then there is no man merrier than he is in his spirits.

The meaning of this often quoted passage cannot be mistaken, namely, that the angler need not catch fish but only try, and he shall have the essential walk in nature. Trying to catch fish distinguishes the angler from other walkers in nature, and, as the angler binds himself by arbitrary rules, to catch fish "with difficulty" is his unique pleasure. The link to the pastoral tradition is not explicit here, as it is in a later school of angling writers (Dennys, *Secrets of Angling,* 1613; Walton, *The Compleat Angler,* 1653). The author of the treatise is interested in placing the angler in his natural setting and differentiating him from others through his particular engagement with nature. So we are told about the rules he adopts, his knowledge of stream life (in time the angler will become a student of nature, even an entomologist), the tackle, ways to fish, and the angler's catechism of good conduct. But the passage quoted above, accompanied in the first printed edition (1496) with a woodcut of the angler beside a stream with a town rising behind him, reveals his pastoral lineage. The cities of Europe declined after the fall of Rome, but they had begun to revive by the time the *Treatise of Fishing* was written. A story emerges: The angler is a townsman returning to his idyll in nature.

Early anglers synthesized their sport from several spheres: professional fishing (the tools), hunting (the idea and aesthetic of sport), and the pastoral tradition. They transposed the dominant style of two of these spheres into its opposite: cheerfulness replaced the melancholy of professional fishing, serenity replaced the epic-heroic spirit of hunting. The legacy of the pastoral, however, is more complex.

Among the many visions and antivisions of nature is the notion that it is animate, and friendly or unfriendly. In one romantic vision, the natural world is a prospect for limitless imagination; in another it is divine. A sea of philosophies surrounds it. Some modern poets, tangling with the branch of philosophy called phenomenology (what the senses take note of) seek in meditations on nature to close the gap between words and things. There is Ruskin's "pathetic fallacy" (i.e., that nature is moody like a person); also Robbe-Grillet's doctrine that the metaphor (e.g., "the village crouches") is a self-inflicted preparation for inevitable separation from the object, hence for tragedy. Others observe that nature is without value until someone values it. Some say simply that the experience of nature is a pleasure. Mary McCarthy is interpreted as saying that nature is dead. Certainly nature is a pain for those who are allergic to earth, air, fire, and water, or for those who remember only crawling ants and blackflies. Einstein wrote in his autobiography that he chose to study the universe because the relationship between man and nature was harmonious. Those who work the earth for a living, or who live by hunting and fishing, experience nature as a distinctive kind of reality to which they are tied by its apparent order.

My father, some time after he had come to the city and had saved enough money, toyed with the idea of buying a farm near town for the summers. But he could not bring himself to, because the idyll which his children voiced in pure joy was counterpoised in his mind by the dour memory of long hard days of work on his father's farm where he grew up. Had he been a poet, he might have written some lines on the happier visions of his rustic youth—from the safe distance of the city. But poets are not alone in these visions; when a city person walks in the country, it's a pastoral. As it was, my father settled for taking the family to the country near the farm in question on Sundays, when we would walk leafy paths and skip stones over the then clear, lapping water of Lake Erie.

Whether love of the earth is natural or not, it has been cultivated from earliest times. Pastoral poetry helps us to understand this love. Formal pastoral art comes relatively late in antiquity and does not quite fit the older tradition of an earthly paradise found (or lost) in a garden. Theocritus, the third-century Greek poet who is credited with the invention of pastoral poetry, was a native of Sicily who became a city man and wrote about walking in nature (Idyll V, 46–50, trans., Gow):

Here are oaks and galingale [an aromatic root]; here sweetly hum the bees about the hives. Here are two springs of cold water, and on the tree the birds twitter, and the shade's beyond comparison.

Nature is without fashion. The setting of a 2,300-year-old pastoral contains the same ideal elements that a pastoral writer of any time would describe: tree, shade, water, animals. About 200 years after Theocritus, his literary disciple Virgil, country-born and a Roman by adoption, wrote (Eclogue X, trans., Putnam):

Here are cool springs . . . here soft meadows, here a grove; here with you I would be eaten away [by love] for my whole life.

They and scores of poets who followed them made no pretense of treating the real life of the country. The pastoral is a pure act of the urban imagination—whether metaphorical, symbolic, or allegorical. Typically it depicts idealized shepherds in idyllic surroundings, walking, reclining at ease, piping, debating, and engaging in innocent contests of song. The pastoral poets wrote fantasies of a golden age of man in the far past, or in the expected future. The poet himself, slightly disguised, was often a participant in the scene. In the creations of Theocritus the idyll is internally self-sufficient and stable, and these conditions are the rule in pastoral art; by implication city and country are harmonic aspects of the human experience. Simichidas (Theocritus) and two friends, on their way to a harvest festival one midsummer day, meet a wayfarer (Idyll VII, trans., Gow):

> His name was Lycidas, and he was a goatherd; nor could one that saw him have mistaken him, for beyond all he looked the goatherd. On his shoulders he wore the tawny skin of a thick-haired, shaggy goat reeking of fresh curd, and round his breast an aged tunic was girt with a broad belt; in his right hand he grasped a crooked club of wild olive. And with a quiet smile and twinkling eye he spoke to me, and laughter hung about his lip: "Whither now, Simichidas, art thou footing it in the noontide, when even the lizard sleeps in the wall and the tomb-crested larks fare not abroad? Art hastening unbidden to some banquet or speeding to some townsman's winepress, for as thou goest each pebble spins singing from thy shoes?" And I made answer, "Friend Lycidas, all men say that among the herdsmen and the reapers thou art by far the best of pipers, and much it glads my heart to hear; and yet, in my thought, I fancy myself thy equal . . . come; the way and the day are thine and mine to share; let us make country song, and each, maybe, shall profit from the other. For I too am a clear voice of the Muses."

When they have sung to an apparent draw, and have reached a fork in the road, they part, the rustic Lycidas giving his stick as a token of friendship to the townsman Simichidas. The latter and his friends continue on to the festival, where they lie down "rejoicing on deep couches of sweet rush and in fresh-stripped vine leaves"; and there follows a lush description of harvest time.

Virgil jolts this concordance. Rome threatens the idyll. This ominous note in two of his Eclogues nearly demolishes the pastoral idea. The pastoral is a delicate frame, with tolerance for internal conflicts (love) resolved in song, but none for intrusion. In Virgil, paradoxes abound. The city that was then the epitome of civilization is described by a shepherd as barbaric. Another story emerges (Eclogue I): Two shepherds meet and talk in a conventionally pastoral setting; one reclines at ease, his way of life protected by Rome; the other, facing exile, is tormented by the prospect of losing his land and way of life. Both, it appears, are dependent on Rome (the canons of the pastoral convention are doubly violated) but with different consequences. The unhappy shepherd addresses his companion:

Fortunate old man, here among streams you know and holy founts you will find cool shade. Here, as it always has done, the hedge along your neighbor's border, whose willow flowers are fed upon by bees of Hybla, will often induce you by its gentle buzzing to fall asleep. Here, under a lofty rock, the pruner will sing to the heavens. Nor then, too, will your pets, the cooing pigeons, and turtle-doves cease to moan from the lofty elm. (Trans., Putnam)

Of his own plight, he says:

Will a blasphemous soldier possess these fields I have so nurtured, a barbarian, these crops? Behold whither strife has led hapless citizens! For these we have sown our fields!

We know, outside the poem, that at the time there was civil war in Rome following the assassination of Julius Caesar; that Virgil's father, a yeoman-farmer, was dispossessed to make way for soldier-settlers (though later, with his son's aid, he managed to repossess his farm); and that Virgil was torn between his love of the peaceful countryside of his youth and his subsequent passion for the glory of Rome. Is this permissible knowledge in understanding the poem? The time is long ago and the poem holds complex levels of meaning, as pastoral art usually does. There is reason to believe that in one sense, the shepherd who is protected by Rome is Virgil himself. A student of Virgil, Michael Putnam (*Virgil's Pastoral Art,* 1970), unearths a deeper meaning in the poem: The peaceful shepherd, who has no interest in practical affairs, "uniquely possesses that ideal we might offer as visual definition of the pastoral myth: leisure and undisturbed intellectual freedom. This individual's life is wholly his own. Another, who speaks for at least a plurality of his fellow citizens, is driven from the land. These situations have as little to do with each other as the different roles which the shepherds assume—the one emblematic of the imagination, of that liberty for which spreading beeches and resounding woods are tangible evidence, the other symbolic of the troubles of rural affairs, vulnerable now to the whim of power politics and military might." Virgil's double vision, involving city and country, thus comes through clearly across the ages.

Pastoral art based on the ancient models thrived again in numerous variations when it was revived by Renaissance writers, among them the pre-Restoration Royalist, Izaak Walton, who wrote pastoral prose. *The Compleat Angler* is often cited as the greatest of English idylls. Many angling writers later tried, but none succeeded in making Walton their literary "father." Even his contemporary and friend Charles Cotton, who wrote the section on fly-fishing for an edition of his work, could not satisfactorily re-create his style. The fragility of the pastoral art is such that it lapses easily into artificiality and so loses the illusion. But the difficulty an angling writer has when he tries to follow Walton is not merely a matter of skill in writing. Walton is unique because of the way he puts the elements of angling together. He made the pastoral element dominant and used angling as a secondary device, thereby reversing the order of the main line of angling tradition. The central impulse of the angler is to engage nature; it is to that end that he observes nature in detail. In the peculiar act of the imagination that distinguishes angling, the balance of things is intricate.

A brief excursion into the origins of modern romanticism throws some light on this balance. When they revived the pastoral art, writers also began to spin theories about it, linking the fantasy to real life (a rather simple formulation of a complexity that includes real-life imagination). In the eighteenth century, the pastoral came into high literary fashion—strangely, just before it vanished altogether as a formal genre. Its meanings were not lost but were absorbed into other literatures and philosophy. The grand spinner of the art was Jean Jacques Rousseau, who laid the foundations of the romantic age.

Rousseau's influence is still with us and may come back strongly again in the near future. To learn something of value from his exploration of the relationship between the imagination and the external world, one does not need to subscribe to his doctrines concerning the corruption of civilized man as a result of our deviations from nature. Christie Vance (*The Extravagant Shepherd: A Study of the Pastoral Vision in Rousseau's* Nouvelle Héloïse, 1972) has shown that Rousseau derived his powerful vision in part from Theocritus, Virgil, and other pastoral poets, and made of their myth both a force in his novel *Julie, or the New Heloise* and an ideal in his personal life.

There is no direct route from pastoral poetry to real life. The road that must be taken leads back through the grounding of the pastoral in the imagination. Rousseau surmised that the human race in moving from primitive to civilized life (from country to city) never escaped its origins but was left with an unresolved tension between the two worlds. Alienated from nature, man has tried to regain his old unity with it through acts of the imagination. The objective is tranquillity. Pastoral poets invoked tree, shade, and water as the verbal symbols of this lost state of being. In their convention, they made no direct observations of nature.

Rousseau, however, according to Vance, broke with this convention. He introduced the botanist, whose exact, empirical observations of plant life are in opposition to the pastoral ideal. Yet it is precisely in the maintenance of this juxtaposition of opposites, together with one's ability to go back and forth between them through the medium of words, that Rousseau resolves the conflict. When Rousseau opens his book of botany, he is transported out of its technical sphere to his pastoral experience. He is no longer concerned with the book's latin-designated categories, but with the gentle-

9

ness of the country and the innocence of its people. "Realistic observation [thus] leads to idealized pastoral memory—fields, water, woods, solitude and repose. One forgets the present ills of society and is thrust into the imaginary world of simple, innocent people."

Rousseau's botany is the angler's entomology (water insects) and knowledge of stream life. As with Rousseau's botany, the angler's observations become his pastoral memory. The angler, however, also relates his observations to action. The English poet John Gay, whose span of life happened to overlap Rousseau's youth, put his angling poetry in a book called *Rural Sports* (1720). He was a precise observer of nature. Yet only Gay the city man, meditating in his study in London, would write this celebrated instruction on how to tie a trout fly:

> When if an insect fall (his certain guide)
> He gently takes him from the whirling tide:
> Examines well his form with curious eyes,
> His gaudy vest, his wings, his horns and size,
> Then round his hook the chosen fur he winds,
> And on the back a speckled feather binds,
> So just the colours shine thro' ev'ry part,
> That nature seems to live again in art.

Most of what we know about Theodore Gordon's single-minded pursuit of the art of angling stems from the trout flies he created—particularly his emblem, the Quill Gordon fly—and the lines he wrote about fishing. His cousin, Theodora Gordon, once told me in her old age that she remembered him at family gatherings as a young man sitting on a high stool, his head buried in a fishing book. He writes of an illness, and we give him the excuse of poor health for retiring to a solitary life beside the Neversink River—not, of course, solitary in mind if we take account of his notes and letters. He did not pretend that angling was more than a recreation for other people, but there is no sign that he felt apologetic for making it his life.

In April 1906, Gordon described the idyll as he conceived it:

It is a bitter cold winter's night and I am far away from the cheerful lights of town or city. The north wind is shrieking and tearing at this lonely house, like some evil demon wishful to carry it away bodily or shatter it completely. The icy breath of this demon penetrates through every chink and crevice, of which there appear to be many, and the wood-burning stove is my only companion. It is on nights such as these, after the turn of the year, that our thoughts stray from the present to other scenes and very different seasons. We return in spirit to the time of leaf and blossom, when birds were singing merrily and trout were rising in the pools. We remember many days of glorious sport and keen enjoyment, and then somehow our thoughts take a turn and leap forward. Spring is near, quite near, and it will soon be time to go fishing. We want to talk about it dreadfully. O for a brother crank of the fly-fishing fraternity, one who would be ready to listen occasionally and not insist upon doing all the talking, telling all the stories himself. But if we cannot talk we can write.

Two years later, in February, he wrote:

The silence of the snows is over all the land, and the bright waters of our trout streams run almost black between icy banks. In our walks abroad we find a few living creatures—a jay, perhaps, or a few half-starved crows. Mother Nature is fast asleep, but will soon awaken . . . we know that there is a good time coming. On a cold, bright day the wintry landscape is dazzlingly beautiful . . . we begin to think about fly-fishing . . . we wish to be as keen as mustard when the trout are open to us at last, and by combining a few recollections of the past with dreams of the future we can arrive at an eminently satisfactory state of mind.

On another occasion he described the river he lived beside (now buried under a reservoir for New York City):

The Neversink is a "white" water stream. No lakes drain into it until it has danced for many miles down the valley and there is not a tinge of vegetable matter in its pellucid rifts or pools. Where in its rapid course it flows over golden sands between woods and meadows the effect is very beautiful. Unfortunately . . .

Gordon had an apprehension. His idyll was threatened by the surrounding world: "Unfortunately in many places great damage has been done by the floods of recent years and there seems to be no effectual way to checking these ravages." Again, writing in the *Fishing Gazette* (London, England), he said:

The country is rapidly being denuded of all the good timber that is to be found scattered here and there. The woods are shrinking and so are the streams. . . . Last year many small trout died for want of water in the little runs and tributaries. It is to be hoped that in the Mother Country you are more farsighted, and are not so fond of killing the goose that lays the golden eggs. Here *progress* is rapid. We will soon have no forests to cut, or would not have had if reforms recently inaugurated had not been considered.

And he feels the pressure of population: "There are too many fishermen on our free waters nowadays . . . for every man to kill all trout he can in every possible way." But he is genial and hopes for the best: "Let us be liberal and kind to one another, trying to smother prejudice and cultivating a spirit of peace and good will among the brethren of the angle rod. We can have a good stock of trout in free waters—that are pure and well stocked with food—if we are not too greedy and obey the laws." Thus for Gordon the harmony of city and country was a possibility if the natural areas were large, well kept, and protected. He saw the rules of sport as one of the disciplines of conservation.

Gordon was unusual in that he made an angling idyll of his life, but his imagination is no different from any angler's in his best moments. As a fly-fisher, Gordon is occupied with the observation of fish and insects, the mimetic art of tying flies to represent insects, and fishing. In the winter, he is conscious of moving back and forth in imagination between memory and anticipation. Reality lies in the words that come to mind and in the belief that he will act again in nature. The element of pastoral myth—a truth of the imagination—is qualified by these essential realities. But it is still present, as it was in the ancient poets, in Gordon's central assumption that the natural environment of stream, woods, and meadows is the ideal setting for harmony and innocence.

There are striking parallels between Gordon's idyll and the view of nature taken by most Americans today. Anglers, pastoral poets, and Americans (most of them) are urban people. Substantial remnants of a once virgin continent—a diverse wilderness of mountain, desert, prairie, forest, stream, lake, and seashore—dwindle before the spread of urban civilization and deteriorate as a result of pollution. Privileged people throughout history have turned to nature for leisure pastimes, and this nation, despite its underworld of poverty, is the most leisured nation on its scale in history. Americans are busy traveling to reach places where they will take their leisure either actively or passively. And the places they head for are usually pieces of protected natural earth or water. It is a paradox of our civilization, and one which Virgil and Gordon also saw in theirs, that from economic gains we got the wherewithal to return to the country, urbanized in mind and thus prepared to see the country as a special place for a special harmonious state of mind. Yet that which made our return possible also threatens to destroy the idyll. "Rome" threatens. Pollution threatens. Neither is natural. Hidden always in the pastoral myth was man's own threat to nature. And the threat is not only to his own physical well-being but also to his imagination.

Until recently, the norm in the United States has been to pollute. Fiduciary agents representing cities and corporations have felt obliged to pollute, since it pays to slough off this part of the cost of production onto others. They will stop only when code or law obliges them to. Sportsmen by the millions pollute; in the absence of code or effective law, why should we not expect a yachtsman to dump his particular waste in Lake St. Clair? Maine lobstermen bring their boats to dock and empty the crankcases. If this norm is really changing, the difference to American society will be revolutionary—and we should not be surprised if the change is in fact occurring. But if society should continue on toward complete urbanization, then it will be caught in self-contradiction. The more urban it becomes, the stronger its need for nature; what is lost is valued more. To be moving toward that which repels one is a fairly common human paradox, the resolution of which will need to be preceded by understanding it. The work of the writers mentioned here, whose minds circled around nature over a span of more than two thousand years, may contribute something to that understanding.

Chapter 2
THE ORIGINS OF ANGLING

The Angler must entice, not command his reward.
GERVASE MARKHAM

The Treatise of Fishing with an Angle set forth the argument, new at the time, that among the four good sports, hunting, hawking, fowling, and fishing, the best is fishing. The novelty of the treatise was not simply that it gave fishing the highest rank among these outdoor sports—though more than one noble hunter must have blinked at the contention—but that in doing so it put fishing in the same class with hunting. Its doctrine is clear: the rule is rod, line, and hook—all other kinds of fishing are set aside—and the proper comparisons are with the hunting sports. With this definition the treatise began the first known codification of the practices of the sport of fishing.[1]

Praising one's favorite sport at the expense of others is an ancient practice in writing, but those who wrote on the varieties of hunting in the Middle Ages had not troubled to mention fishing even negatively. Sport fishing was

1. A sport or game may be thought of as the set of rules that describes it. The rule of rod, line, and hook has been widely accepted since sport fishing was described in the *Treatise of Fishing.* Whoever has fished with a hand line will rightly take exception. The sport is also divided into schools according to different forms of disguise, such as bait, spinning tackle, and artificial flies. The real objection today to the poacher with net, spear, or dynamite is not simply that he removes fish, but that he disturbs the morale of the angler who abides by the rule of the disguised hook. Professional fishing may be viewed as a game in which the rules are those of economics. But sport obviously suggests also a pastime rather than the purpose of making a living, though this concept needs modification to make room for the professional sportsman. The word "angling," since the time of the treatise, has come to be a writer's word for the sport. In speech, at least in the United States, one "goes fishing," no matter what kind of fishing it is or what its purpose is.

not recognized in writing until the fishing treatise suddenly appeared, very like a hunting treatise, but gently mocking the heroic sports. The hunter's lips blister from the horn; after laboring and sweating he finds his hare to be a hedgehog; the author does not even dare to report the hunter's griefs in full for fear of giving offense. The hawk ignores the hawker's shouting and whistling and is often sick from the diseases of birds. The fowler returns from his snares cold, wet, and empty-handed. But fishing with an angle rod brings good spirits and a fair old age. And if the angler does not catch fish, he will have had his walk in nature, among the plants and flowers and "the melodies of birds . . . which seems to me better than all the noise of hounds and blasts of horns."

Sport fishing thus was introduced to a reading audience in the early fifteenth century on a cheerful, nonheroic note, which since then has been characteristic of the sport, except perhaps for big-game fishing. The humor of the treatise had a clear target. For medieval hunting and hawking were chivalric sports, held to be good pastimes for warriors and practiced by noblemen and others who aimed to be like noblemen. Indeed, hunting ranked with love, combat, and religion as a kind of branch of chivalry, and in the fifteenth century the language of hunting was still a sign of that tradition. Knights, real and fictional, were usually hunters, employing terms supposedly invented by the legendary Tristram, ideal hunter, lover, and warrior. Hawks were bred by rank according to the orders of society; first was an emperor's hawk (gerfalcon) for an emperor's wrist. King Arthur was often hunting while his knights engaged in more strenuous adventures. Such immortal tales as Chrétien de Troyes's *Eric and Enide* and the anonymous *Sir Gawain and the Green Knight* would lose important elements in their plots and backgrounds without falconry and the chase. But chivalry had become decadent and nostalgic by the time the fishing treatise was written. The special literature of hunting, essential to a noble education, had been refined to such an extent that a hunting treatise could be more a play on words than practical instruction. Other moods were rising in the fading Middle Ages, among them a feeling for individual, private serenities to be sought in nature. Angling meant retirement, in spirit far from the restless passion and triumphs of medieval hunting.

From hunting, however, the angler obtained the art of the sporting treatise. The medieval hunting treatise—derived, it appears, from the ancients—was constructed essentially in two parts: first the argument and elevation of the subject, and then the instruction in technique. These two elements reflect respectively aspects of chivalry and learning, two forces of mind that have given a character to modern culture. Likewise the fishing treatise—out of hunting and so, indirectly, out of chivalry—is a manual of ideals and deportment as well as of the technique of fishing. It teaches a style of life. The aristocratic ideal was knightly. In fishing, the formalism of

15

late chivalry was transformed into a code of good and quiet manners. The *Treatise of Fishing* is not addressed to noblemen but to all who are "virtuous, gentle, and freeborn." In a world then divided into conditions of serfdom, freedom, and nobility, the angler was something fairly new, a plain gentleman.

It is difficult to believe that the fishing treatise can be so novel as it appears. Cultural events do not usually happen suddenly. And as knowledge of the past is subject to interpretation and to future discoveries, a reservation is called for. The author of the treatise actually mentions the existence of "books of credence," a phrase which has suggested the possibility of earlier, now lost writings on the sport. The possibility is real but bare. Writers in the Middle Ages preferred to claim learning by books rather than by experience; and the treatise does not say its authorities were fishing books, let alone books on sport fishing. The medieval scholar Charles H. Haskins made a special search for writing on sport in the Latin language (*Studies in Medieval Literature*, 1929). He found no works on hunting or fishing by the Romans, however; if they read anything on sport they read it in Greek. Haskins found little record of any sport in the early Middle Ages, but in the twelfth and thirteenth centuries Latin writing on sport appears in considerable body.

This medieval "Latin period," preceding the early French and English vernacular periods, brings in the renaissance of writing on sport; we shall later look at its prize piece of work—a treatise on falconry—for its bearing on the *Treatise of Fishing*. But Haskins found only one work in this period touching on fishing, a manual on country life by Petrus de Crescentiis (c. 1300), and that "hardly sporting." Medieval literature before the *Treatise of Fishing*, though abounding in scenes and symbols of hunting, ignores sport fishing, so far as one can tell. The historian of fishing W. J. Turrell (*Ancient Angling Authors*, 1910) found no mention, except in a few statutes, of fishing of any kind in English literature between the tenth and fifteenth centuries. Some notices of fishing that was not just utilitarian may turn up in descriptions of rural life (a conjecture made by the medievalist R. W. Southern in a letter to the author); but as it is, to the testimony of Haskins on Latin and Turrell on English must be added the silent testimony of generations of medieval scholars who have reported nothing tangible on the sport from their reading of masses of medieval manuscripts in French and English.

It would be absurd, of course, to suppose that people have not fished for pleasure since the hook was invented in prehistoric times. Fishing is instinctive; you don't have to read to enjoy it. And so experienced is the *Treatise of Fishing* in the delights of making a rod, coloring a line, dressing a trout fly, and taking a fish, that there can be no doubt of the existence of an older oral tradition of the sport. But as the treatise has no known antecedent in fishing history and asserts for the first time distinctive sporting attitudes toward fishing, it serves as the point of origin of modern angling. For most of two centuries after it was written it was the sole authority on angling in England, along whose streams the sport was developed. Thereafter it shaped the general outline of the large body of writing about sport fishing which has come into existence.

Yet the *Treatise of Fishing* doubtless had literary antecedents of some kind, since writers learn from writers as well as from other experience. The basic tackle and technique of sport fishing clearly come down through the main line of professional fishing tradition, oral, pictorial, and written.[2] The literature of professional fishing, however, which has an old and fairly continuous tradition to which *Moby Dick* and Hemingway's *The Old Man and the Sea* belong, has not only no connection with sport but an incompatibility with it. The *Treatise of Fishing* prescribes sport fishing for the avoidance of melancholy; for the ancient writers melancholy was the dominant mood of professional fishing.[3]

A funereal epigram by Sappho written about 600 B.C. has long been accepted by fishing historians as the key to the old writing on fishing. The Greek epigram of this kind is a literary feat, telling a whole story in a couplet, and so can hardly be translated with the virtuosity of the original. Sappho says something like this: "To the fisherman Pelagon, his father Meniscus has put upon the Altar [or on the wall or other place in a small local shrine] his son's wicker fish trap and single skulling oar as a memorial of a poor unhappy life."

This feeling appeared again in a famous sea idyl by Theocritus. Turning from shepherds to fishermen, he told a spooky story that has influenced the entire poetic history of fishing. Asphalion (the fisherman) wakes up in the night in his lowly cabin and tells his friend a dream. Fishing from a rock with a rod, he had hooked a big fish and when he landed it, after a tremendous struggle, he found that its scales were made of gold. Fearing it might be the favorite of a sea god, he dragged it on shore and swore never to go to the sea again but to stay on land with his treasure. When he awoke, he was dismayed and terrified by his rashness at having sworn the oath. His friend advised him that dreams are lies and that he should go back to work or he would starve.

The form of this poem, a conversation among professional fishermen called a "piscatory eclogue"—an approximation to the pastoral, in which fishermen rather than shepherds are the speakers—was used by poets for two thousand years. In the eighteenth century an English writer, Moses

---

2. The artificial fly, like the trained falcon, tempts one to imagine it was the invention of sport; but the falcon at one time was probably the most effective way of capturing certain game; and the fly in season will certainly outfish bait, when the object is trout, salmon, grayling, whitefish (Rocky Mountain), and other risers.

3. Ovid cited fishing as a remedy for love. Plutarch, on the other hand, had Cleopatra angling for Antony. This playful tradition has come down through John Donne and Shakespeare to the present without having much to do with catching fish.

Browne, wrote on angling in this manner and his work had a vogue for a while, but the eclogue genre failed to convey the moods of the sportsman as it had those of the shepherd and the professional fisherman with his terror, toil, and dreams.

One might wonder whether the water poets imposed their melancholy theme on the ancient fishermen—certainly Italian fishermen today sing gaily with their families on Sunday boat picnics, and Maine fishermen are unable to speak without wit—but the old popular myth of the fisherman Glaucus suggests that the poets were in touch with a peculiar reality of the minds of men at sea. Readers of Ovid and other old storytellers will recall how Glaucus, upon seeing his catch of fish eat a magical herb on the ground and return to the sea, tasted the herb himself, followed them into the water, and became a sea god with eyebrows of bristle, seaweed hair on his chest, and a fish's tail; how he pursued the nymph Scylla, who eluded him, and on appealing to a divinity, Circe, to intercede in his favor, saw her instead in jealousy change Scylla into a sea monster—now, of course, the rock off the Italian coast. In Greek poetry Glaucus was the principal fisher hero, ranking with the shepherd hero Daphnis who, being mortal, died of a broken heart for his elusive nymph.

In Greek writing on fishing, there was, however, also a didactic branch, much of which is known to have been lost. The best surviving work of this kind is Oppian's *Halieutica* (A.D. 169), a Greek hexameter poem in five books, two describing many fishes of the sea, and three the art of fishing with a wide variety of "arms" (hooks, several kinds of nets, a trident, and other tackle). Oppian begins by comparing hunting and fishing. The hunter sits comfortably in a cave during a storm while the fisherman is out in a leaky boat braving the elements. The sea, however, has its charm and there are pleasures in fishing, but—curious argument for fishing—the hunter has more pleasure than toil. *Halieutica* is part sea pastoral and part manual of instruction, and as one of its readers has said, it has "the right spirit of enthusiasm." Oppian's dolphins are divine and his descriptions of the mysteries of the sea inviting, yet his fishing seems to be regarded as work. There are in *Halieutica* also elements of the art of the sporting treatise; its argument against hunting, for example, serves to provide an opposition between land and sea, to the advantage of the latter. But since few medieval writers knew Greek literature before it was translated in quantity into Latin in the Middle Ages, and since, as we have seen, there is nothing on the sport in earlier Latin, it is unlikely that Oppian had any influence on the origins of modern writing on sport.[4]

---

4. The fish has been a symbol of the Christian faith since the time of the catacombs. Fish symbols, however, are common to all ages and faiths. There is no sign that sport fishing had religious origins, though medieval monks, who usually lived near water and took fish for food, presumably enjoyed catching them.

The first English (Anglo-Saxon) text on fishing is the *Colloquy on the Occupations*, a late-tenth-century book by Aelfric the Abbot, the great writer and teacher of his time. Aelfric mentions the use of nets, fishhooks, and bait by professional fishermen, the kind of fish caught, how they were sold, and the like. His fisherman speaks for himself as to what he is about. A fragment goes as follows (P stands for Piscator; M for Magister):

M. What trade are you acquainted with?
P. I am a fisherman.
M. What do you get by your trade?
P. Food, clothing, and money. (Trans., W. J. Turrell)

No sport here. And after Aelfric's *Colloquy* follow the remarkable centuries of near silence on fishing until at the beginning of the fifteenth century the *Treatise of Fishing* describes the ancient occupation for the first time in history as a sport.

Compare hunting. The sport goes far back in antiquity—falconry, it is said, as far as 2000 B.C. in China. Among the ancient Greeks it was well regarded. Xenophon, historian, general, and sportsman, begins his treatise on hunting (c. 400 B.C.?) with the assertion that the art was invented by the gods and was the care of Apollo and Diana. "I therefore exhort the young," he says, "not to despise hunting, or any part of liberal education; for by such means men become excellent in military qualifications, and in other accomplishments by which they are necessarily led to think, act, and speak rightly."[5] After developing this theme at some length, he describes in the body of the treatise the qualifications of the hunter, his dogs, his equipment (nets, javelins, snares, and spears), and the technique of hunting hares, deer, boars, lions, leopards, and other animals; and then, in Chapter 12, restates the merits of the sport: "1. Concerning the modes of proceeding in the chase I have now spoken. Those who are fond of the pursuit will receive many benefits from it; for they will secure health for their bodies, greater keenness of sight and hearing, and a later old age. 2. It is also an excellent preparation for the toils of war." He shows in detail how the rigors of the chase train a young man in real action and keep him from viciousness or excessive pleasures of the senses. In a vein he may have learned from Socrates, of whom he was a disciple, Xenophon then makes a characteristically intricate Greek observation. Men love virtue, he says, but attain it only by labor. They will not neglect it if they see it bodily, "for everyone, when he is in sight of the object of his love, conducts himself better than at other times, and neither does nor says anything unbecoming or wrong, lest it should be seen by that object." Thus hunting makes a good soldier and a good leader.

5. *Xenophon's Minor Works,* translated by J. S. Watson (London: Bohn Library, 1857), p. 332 *et seq.*

That Xenophon was read with interest for a long time is evident from a hunting treatise by the Greek writer Arrian, in the second century. He wrote a supplement to Xenophon, on coursing, beginning with a summary of "the advantages that accrue to mankind from hunting," as related by Xenophon.

When hunting literature reappeared in medieval Europe, it described what had become one of the most prominent features of the life of the nobility, and a protected privilege. "The noble of every age," said Balzac, "has done his best to invent a life which he and he only can live." Hunting, in addition to its inherent pleasures, performed that service. Men of noble rank not only hunted but also wrote about it, and it is from the tradition of their writing, rather than from fishing's own literary history, that the *Treatise of Fishing* emerged.

Because they were at the beginning of modern writing on sport and under the influence of the ancients, early writers of hunting treatises tended to be systematic and doctrinal; their observations on nature have been given a place in the history of science. On one level these writings went no further than such matters as the diseases of hawks; one work of this kind was written in England about 1200 by a mathematician and natural scientist, Adelard of Bath. On a higher level they dealt with all the elements of sport, including its place in the general scheme of things. Earlier in this chapter we advanced the thesis that the sporting treatise brought together the forces of chivalry and learning, chivalry in the high-minded argument for a sport, and learning in the manual of instruction. The aspect of chivalry needs explanation.

We often today think of chivalry as exaggerated courtly manners in comparison with our own manners, or with those of ancient Greece, where they were incorporated less conspicuously in the way of life. The characters in the romantic literature of the Middle Ages often seem like children beside the Greeks. The writers of the Middle Ages—whose historic role is said to have been to tame the ferocity of medieval knights—celebrated courtesy, service, sacrifice, courage, honor, piety, heroism, compassion, fidelity, justice, love, and other qualities of mind and heart; and though this hardly gave a true picture of life outside the books, the chronicles indicate that it displayed the ideals of life as well as the state of mind of writers for several centuries. Chrétien de Troyes, the most celebrated poet of the twelfth century and the most influential upon later writers, whose manuscripts are the earliest extant in the Arthurian tradition, stated the case precisely in the little prologue to his story *Cligès*:

> Our books have informed us that the pre-eminence in chivalry and learning once belonged to Greece. Then chivalry passed to Rome, together with that highest learning which has now come to France. God grant that it may be cherished here, and that it may be made so wel-

come here that the honour which has taken refuge with us may never depart from France: God had awarded it as another's share, but of Greeks and Romans no more is heard, their fame is passed, and their glowing ash is dead. (Trans., W. W. Comfort)

In this passage the medievalist R. W. Southern found the "secret revolution" of the eleventh and twelfth centuries: "all that we comprehend in the word 'civilization.'" (*The Making of the Middle Ages*, 1961)

It is not surprising that the same elements should crystallize at the same time in the literature of the ideal life of sport. Writers have rarely viewed sport as recreation without meaning. As the Greek Games were an expression of religion and love, modern sport is an expression of a secular code of chivalry and learning. The idealism of modern sport is identical with the ideals of chivalry, and chivalry is its apparent source. In sport, unlike life outside of sport, the rules are both understood without ambiguity and accepted without reservation; when one is broken, either there is an established penalty (another rule), or the game is over. Hence sports writers have always been moralists par excellence. Three hunting treatises in the two centuries preceding the writing of the *Treatise of Fishing* show the course of this tradition.

If modern writing on sport had only one originating point—unlikely as that assumption might be—a claim to it could be made on behalf of Frederick II's *Art of Falconry*, which he completed in Latin not long before he died in 1250. It is in any case the high point of treatise writing in the early Middle Ages and the earliest complete model known in Europe. As the invention of the sonnet and the beginning of Italian poetry are attributed to Frederick II's court at Palermo, Sicily, it is appropriate that the beginning of the art of writing about sport in modern times should be found in that workshop. The Holy Roman Emperor, King of Sicily, King of Jerusalem, etc., who altered the history of Europe with the secularization of the state (and literature), was a great hunter, obsessed with the ancient royal sport of falconry: he says in his prologue that he prepared himself for thirty years to write the treatise. For his study of the art, he brought master falconers from "the four corners of the earth." The twelfth and thirteenth centuries were "the centuries of Aristotle," and Frederick gave himself to this influence. He caused Aristotle's zoology and two Arabic works on the diseases of hawks to be translated. From Aristotle also it is apparent that he learned the sense of logical order which the ancient philosopher gave to the medieval mind. Frederick II's treatise of falconry, however, rests upon direct observation and experience and is good enough to be considered the earliest modern scientific work on ornithology.

As the ruler of a large kingdom and an extensive empire [Frederick writes] we were very often hampered by arduous and intricate governmental duties, but despite these handicaps we did not lay aside our self-imposed task and were successful in committing to writing at the proper time the elements of the art. *Inter alia,* we discovered by hard-won experience that the deductions of Aristotle, whom we followed when they appealed to our reason, were not entirely to be relied upon, more particularly in his description of the characters of certain birds.[6]

To this comment on the limitations of logic, he adds the observation—as if he had expected more—that "the Prince of Philosophers . . . was ignorant of the practice of falconry." What inspired Frederick to lay down this model for the organization of a sporting treatise is not known, but it appears to be in the tradition of Xenophon.

> Our main thesis, then [Frederick says], is *The Art of Falconry*; and this we have divided into two cardinal sections. The first contains the argument, by which we mean contemplative thought, or theory; the second illustrates practice, which portrays experimental action. In addition, a third subsection contains a part of the argument and includes certain data pertaining to both theory and practice. Our purpose is to present the facts as we find them. Up to the present time the subject of falconry has been devoid of both artistic and scientific treatment.
>
> The medium we have chosen for this monograph is prose, with prologue and text.

This design for writing a sporting treatise, providing a place for discussing the meaning of sport before dealing with the art and science of it, has never been superseded. And each of these places Frederick filled with memorable content. He had a high degree of consciousness of the nature of sport: "Hunting itself," he says, "is nothing else but a form of bodily exercise and practices employed to capture animals." And (in the Mazarine Library version of his treatise) he takes one through a 589-page mental exercise in zoology, the breeding and care of falcons, lures, gerfalcons catching cranes, and a discourse on herons and river birds. He justifies this activity with the argument that falconry is the most noble of the several branches of hunting. From it one learns the secrets of nature. To practice it one needs to be skilled, for birds of prey are difficult to train; and the interesting problem is the training of the bird rather than the hunt itself. It is more noble to employ animals than artificial instruments in the hunt; and birds of prey are more noble than four-footed animals (presumably hounds used in the chase). In conclusion he turns to the medieval doctrine that noble qualities are associated with a noble class:

6. *The Art of Falconry,* translated and edited by Casey A. Wood and F. Marjorie Fyfe (Stanford University Press, 1943). This magnificent work sums up present knowledge of Frederick's treatise and its background. It was inspired by the earlier studies of Charles H. Haskins: see especially the *English Historical Review,* July 1921, pp. 334–55; and *Romanic Review,* Vol. XIII, 1922, pp. 18–27.

Here it may again be claimed that, since many nobles and but few of the lower rank learn and carefully pursue this art, one may properly conclude that it is intrinsically an aristocratic sport; and one may once more add that it is nobler, more worthy than, and superior to other kinds of venery.[7]

The early writers on sports, like Frederick, codifying their practices for the first time, thus were explicit about what they considered to be the sporting state of mind. Frederick's values—knowledge, skill, preference for the animate, belief in the myth and symbol of the hawk and in something intrinsically aristocratic (things perhaps learned from his Greek models and Arab contemporaries)—are devoid of romantic sentiments. He is disciplined about the nature of sport, raising it above mere exercise, but his emphasis falls chiefly on the values of skill and learning. His chivalry was part classical, part Oriental, and part medieval European. His learning was scientific in the modern empirical sense.

The Art of Falconry was the most important and most influential treatise on hunting in the early Middle Ages. It was circulated during the second half of the thirteenth century and translated into French. Several old books on falconry derived from it.[8] We are not concerned here, however, with the direct relationships between manuscripts, but with tradition.

In this sense Frederick's argument was "answered" in another treatise, a didactic poem, *La Chace dou Cerf*, written about the mid-thirteenth century by an unknown author. This is the oldest treatise on hunting in French. Following the form of argument and instruction laid down by Frederick, it sets forth the case for a different branch of hunting (the chase *vs.* falconry) and raises equally high but quite different values. It brings medieval chivalry into sport with the words *honor, love,* and *faith.* And while the author upholds the royal rank of hunting, he also makes a bow to equality. His prologue is brief:

> There are some who attempt to rime and take much trouble about it; some do it to gain honour and others to gain money. Some concern themselves with love; many knights also go to tournaments to advance themselves; one draws (the sword), the other jousts with the lance. A loyal heart delights in many things; his faith guides him. There are such as love falcons, sparrow hawks, and merlin hawks, but some carry them on their wrist who in their hearts care little for them. He who meddles in a sport if he does not love it, whatever pains he takes can profit and avail little. If there is anyone who wishes to learn of a sport which surpasses others (whoever learns well is not easily wearied) I much wish to make you understand it. No man is the worse for learning well. The sport is so royal that there is neither king nor

7. Frederick also begged nobles everywhere to have his treatise read to them. Few of them would have been able to read Latin, if they read at all.
8. *Romania,* ed. by Paul Meyer, Vol. XV, 1886, p. 278.

count nor [even] Gawain, if he were alive and loved it well, who would not be more honoured for that reason by all who understand it.

"Good Sir, if all knew it, would it be less honoured than it is now?"

"Nay, rather it would be more honoured, fair gentle friend, know it well."

"Wherefore I pray you that you would say before all what it is."

"Certainly, fair sweet friend, it is the amusement that one has from running hounds." (Trans., H. E. L. and Alice Dryden)

Little about actual incidents in the hunt, or stories of hunting, can be learned from treatises; but writing about hunting in the Middle Ages was not confined to a specialized literature. Hunting was a large and significant part of life—for many it was all of life that was not war—and a literary subject. An incident in the noted English romance *Sir Gawain and the Green Knight*, a narrative poem written by an unknown contemporary of Chaucer, gives some idea of what is meant by the lofty cliché "mighty hunter." There are three hunts in the story on three successive days, for the deer, the boar, and the fox, respectively, each vividly described in minute detail and with a symbolism in the story which is not of concern here. After a hard chase, on the second day, the boar is wounded and at bay (the climax of a boar hunt); the professional huntsmen are afraid and stand back and we see how the ideal medieval hunter goes in for the kill:

But then came the lord himself, spurring his horse, and saw the boar standing at bay. He got down from his horse, and left it standing there, and drew his bright sword, and went forward with long strides, passing through the ford to where the grim beast was waiting for him. The boar watched him coming with his weapon in hand, and his bristles rose and he snorted so fiercely that many feared for the knight. The boar made straight at him and the man and beast fell locked together and the water swirled about them. But the beast had the worst of it, for the man watched his mark well at the first charge, and drove the sharp steel firmly into his throat, right up to the hilt, and pierced the heart. The boar snarled and gave up the fight and made away across the stream, but a hundred hounds fell on him, biting furiously, and the men drove him to open ground where the hounds finished him off.

Then there was a loud hollaing, and the blowing of the kill on the loud horns, and the hounds bayed over the boar as their masters bade, they who had been the chief huntsmen in that long chase. Then one who was wise in woodcraft unlaced [i.e., cut up] the boar. He cut off the head, and fed the hounds with some of the flesh. Then they slung the carcase on a stout pole, and set off for home. The head was borne before the lord himself, who had slain the beast in the ford by the skill and strength of his hands. (Trans., M. R. Ridley)

About the time this was written—a little more than a hundred years after Frederick II died—there lived such a mighty hunter as this in France, who, as it happens, wrote the most famous of all hunting treatises, *Livre de Chasse*. This man was Gaston de Foix, a feudal lord who from his court at Orthez ruled over two principalities in the Pyrenees. His fame—and nickname, Gaston Phoebus (which also is given to his treatise)—was established by the medieval chronicler Jean Froissart, of whom he was patron, the celebrity of the two men, as a result, to some extent brushing off on each other. Much lore has gathered around this point in history. Sir Kenneth Clark (*Landscape into Art,* 1949), for example, discovered that natural observation in landscape painting began in illustrated manuscripts on sport—*Livre de Chasse* one of them—a circumstance that led Clark to remark on the paradox that through the instinct to kill man achieved intimacy with nature. Gaston Phoebus has also been celebrated by his English biographer-editor W. A. and F. Baillie-Grohman, and by Theodore Roosevelt, who wrote, under a White House dateline in 1904, a remarkable essay on Gaston Phoebus and related matters, lauding him as "a mighty lord and mighty hunter, as well as statesman and warrior." Gaston Phoebus surely deserved superlatives, but an account of the chilling episodes of his life does not belong here. He died of apoplexy in 1391 after an all-day bear hunt.

Fourteen years later, Edward, Duke of York, grandson of Edward II, conspirator against two kings, and a famous hunter, was put in prison by Henry IV. There it is surmised he performed his work of translating Gaston's *Livre de Chasse* into English, with five new chapters, under the title *Master of Game*. Gaston's treatise thereby achieved the new distinction of being the first hunting treatise in the English language.[9] In 1406 Edward was freed and appointed to the office of Master of Game under Henry IV. He died, a hero, in the English victory over the French at Agincourt in 1415; though, according to one account, he suffocated from the heat in his suit of armor. The author of the *Treatise of Fishing* acknowledged *Master of Game*, as follows:

> I will now describe the said four sports or games to find out, as well as I can, which is the best of them; albeit, the right noble Duke of York, late called the Master of Game, has described the joys of hunting, just as I think to describe (of it and all the others) the griefs.

The treatise *Master of Game*, like its French original, follows the now familiar form of argument and instruction. Hunting (i.e., the chase), the author says, is better than hawking. It is so noble as to be called the "Master of Sports." And he writes:

9. Twici's *The Art of Hunting* was written in England in the early fourteenth century in Norman French. The author was huntsman to Edward II. His treatise, curiously, lacks a preliminary argument. It was translated into English about 1425 and was very influential in the hunting literature that followed.

QUILL GORDON

I will prove by various arguments in this little prologue that there is no man's life, of those that engage in noble games and sports, that is less displeasing to God than is the life of a fully trained and skillful hunter, nor any such life that more good comes from. The first argument is that the sport often causes a man to avoid the Seven Deadly Sins. Secondly, men are better horsemen, more just and intelligent, more accomplished, more gracious, more enterprising, and better acquainted with all districts and all routes, both short and long. All good habits and manners come from it, as well as the health of a man and of his soul.

The hunter, he says, will avoid sins because in hunting he will not be idle; for idleness leads to lust and pleasure, dreams and evil imaginings. The author will prove how hunters live more joyfully than anyone else. "For when the hunter rises in the morning, he sees the sweet and fair morning and the weather clear and bright, and he hears the song of the small birds, which sing sweetly with great melody and full of love." He will prove, he says, that hunters live longer than others. "For as Hippocrates says, full repletions of food kill more men than any sword or knife. But hunters eat and drink less than any other men of this world. . . . And since hunters eat little and [sweat] often, they should always live long and be healthy." He does not overlook war. "For if he [a man who is not a hunter] were in need or at war, he would not know what to do, for he would not be used nor accustomed to toil, and so another man would have to do what he ought to do."

Now, in the early fifteenth century, we come to the *Treatise of Fishing*, which has no model in fishing history. The famous woodcut accompanying its first printed version (1496) showed the solitary, animated, and intent angler playing a fish with his rod held high in his left hand, his catch in a tub beside him on the bank of a stream. The town in the background suggests that he came out from there to the country for recreation. Today he might be a bank president on the Beaverkill, or a Butte, Montana, copper miner on the Big Hole. In those days he was likely to have been a merchant; very likely not a noble and not a landowner, since fishing had none of the dignity, ceremony, and hierarchal associations of medieval hunting. If he read the *Treatise of Fishing* it would have been for reflection and practical instruction on the sport, and not to learn the language and manners of an aristocrat. Fishing was an inexpensive sport, and, though sophisticated in technique, it was not yet divided into specializations. A man could do it all with his hands: a good part of the *Treatise of Fishing* is occupied with instruction on making your own tackle. But that is not all he would have learned from his reading.

The *Treatise of Fishing* is formed in three parts: (1) the argument, (2) the instruction, and, in the complete 1496 version, (3) further argument

26

establishing the concept of the angler through his moral qualities. The treatise begins, as we have seen, by defining the sport with the rule of rod, line, and hook, and lauds it above other good and honorable hunting sports in which there is pleasure without repentance and which lead to a fair and long age. The good life derives from merry thought, moderate work, and moderate diet, as opposed to contentious company, an uncongenial occupation, and places of debauchery. Rise early, as the angler does, and according to the adage you will be holy, healthy, and happy. Therefore, learn your fishing tackle, how to fish (at each level from the bottom to the top of the water), the kinds of fish, the weather, and baits, hooks, artificial flies, and rods, and how to make them, as the treatise shows. In conclusion, the author gives the order to anglers, in a form which is possibly a take-off on official proclamations: "I charge and require you in the name of all noble men that you do not fish in any poor man's private water . . . without his permission and good will." Don't break a man's fish traps. Don't break a hedge. Shut the gate. Fish not for material gain but for solace and health of body and soul. This way you will avoid the vice of idleness. Don't take too many fish, a rule you can easily observe if you fish according to the instructions. Conserve the fish in the water. So enjoined, you will have the blessing of God and St. Peter. From this beginning the angler with his rod and pursuit of pleasure was in time to be identified in a vast number of writings as philosopher, scholar, and teacher, and his sport as gentle, solitary, contemplative, passionate, cheerful, and innocent.

Did the author learn the design of the treatise and some of these sentiments from *Master of Game*? The great scholar of the second edition of the *Book of St. Albans*, Joseph Haslewood, commented in his book in 1810 that the commendation of hunting in *Master of Game* "awakened the jealousy of the author of the Treatise upon Angling." The historian of fly-fishing J. W. Hills, upon seeing the relation of the two treatises in 1920, had the brilliant insight "that all sport is one." Both the first hunting writer and the first fishing writer in English apply the measure of what is noble. Both speak of skill and the avoidance of idleness, of living longer with good diet and exercise, of joy in the presence of nature, and of other benefits to body and soul. The hunter is more just, intelligent, accomplished, gracious, enterprising, learned, and well-mannered; and the fisherman more specifically respects his neighbor. In a word, both are chivalrous and learned. But they also differ. Hunting is worldly; it is good training for the warrior. Fishing is solitary and reflective. Even the rod is designed to be used also as a walking stick that will keep secret where you are going. And though you should catch fish if you fish according to the instructions, it does not matter if you do not. Thus though the two treatises are similar in sporting sentiment, they part widely in the experiences peculiar to each sport. Whether the *Treatise of Fishing* drew upon *Master of Game,* as it

27

seems, or upon another source, does not matter. The simple facts are that the modern history of writing about hunting has its first classic in Frederick's treatise on falconry, and the modern history of writing about sport fishing has its first classic and its first known writing in the *Treatise of Fishing*, and the two treatises have in common their aesthetics and the state of mind called sport.

The *Treatise of Fishing* presumably appealed to an audience wider than that of privileged hunters. Language alone suggests different readers for *Master of Game* and the fishing treatise. *Master of Game*, and other early hunting treatises in England, employed a hunting terminology that was largely Norman French, the language of the court and the official language of England after 1066. The English of the *Treatise of Fishing* is the language of ordinary people. It is simple native prose with few long words: most are of one syllable, and most of the remainder are of two syllables—not a language for discussing Aristotle, but good enough for love and war and hunting and fishing. The *Treatise of Fishing* is one of the best pieces of prose writing of its time.

Courtly literature of sport was written for a knightly class which had extraordinary leisure and aspired to make a way of life of it. Later on, unchanged in essence, the literature of sport was written for an ever widening audience until we come to the millions of sportsmen with their new leisure today. The *Treatise of Fishing*, while first in fishing, also marked a turning point in the general history of sports writing, both in style and in its probable readers. The treatise was available in manuscript during the fifteenth century, was transcribed no one knows how many times, and when it made its first appearance in print in the second *Book of St. Albans* in 1496, was in a hunting context. As hunting, hawking, and heraldry were interests of the nobility which could be acquired, the *Book of St. Albans* served as a handbook for gentlemen. But the author of the *Treatise of Fishing*, writing near the beginning of the century for all who were "virtuous, gentle, and freeborn," cannot be held responsible for the less felicitous advertisements introduced into the book by its first printer near the end of the century. Wynkyn de Worde made no bones about selling the social merits of sport. At the conclusion of the treatise of coat armor, he or his shop editor entered the following notice:

> Here we shall make an ende of the moost specyall thynges of the boke of the lygnage of cote armurys: and how gentylmen shall be knownen from ungentylmen. And consequently shall folowe a compendyous treatyse of fysshynge wyth an angle whiche is right necessary to be had in this present volume: by cause it shewyth afore the manere of hawkynge & huntynge wyth other dyvers maters right necessary to be knowen of noble men and also for it is one of the dysportes that gentylmen use. And also it is not soo labororyous ne soo dishonest

to fysshe in this wyse as it is w^t nettes & other engynes whyche crafty men done use for theyr dayly encrease of goods.[10]

In an epilogue to the fishing treatise, de Worde explained why he included it with the other treatises in the book:

And for by cause that this present treatyse sholde not come to the hondys of eche ydle persone whyche wolde desire it yf it were empryntyd allone by itself & put in a lytyll plaunflet therfore I haue compylyd it in a greter volume of dyuerse bokys concernynge to gentyll & noble men. to the entent that the forsayd ydle persones whyche sholde have but lytyll mesure in the sayd dysporte of fysshying sholde not by this meane vtterly dystroye it.

It has been inferred from these expressions of the printer that literacy in the fifteenth century extended to classes regarded by de Worde as lower than that embraced by the term "gentlemen" (though he did later, in 1532, yield on exclusiveness by publishing a separate edition of the fishing treatise). More to the point here, however, is the implication that at the end of the fifteenth century hunting and fishing were an acceptable combination within the same covers, needing only a mild apology for their connection. In the following century the hunting and fishing treatises of the *Book of St. Albans* were often published together, from which one may conclude that fishing had become a fashionable sport. Yet the *Treatise of Fishing*, though a best-seller, attracted no known literary competition for most of the two centuries.

During the 157 years between the first printing of the *Treatise of Fishing* and the first edition of *The Compleat Angler*, the few angling writers who appeared went on to develop the concept of the angler. Only five angling books worthy of note—exclusive of the sixteen or more reprints of the *Treatise of Fishing*—are known to have been published in this period in the English language. The second book on angling, *The Arte of Angling*, was first issued in 1577 by an anonymous author and was apparently known to early fishing writers—including Walton, who borrowed from it but never mentioned it. The book was lost to angling history until a single surviving copy was recently discovered in an attic in England, brought to the United States by the collector Carl Otto von Kienbusch, and printed at Princeton in 1956. The *Arte*, the first writing on the sport in prose dialogue, has two characters, Piscator and Viator (Wayfarer).[11] Piscator (the pupil in Aelfric) is the teacher, Viator the student. The *Arte* is a fine little book, the

10. By "labororyous," the printer meant professional, that is, not sporting; and by "dishonest" he meant, in this context, ungentlemanly.
11. Adopted by Walton, who after his first edition changed "Viator" to "Venator."

best use of dialogue on the subject of angling outside of Walton's. Piscator is testy but hospitable. He treats angling as an art and a science, and "as of that pleasure that I have always most recreated myself withal, and had most delight in, and is most meetest for a solitary man, and is also of light cost." He speaks of the fellowship, ruling out, however, "the sluggard sleepy sloven," the poor man, the angry man, the fearful man, and the busybody, who can stay at home or, if they like, hunt or hawk. The character of the angler is described in thirteen "gifts":

Vi[ator]. Why then, I pray you, what gifts must he have that shall be of your company?

Pi[scator]. 1. He must have faith, believing that there is fish where he cometh to angle. 2. He must have hope that they will bite. 3. Love to the owner of the game. 4. Also patience, if they will not bite, or any mishap come by losing of the fish, hook, or otherwise. 5. Humility to stoop, if need be to kneel or lie down on his belly, as you did today. 6. Fortitude, with manly courage, to deal with the biggest that cometh. 7. Knowledge adjoined to wisdom, to devise all manner of ways how to make them bite and to find the fault. 8. Liberality in feeding of them. 9. A content mind with a sufficient mess, yea, and though you go home without. 10. Also he must use prayer, knowing that it is God that doth bring both fowl to the net and fish to the bait. 11. Fasting he may not be offended withal, but acquaint himself with it, if it be from morning until night, to abide and seek for the bite. 12. Also he must do alms deeds; that is to say, if he meet a sickly poor body or doth know any such in the parish that would be glad of a few fishes to make a little broth withal (as often times is desired of sick persons), then he may not stick to send them some or altogether. And if he have none, yet with all diligence that may be [he] try with his angle to get some for the diseased person. 13. The last point of all the inward gifts that doth belong to an angler, is memory, that is, that he forget nothing at home when he setteth out, nor anything behind him at his return.

The third book on angling is Leonard Mascall's *A Booke of Fishing with Hooke and Line* (1590), which has some distinction in the field of fish conservation but is otherwise little more than an edited version of the *Treatise of Fishing.*

The fourth[12] is John Dennys's treatise in verse, *Secrets of Angling* (1613), the first angling poem. He begins with a play on the elevated opening line of Virgil's *Aeneid* (*Arma virumque cano:* Of arms and the man I sing):

> Of Angling, and the Art thereof I sing,
> What kind of tooles it doth behove to have;

12. We omit John Taverner's *Certaine Experiments concerning Fish and Fruite* (London, 1600), which fishermen read for its remarkable observations on water life.

> And with what pleasing bait a man may bring
> The fish to bite within the water wave.

Dennys confesses:

> Not that I take upon me to impart
> More than by others hath before been told;
> Or that the hidden secrets of this art,
> I would unto the vulgar sort unfold.

It is not known who all the others are by whom this knowledge has been told, but the author of the *Arte* is one of them. From him Dennys appears to have taken the thirteen gifts of the angler, calling them "The Qualities of an Angler." He gives twelve instead of thirteen; the odd one, alms, he combines with love. Dennys appears to be the first in didactic angling literature to draw explicitly upon the ancient pastoral and piscatory, which he acknowledges by paying farewell respects to Neptune and all his monsters on entering Arcadia and the gentle haunts of perch and trout. To the second edition of *Secrets of Angling* the editor, William Lawson, added this now established gift of the trout to the angler: "The trout," he said, "makes the angler most gentlemanly, and readiest sport of all other fishes."

The year after the poem was first published, Gervase Markham set it back to prose (with a few additions from the *Treatise of Fishing*), in a work entitled *The Pleasures of Princes*, the fifth known book in the history of angling. He also had some new and original ideas on the angler. The twelve "inward qualities of the mind" were not enough, he said. The angler must also be a general scholar, knowledgeable in the liberal sciences, a grammarian, a writer "without affectation or rudeness," sweet of speech "to persuade, and intice other[s] to delight in an exercise so much laudable"; he must have strong arguments "to defend, and maintain his profession against envy or slander"; he should know the sun, moon, and stars, from which to guess the weather; he should be versed in countries, highways, and paths to lakes and streams; he should know geometrical angles so as to describe the channels and windings of rivers, and the "art of numbering" so as to be able to take soundings; he should be able to make music to dispose of melancholy.

Thus the angler emerging from the Elizabethan Age could be told from an "ungentleman." It is not far from here to the personification of this image in *The Compleat Angler* in 1653. One writer, however, intervened with the sixth book on the sport. He was Thomas Barker, a cook by profession, who wrote a rare little treatise which he called *The Art of Angling* (1651). So well established had the literary image of the angler become in his time that Barker felt constrained to apologize: "I do crave pardon," he said, "for not writing scholar like." But Barker was an able fishing writer, the first to proceed directly to the kill, to speak of a reel, and to invent new trout flies. By Turrell's conferment he is the "father of poachers." Walton acknowledged Barker alone among the angling writers before himself.

Walton merged the basic outline of the *Treatise of Fishing* with the dialogue technique, the characters, and some of the content of *The Arte of Angling* (1577), and with elements of the pastoral. Together with everything he could find in classical, Biblical, and medieval traditions, he brought along his contemporary "band of musicians," the great poets who were his friends and neighbors. In his fifth edition he also got Charles Cotton to make the book actually complete with a treatise on fly-fishing, the first specialized treatment of that subject, and still one of the best. Into the pleasant ensemble Walton breathed his personality and idyllic mood. The effect of this most popular of English idyls upon writing on the sport of fishing was both inspiring and disastrous.

For seventy-four years after his fifth edition, Walton was in eclipse; then, with the benediction of Sam Johnson, he was revived and, even before the nineteenth-century renaissance of angling, was canonized as the model of the angler. Although he had warned of the limits of making "an angler by a book" alone, Walton, the least imitable of angling writers, for a long time thereafter was closely imitated with idyls upon an idyl. One of the first to see the danger was Sir Walter Scott, who said: "The palm of originality, and of an exquisite simplicity which cannot, perhaps, be imitated with entire success, must remain with our worthy patriarch, Izaak." (Scott also defended Walton against Byron, who condemned Walton for his posture of innocence in a blood sport.)

Up to this time there were fewer than a hundred titles in angling literature; they were soon to begin multiplying into the thousands of books that today constitute by far the largest library in sport. Most of the classics were from the seventeenth century; the eighteenth produced little. On the eve of the great developments of the nineteenth century, two courses presented themselves to the angling writer: one the Waltonian tradition, the other a more direct, empirical approach to the sport. Each course was taken by large numbers of writers. In England Walton ruled, at least formally—ninety editions of his book were reported by Westwood and Satchell in their angling bibliography in 1883—though the best writers went their own way.

The difficulty of imitating Walton in America was described by Washington Irving in his sentimental travesty "The Angler," one of the sketches published in 1819. He and a group of friends read Walton one winter and determined to become anglers like him. As soon as the weather was good they went up to the highlands of the Hudson, "as stark mad as was ever Don Quixote from reading books of chivalry." One of the party, fully harnessed for the field with all the angler's equipments, "was as great a matter of stare and wonderment among the country folk, who had never seen a regular angler, as was the steel-clad hero of La Mancha among the goat-herds of the Sierra Monera." Irving hooked himself instead of the fish, tangled his line in the trees, lost his bait, broke his rod, and in a short while gave up fishing, lay down under a tree, and spent the rest of the day reading Izaak Walton, "satisfied that it was his fascinating vein of honest simplicity and rural feeling that had bewitched me, and not the passion for angling." With a bow to Walton for his idyl and another to the *Treatise of Fishing* for its maxims, Irving concluded that angling was suited neither to him nor to America, but only to England, where there is "rule and system" and where "every roughness has been softened away from the landscape." Walton had misled him.[13]

The American continent, as it happened, was explored in detail in the century that was dominated both here and abroad by a romantic view of nature. Most writing on fishing in England in the nineteenth century was immersed in that romanticism. In the United States sport fishing did not become prominent until the middle of the century. George Washington Bethune, a Reformed Dutch clergyman and scholar, in 1847 introduced Walton (keeping himself anonymous for fear of censure) with one of the notable editions of *The Compleat Angler*, and the influence of Walton grew until the turn of the new century, when it declined. Bethune also discussed and quoted from the *Treatise of Fishing*, although an edition of it was not published in the United States until George W. Van Siclen's in 1875.[14]

A new spirit, however, came early into American fishing. On the frontier men had hunted and fished not as a recreation but to live. The act of going to the wilderness was itself a sought-out adventure with its own romanticism, and as sport began to flourish, hunting and fishing absorbed this new sense of frontier excitement, which in the United States has never died out, especially in the West. So we have two literatures of fishing, one of retirement to old meadows, the other of going out to new waters. The *Treatise of Fishing* produced no cult, as Walton did, and by its nature could not. What the treatise did was to establish the sport in its pastoral setting, to form its character out of the elements of rule, courtesy, and learning, and to find in it a tolerable state of mind.

13. He did not mislead his leading disciple in angling today. Though inspired by Walton, Arnold Gingrich (*The Well-Tempered Angler,* 1966) is the most natural of angling writers.
14. The notable editions of *The Treatise of Fishing with an Angle,* after the numerous reprints of the sixteenth century, were Haslewood's in 1810, William Pickering's (Baskerville) in 1827, and M. G. Watkins's in 1880. Van Siclen reprinted the edition of 1827. Thomas Satchell printed a transcript of the manuscript in 1883.

Chapter 3
GORDON AND AMERICAN FLY-FISHING

The best thing about Gordon the man is that he wrote well and with re-markable knowledge about contemporary fly-fishing. As the principal creator of the structure and style of the American imitation trout fly, and as the angler who introduced and adapted the dry fly to the United States, he also occupies a unique position in the sport. Despite the fact that he died in 1915, his work has a direct connection with our present practices, for it was he who developed much of what we now do. Time moves slowly in fly-fishing. The last time it moved in a large way in the United States was with Theodore Gordon.

Gordon was a flytier as well as a fly-fisherman and a journalist of the stream. He began publishing in the late nineteenth century in an English journal, the *Fishing Gazette,* and until his death he was widely regarded here and in England as the leading American angling authority (in fishing, "authority" is a manner of speaking). Since then he has become legendary. I should like to try to describe the condition of fly-fishing—particularly with reference to the trout fly—when Gordon appeared on the scene.

The trout fly of today grew out of the trout fly of yesterday. From a dim ancient and medieval background it emerged in the late Middle Ages, multiplied, and divided into schools from which the flies of today take their character.

Fly-fishing has three elements: equipment, knowledge of stream life, and presentation. The equipment centers on the artificial fly; knowledge of stream life encompasses insects and trout; presentation is skill, acquired and magical, in presenting the fly to the trout. Fly-fishing argument, which is fabulous, revolves around the comparative value of these elements. At the heart of the argument is the trout fly, its patterns and forms giving tangible expression to fly-fishing theory. Most trout flies are either *imitation*, resembling natural insects, or *fancy*, resembling in their abstract patterns merely the generality of insect life.

In its classic form, the trout fly is modeled on an insect. Like an insect, it has, in full regalia, wings, body, legs (called *hackle*), and tail. Trout-fly-fishing began, according to the lore, in antiquity, when some angler, seeing a fish rise up to take an insect off the water, dropped his worm and tried to use an insect as bait. It did not work very well, of course, the insect being too fragile to remain on the hook during the necessary casting and manipulation—and so began the historic, irreconcilable split between fly- and bait-fishing. (*Dapping*, the delicate art of fishing with natural flies, is little known and seldom practiced any longer.) Certain bird feathers were found to be similar to insects in color, marking, texture, and weight. Tying a feather on a hook to represent insect wings, spreading the fibers of another as legs, attaching strands of the fiber for the tail, and winding fur around the hook for the body, the ancient anglers produced a sufficiently delicate yet sturdy likeness of an insect.

The trout fly is either wet or dry. The wet fly is relatively flat, two-dimensional, with soft, flowing hackle. It is fished literally *wet*, that is, below the surface. The dry fly is three-dimensional and can be stood up on its stiff hackle and tail. It is fished literally *dry*, often with the aid of waterproofing, and cocks up like an insect on the water. The dry fly is almost always fished upstream (under most conditions downstream, it would quickly drag); the wet fly is fished up, down, or across. Once the subjects of controversy, both the wet and dry fly are now generally found in the equipment of the experienced angler.

The angler's problem today, as always, is in his choice of flies. Most fly-fishers use only a small number, perhaps not more than fifteen or twenty. But which ones and why? Some 500 *standard* patterns in the United States have been listed by the *Sporting Goods Dealer*. Mary Orvis Marbury (*Favorite Flies and Their Histories*, 1892; reprinted 1955), member of a celebrated flytying family of Vermont, eighty years ago expressed "perplexity" and "dismay" at the "accumulation of the ages"—and that was before the dry fly was really known in this country. Today it probably accounts for half of our trout flies. Standard and nonstandard patterns together run into many thousands.

This number and diversity represent various approaches to fly-fishing. Every new thought or method has inspired new flies, even where conditions have remained constant, as in the chalk streams of southern England. Consider then the provocative inconstancy of the North American continent and its inhabitants; its waters wild and domestic, varying in altitude,

35

temperature, movement, food supply, and species of trout; its regional habits embodied in fishing traditions expressed by the fancy yellow-white-scarlet Parmachene Belle fly of Maine, the precise, subtle, bronze-blue-gray Quill Gordon of the Middle Atlantic states, the roughly delicate, mottled brown-and-gray Adams of Michigan, the coarse, durable, hair-woven Mite family (a relatively conservative symbol of the West), and others that we shall come to. The important thing for the angler is to understand enough about fly theory to know what he is doing. A million flies will not confuse the sound angler. He begins where fly-fishing began, with nature.

Imitation of the Natural

The relationship of trout flies to natural insects is the rule, the first principle of fly-fishing—exceptions afterward. The primary food of the trout is the insect life of the stream. Underwater food has been called the trout's beef, the winged fly its caviar. And it may be so, for many fishermen have seen that a trout taken on a fly may already be full to bursting—an experience which suggests that the trout may have either a sporting or an Epicurean instinct, in addition to ordinary hunger. This observation may serve also as a tip that fly-fishing information is highly speculative.

Early fly-fishers pioneered loosely in entomology, vaguely studying insect forms and colors. Science later identified insects by form in black and white. The fly-fisher, with his special interest in color, could have paid more attention to scientific discipline, for he got himself into such an unholy mess with his beautiful language of watery duns, pale evening duns, hare's ears, and March browns that he was not able to speak clearly across the centuries, as the scientists could with their Latin and Greek, or across the Atlantic, or even between the states.

The big five of trout-stream insects—the May fly, caddis fly, stone fly, true fly, and alderfly—and their several stages of life are not of equal value to the fisher. In their preadult stages (nymphs or larvae), these insects live under water, where their herbivorous appetite performs the service of converting plant into animal life. The stream bed is generally littered with larvae and nymphs, and trout spend most of the year rooting among them for the better part of their food. In this century fly-fishers have shown an increasing interest in the nymph, and it may be that the wet fly is often taken by the trout for a nymph or a minnow rather than a winged insect. The chief interest of fly-fishers, however, is in the adult winged flies that appear in spring and summer, especially in the East, between the lilac and the laurel, the heart of the fly-fisher's season. Most trout flies represent winged insects.

Two groups of winged flies are favored by the trout: the May fly and the caddis fly. The latter, unfortunately, does most of its hatching near or after nightfall and so is usually on the stream after the fly-fisher has gone home. Therefore, beyond but by no means to the exclusion of all others, the trout fisher has traditionally prized and copied the gorgeously hued aristocrat of the stream, the May fly. The May fly lives most of its life, which lasts a few weeks to more than a year, under water as a nymph, and gets its scientific name, Ephemeroptera, from its fleeting adult life. As an adult it goes through two further stages: the fly-fisher's dun (in scientific terms, *subimago*) and spinner (*imago*). Sometime in the fly-fishers' season the May fly nymph makes a dash for the surface, often with a trout in swift pursuit, splits the nymphal shuck, airs its wings, and takes off for the woods as a dun. In this form the fly-fisher knows many species. Some anglers prefer the dun to all others, as it is found so frequently on the stream. The dun is a great and historic fly, progenitor of countless trout-fly patterns. John Waller Hills (*A History of Fly Fishing for Trout,* 1921) has traced the artificial duns of Berners's fifteenth-century treatise down to the present century. The dun is out in profusion each month of May.

After spending a few hours or days in nearby trees, the May fly dun molts and is transformed into a spinner, more brilliant than the dun and slightly altered in size and shape. The spinner returns to hover over the stream in a rhythmic mating dance of birth and death. Before the end, the female deposits her eggs in the water, caviar in truth for the trout.

Duns and spinners vary by country, region, stream, and season. Fly-fishers often get to know them on their favorite stream, though the date of hatch is unpredictable. It is not always possible to match the natural insect, even from a full fly box. The strict use of imitation flies is the ideal of a number of anglers. But because of the many difficulties, including the problem of obtaining good floating materials in certain colors, anglers are generally satisfied to use a fly that at once resembles several species. This traditional practice of matching a single or similar species accounts for the largest number of trout flies.

No matter how flies are chosen or fished, some kind of speculative under-water view is implied. Man lives in air, trout in water, and the surface of the stream is like the borderline of metaphysics. The theory of strict imitation, asserted or hidden in simple practice, assumes that the trout has a fine sense of color, form, and size. The imitators uphold one or another of these capacities. Their rather formidable assumption is notably challenged by P. B. M. Alan (*Trout Heresy,* 1936), who submits that "the trout has no more brain than a lizard," and that as, say, between the shades of an olive dun, it has "no powers of discernment whatsoever." To Alan the legend of the wise trout is man's conceit, "for if trout can outwit us, the lords of creation, he must be superior to us in cunning."

.   .   .

QUILL GORDON

Fancy Flies

Skeptics where the wise trout is concerned often fish with fancy flies such as the Scarlet Ibis and Parmachene Belle, suggestive not of species or group but merely of fly life. One can get entangled here, however. The Parmachene Belle, for example, was created in the 1870's to imitate the fin of a brook trout; no one will ever know what the trout has been taking it for all this time. Fancy flies are fished without regard for the insects on the water. Both fancy and imitation flies take trout, yet the reconciliation of the theories behind them would be the most revolutionary event in the history of fly-fishing. It would be easier to reconcile Plato and Aristotle. Ray Bergman (*Trout*, 1938) takes the genial view that any standard pattern will do. Another authority, Lee Wulff (*Leaping Silver*, c. 1940), believes that the trout sees not color so much as a silhouette, and Wulff fishes his flies accordingly. Charles M. Wetzel (*Practical Fly Fishing*, 1943) is a color imitationist. The late Ray Camp of the *New York Times* used to like to try out new flies. Charles Fox advises us to fish the fly that suits the conditions of time and place. The fine Western flytier Dan Bailey prefers flies for streams. Jim Deren fishes all the angles. By all accounts these master fishermen have taken many fish. From this one ought to arrive at a skeptical conclusion. But be careful: belief inspires confidence, and confidence inspires the angler.

Basically there are but two schools of fly-fishing—imitation and presentation, both closed systems of thought. They work this way: The imitationist, making due allowance for the fisherman's skill, believes that his trout rise to the naturalness of his flies. He explains the basket of the presentationist as the result of trout mistaking the fancy or unnatural fly for some known insect. In extremity, he will deny that there is any such thing as a fancy fly; all are imitations in one way or another, and the basket would be fuller if the presentationist paid more attention to the insects. The presentationist, on the other hand, graciously attributes the basket of his adversary not to his flies but to his fishing skill. The tallest tales of fishing experience will not crack the logic of these views.

Regional fly practices defy all theory. Dry flies are predominant in the East after the snow water and April freshets have run off, but toward the West flies grow wetter and wetter. Imitation flies have prevailed for seventy-five years from the Beaverkill in New York to the Brodhead in Pennsylvania. They turn fancy north along the Seaboard to Maine and Canada. In the whole sweep of the Rockies, flytiers are wonderfully enterprising and unorthodox. They often abandon the delicacy of fur and feathers for the durability of hair, squirrel tail, and bucktail. Large, rough, and radically spectacular, their flies express the directness and enthusiasm of wild-country fishing.

The Old Master

The main tendencies of modern American flytying largely stem from Theodore Gordon, the old master of American fly-fishing, familiar to most fishermen through his Quill Gordon fly. Gordon's influence was consciously passed on by the generation immediately following him, the peerless school of Sullivan County (New York) flytiers, standard-bearers of the imitation fly: Reub Cross, who attributed his learning to Gordon's tutelage; Roy Steenrod, creator of the Hendrickson fly, and Herman Christian (both Gordon's fishing companions); the Walt Dettes, man and wife; and the Harry Darbees. In delicacy, precision, and style, the craft of the flytying masters is out of the old master, Gordon. He died in 1915 and was swept from sight like a spent spinner. But we know his work and his angling life from his surviving letters and numerous "Little Talks on Fly-Fishing" in the files of *Forest and Stream* and the *Fishing Gazette,* of which he was the American correspondent from 1890 (*The Complete Fly Fisherman,* 1947).

Gordon was born in Pittsburgh in 1854 with a silver spoon in his mouth and fly-fished the limestone creeks of Pennsylvania from the age of fourteen. He lived a remarkable life, unheard-of in our day. A man of taste and intelligence, he was a good, restrained, yet warm and exciting fishing writer, a reader who knew Chaucer as well as Walton and Thoreau, Thad Norris (*The American Angler's Book,* 1864) as well as Frederic Halford (*Dry-Fly Fishing in Theory and Practice,* 1889), and a devoted follower of the great Francis Francis (*A Book on Angling,* 1867). When he fled civilization for his retreat on the Neversink, he put only one thing into his mind—the stream—and sustained it there unflaggingly for many years. An inexplicable performance, probably never duplicated by anyone anywhere. Gordon made an elegant backwoodsman. His one fishing photograph, taken around 1895, suggests a more than ordinary discrimination in clothing and equipment. He spit blood during his last three years and died presumably of TB. What we really know of him is that he lived a sweet, good life, and was perhaps the only man ever to express with his entire existence the ideal of the anglers' brotherhood.

Gordon did not entirely succeed in escaping the civilization from which he fled, and his early writing is more cheerful than his last. The destruction of forests, bringing ice jams and floods, and the pollution of streams, all of which killed the trout, bothered him more and more. He felt that the increasing purchase of riparian rights and the consequent closure of long stretches of streams for private use was a violation of the anglers' code. And although his fame brought him many invitations, he usually turned away from posted and specially stocked waters with the remark that they were too easy to fish and no test of skill. He respected the clubs for their role as trout preserves. But he loved difficult fishing, and he most enjoyed the days when the trout, especially the big ones whose lairs he knew, were elusive.

A Fish Story

Gordon is the subject of many anecdotes. His small, slender figure was beloved by the people of Sullivan County, where he and his rod were most often seen bobbing along paths and streams. His haunts were the Neversink, the Beaverkill, the Willowemoc—the big three of Catskill trout streams —and the Esopus and Big Indian. But he had also fished in the dear Brodhead of Pennsylvania, and in streams south to Florida, north to Maine, and west to Ohio, Michigan, and Wisconsin. Gordon himself told a fishing story that reveals his stream manners. In the early spring of 1907, when the water was too high and roily for flies in the main stream, he turned off into a tributary (a useful hint for early-season fly-fishers) and soon came upon a little Negro girl fishing a pool with stick and string. He was stalking and she did not notice him. He intended to signal her: "I did not wish to poach upon her pool, but, as a matter of form, dropped my fly at the edge of the stone and not three feet from the small maiden's toes. It was seized at once by a half-pound native trout, which had been lurking under her pedestal, and I am not sure who was more surprised, the child or myself."

As a craftsman and an innovator, Gordon came upon the scene at an opportune time for a great man, and he lived up to the occasion. In 1890, two disparate traditions that today make up the central course of our flytying and fly-fishing were operating independently of each other. The first was the long tradition of English fly-fishing known since the fifteenth century, which was then undergoing its greatest turn with the development of the dry fly. The other was American fly-fishing, which was then still locked into the wet fly, used mainly either in indigenous fancy patterns or in imitation patterns tied on British models. Gordon brought about the juncture of these traditions.

On the English side, trout flies go back to the fifteenth century. We know from Hills's ingenious and masterful history that eleven of Berners's twelve flies, the first on record, can be traced down to the present time. They were wet, and strictly imitative. Other equipment consisted of long rods and twisted hair lines. From the early fifteenth century to Cotton in 1676 (Walton was not a fly-fisher) there was practically no change except for the addition of a number of flies. The seventeenth was a literary century, lit up by Walton, Cotton, Wotton, and other great fishing writers. Fly-fishers in the eighteenth century stopped writing, with the exception of occasional brilliant pieces such as Gay's verses, and got to work supplying the tackle essentially as we have it today: short rods, reels, silk lines, and drawn-gut leaders. It was a technical century; the artistry of flytying stood still.

Action Upstream

The nineteenth century was the fly-fisher's epoch. Literature and fishing came together in the romantic appreciation of nature. The study of science led to the publication of fly-fishers' entomologies in color, notably Alfred Ronalds's monumental work, *The Fly Fisher's Entomology*, in 1836. Flytiers set to work with their models drawn in front of them and expanded their range with numerous species of insects. In 1841 George Pulman (*Vade Mecum of Fly-Fishing for Trout*) pulled the dry fly out of his hat complete, though for all anyone knew it might as well have been a rabbit. It was an extraordinary achievement, but a little ahead of its time.

Then came W. C. Stewart (*The Practical Angler*, 1857) and the first leap forward in fly-fishing history since its origin. Until Stewart, fly-fishers relied on the color and shape of flies to catch their fish. Stewart introduced *action*. How did he do this? By turning upstream. Some fly-fishers had been upstream men since Cotton's time, but Stewart went upstream and made an argument for it. Upstream fishing, wet or dry, is superior fishing for many reasons, but essentially for one: Facing upstream, the fisher controls the position of the fly; therefore the fishing is more precise and the element of luck greatly diminished.

The Dry Fly

The effect on fly-fishing was profound, for upstream fishing was a prelude to the dry fly. The dry fly must float naturally, an effect almost impossible to obtain downstream. From Pulman, who first held it up, to Frederic Halford, who quit his business, took off his coat, and fought thirty-five years for its *exclusive* use, the dry fly had a rapid and spectacular development. During the late nineteenth century it came to maturity. Color and form were debated all over again. Halford wrote the second great entomology (*Dry-Fly Entomology*, 1897), with numbered color plates to identify tints and shadings. After Halford had done his work, a wet-fly fisher on a chalk stream in southern England "skulked like a poacher." Hills was a man of moderate judgment, yet here is his summation of the dry fly: "It altered both the practice and the temperament of the angler. It called different qualities into request. It has a charm and an allurement which the older sport did not possess. In what does its charm lie? Partly in the fact that all the moves in the game are visible."

The dry-fly rage was on in 1890 when Halford received a letter from Theodore Gordon inquiring about this new phenomenon. In his reply Halford enclosed a full set of his dry flies, each carefully identified in pen and ink; and the dry fly winged its way to the New World.

QUILL GORDON

In the United States, sport fishing had been practically unknown before 1830. Fish was food. The fly was discussed in a few books—John J. Brown's, George Washington Bethune's, and Frank Forester's—in the 1840's, but was not widely used until the 1860's, when it suddenly bloomed. The Americans had learned most things from the English, who on their chalk streams lazily "fished the rise," that is, waited until the trout showed itself and then cast over the rise. But the Americans typically strode their fast-water streams and went after the trout wherever they lay, rise or no rise. The fishing was good—too good—and the fancy wet fly was often sufficient to the occasion until the 1870's, when the native brook trout of the East were suddenly fished out.

The great American fisher of the century was "Uncle" Thad Norris, learned in fishing literature and experienced in native practice. He knew about everything there was to know in his time, put it all down in 1864, and thereby equipped the school of early American fly-fishing with a rounded theory and practice. Like Stewart, from whom he may have learned it, he was fishing upstream, sometimes even drying his wet fly in an effort to make it float. That was the nearest an American came to getting in on early dry-fly development—a gesture.

By 1879 the brook trout were all but gone, and the hardier brown trout had not yet been transplanted from Europe. The editor of *Forest and Stream* threw in the sponge with a long editorial dirge, ending, "This is probably the last generation of trout fishers." Norris's crowd had got all the trout, and the following generations had to learn conservation. Eastern fishing, which was the larger part of early American fishing, increased in difficulty for more reasons than one. The immigrant brown trout was wiser than the native brook. Neither fancy flies nor wet flies were enough. Fly-fishers of the nineties faced upstream and waited for something to happen.

The Modern Fly

It was a historic moment, then, in 1890, when Gordon opened Halford's letter and fingered his flies. Gordon was already immersed in the brief tradition of American fly-fishing. The first practical book he had used was Norris's, from which he learned to tie his first flies. Like Norris and his predecessor Stewart, Gordon was an upstream man. He had fished through the decline of the brook trout and the rise of the brown, and so cherished the native species that he refused to accede to its scientific designation, charr. It was a *trout*. He had seen sights rarely seen by the modern Eastern angler: "water covered with dimples made by the rising trout as far as my view extended."

The significant thing is that Gordon had fished the wet fly dry, the natural outcome of an acute upstream man fishing over rising trout. Instinctively he had dried the fly, as Norris had done; but the construction of the fly was wrong. At best the wet fly keels over when dry and floats inert on the surface. It was natural that Gordon, a man consecrated to angling and a reader of English as well as American books, should have heard the echoes of Halford's crusading din across the water.

Gordon saved Halford's flies as models of construction for tying his own flies. But his job had just begun, for Halford's flies imitated English insects, which are different from ours. Gordon set out to correct this in his own way. Lacking any kind of formal fly-fisher's entomology, he studied what entomological information there was and began to observe duns and spinners on the water. It is thus owing in part to the lack of American color-printed entomologies that he observed flies under natural conditions and, tying imitations on the spot, initiated our contemporary style of American flies—cocky, pretty, subtle, and impressionistic.

He became for a time a strict imitationist—that is, he tried for an impression of individual species. Although he grew so well acquainted with insects in his long sojourn by the stream that he could carry hundreds of them in his memory, he gradually turned moderate—partly the effect of becoming a professional flytier. He came to believe that under all but the most difficult circumstances, an imitation covering a group of species was sufficient for good fishing. Gordon regarded his Quill Gordon as a pivotal fly that was subject to different dressings. This famous standard fly apparently was not meant to represent a single insect. "I can vary them to suit," he said.

A further contribution of Gordon's grew out of the fast stream: the English, fishing the rise in quiet water, can afford to use a softer hackle than Americans, whose flies are always being ducked by whitecaps, froth, converging currents, and other movements of the stream. Gordon sought a stiffer hackle, which was a matter of being more selective in cock necks, and tied it as sparsely as the conditions would allow. From this the fly developed greater delicacy and buoyancy. The key to the American dry fly today is still buoyancy, and assuming you start with a light wire hook, that means hackle. American flytiers now use stiff hackle in their flies even at the cost of departing from the exact color of natural insects.[1]

Other men in the early years of this century made important contributions to American fly-fishing. Since Gordon did not himself put his work

1. Only in two important instances is Gordon outdated: in the trend in the East away from his long, heavy rods, and in the trend away from the use of many bird feathers in flies. The crux of the materials problem, which to this day shows no hope of solution, is the difficulty of obtaining certain feathers. Dry flies fished in fast water must float on tiny, stiff strands of feather hackle obtained from rooster necks. But poultry raisers usually kill roosters before they are two years old, the age at which some of them might develop prized neck feathers; and flytiers generally cannot afford the cost of raising poultry exclusively for feathers. Rarest of necks is the blue dun; flytiers have made reputations on their blue-dun hackles.

between covers, the laurel for the first book on the dry fly went to Emlyn M. Gill, whose *Practical Dry-Fly Fishing* hatched out the dry-fly cult in 1912. Here, as in England, the cult put on a great, if belated, campaign to sink the wet fly forever. Their titular leader was Gill's friend George La Branche, whose book *The Dry Fly in Fast Water* (1914) is regarded by many as the American classic. La Branche made a unique contribution to the technique of fast-water fishing: the decoy method of floating a fly many times over the supposed lair of a trout, for no less a purpose than to create an *entire artificial hatch*. His celebrated fly is the Pink Lady. Yet Gordon, who fished the dry fly from 1890, tied it, talked it, wrote about it, and preferred it when the conditions were right, never joined the cult or turned away from the art of the wet fly fished upstream. When the dry-fly rage came on, he resisted it. In England the "wet" man G. E. M. Skues (*Minor Tactics of the Chalk Stream*, 1910) had fought the "dry" man Halford, and together they produced a balance. Gordon's range was wider: he performed the joint services of a Halford and a Skues.

In brief, then, the classic American trout fly of today descended to us in the English line from Berners through Cotton (Walton's disciple) to Stewart, to Halford, to Gordon; and in the American line from Berners through Cotton to Stewart, to Norris, to Gordon. It continued down to us from Gordon through the creations of contemporary flytiers, some of whom have been mentioned here.

Whatever your preference in trout flies, take Gordon's advice and "cast your fly with confidence."

Chapter 4
THE BERGDORF GOODMAN FLY

Theodore Gordon was a prophet as well as a prime mover and historian of fly-fishing. In 1902 he wrote: "We used No. 3 [flies] in 1885 and Mr. Henry P. Wells, in his well known work 'Fly Rods and Fly Tackle' recommended No. 2 for big trout. We will probably go to the other extreme now. Nothing but midges will do. We will have to take record fish on three-ounce rods and infinitesimal or imperceptible flies if we wish to be honored."

We have, of course, done just that, creating a new and delightful aspect of the sport on its margins, particularly in extending the extreme range on the small side. When Gordon foresaw the 3-ounce rod, he was using a 6½-ounce Leonard ("a poem") and a 10-ounce, 10-foot 3-inch English rod, which he never found fatiguing "although I am not a strong man." Lee Wulff in recent years has rendered Gordon's prediction conservative by taking large trout and thirty-pound salmon with a 6-foot, 1¾-ounce rod (now manufactured by Orvis to Wulff's specifications). Perhaps one day soon he will be discovered with just a reel in hand, threatening the definition of angling in *The Treatise of Fishing* as fishing with a rod, line, and hook. Likewise, Joe Brooks has been seen on a Montana spring creek scissoring a No. 22 Light Cahill down to imperceptibility; Sid Neff has a positive preference for No. 28's, smaller than the head of a tack, fashioned by his own hand; and Sparse Grey Hackle (*Fishless Days and Angling Nights*, 1971) reached Lord Grey's spiritual ideal by more or less the same route.

There may be a practical limit to this course, but there is no reason not to pursue it infinitely in imagination. Yet we have given so much attention

45

for some years to approaching the vanishing point that it might be time for a little plop fishing—nothing demoralizing; strictly fly. A start has been made by Joe Brooks—the Florida influence—who has raised big cutthroats on the Yellowstone with streamer flies, size 3/0; that is, four sizes larger than Wells's No. 2, the largest Gordon could muster out of experience or reading memory. But of course, a really new fly at the large end of the scale would have to be dry. There is nothing really new about a big wet or streamer except for patterns, and these have long been extravagantly explored to great advantage in the Northwest. Gordon's No. 3 and Wells's No. 2 would have been wet, as neither were familiar with dry-fly structure in 1885. Dan Bailey ties a Salmon Wulff No. 2 dry for Montanans, but even that must be considered within the convention of the unconventional West. We must go further, and for a starter I have a model to suggest based on a chance experience.

This is the Bergdorf Goodman Fly, whose name expresses its actual origin. Long enough ago to be called once upon a time, Dan Bailey lived in New York, taught physical science at Brooklyn College, and camped all summer on the Ausable. Bailey, like his streamside neighbor and friend, Lee Wulff (and like Gordon before them), had it in mind to spend his life fishing if he could find a viable way of doing it. The known way was to tie flies for a living, so he started tying at night after school. It was immediately apparent that he had the gift. But with the finest Quill Gordons in those Depression years selling at $1.50 a dozen, the prospect of subsistence was doubtful even in a wattled hut by the Madison. Bailey and Wulff therefore combined forces to open a school for amateur flytiers.

The schoolhouse was a room in back of Lee Chumley's restaurant in Greenwich Village; the rent was free—a side benefit that came with the price of dinner. With one prospective paying student, the school was in business. But as a class with two teachers and one student lacked educational balance, Bailey and Wulff engaged two shills, serving without pay, to fill it out. The latter were Ray Camp and this writer. The student was John Jay McCloy, a lawyer who had a job. After dinner the class was convoked at a round table, fur and feathers in the center, vises and other equipment in front of each member. A great deal of learning was imparted by the masters in a jovial fishing evening.

Thereafter memory of the school fails; in any event it did not solve the problem of Bailey's career. He turned to another venture, reluctantly bastardizing the art by tying some large dry flies destined, he hoped, not for the stream but for ladies' hats. He offered these first at $1, later, as demand improved, $2 each. The buyer, Bergdorf Goodman, made a little fashion out of them in 1937. But success put a strain on Bailey's resources of time, raising the specter of a career of digression. After tying about two hundred resplendent May flies the size of Luna moths, he quit, moved himself and his wife to Montana, and starved, except for trout, berries, duck, geese, deer, and antelope, and no more was seen of the Baileys in the East.

That spring, in a Catskill cabin which had been shared by the Baileys and McDonalds, I picked up a discarded hat of Mrs. Bailey's and found one of the fashion flies attached. I pulled it off and put it into a vest pocket to keep as a souvenir.

The place, still on New York maps, was a ghost town which was named Liebhardt owing to the fact that it had been inhabited by the Brown family, lumbermen, since the Civil War at least. It had been called Brownsville in its thriving days, but as there were two Brownsvilles in New York State, the postman asked the Browns if they would mind changing the name of the village. Although willing to oblige, they couldn't think of a new name. After considerable head scratching, one of the Browns asked the postman what his name was; he said Liebhardt, so they said let's call it Liebhardt.

One of Liebhardt's distinctions is a creek, formerly the source of power for the sawmill, that flows through the little valley there. We called it Liebhardt Creek. It is a small pocket stream, its average normal width about 20 feet, flowing out of High Point north of Kerhonksen, and it gave the best small-stream trout fishing I have known. At the abandoned sawmill was a 15-foot dam. In the spring the water came over wide and full, plunging into a deep pool with a complex structure resulting from immense sunken rocks alongside the mill. Ordinarily I would start at the mill and go up or down from there—fishing, say, down a mile or two wet and back up dry, and concluding the day in the twilight at the dam.

There, as the evening rise died out once in late June, I broke off my fly, a No. 14 spinner of a pattern I have forgotten, and stood hypnotized by the falling water and the suddenly flyless and seemingly fishless swirling currents. I reached for a cigarette and felt the big fly in my pocket. I took it out and looked it over: It was all black, at first glance something like a transmogrified Black Gnat. The Black-Gnat impression, however, was lost in its fan wings. Out West it might have been a variation on a Deer fly if the wings had sloped backwards. But the wings—black-dyed goose quill feathers from M. Schwartz & Son, New York millinery wholesalers—flared out, so the fly could be placed only in the fan-wing family. Inside and on top of the goose quills was a smaller pair of barred silver-grey Amherst pheasant breast feathers (like those on the Grey Ghost streamer). The body was wound black silk, spiraled with silver tinsel; the tail a few strands of saddle hackle, dyed black. The hackles, also black, were the largest fibers from the neck of the barnyard rooster. The hook was a long-shanked No. 1. But with the wings 1½ inches wide and soaring up 3 inches high, and the hackles spreading 1½ inches down, the total effect was that of a 3/0 fly, certainly the largest authentic dry fly I have ever

47

seen. (My powers of observation and memory are not this good. Recollection of the dressing many years later was assisted by the original flytier.) It felt like a small bird in my hand.

I had no inclination to fish this fly, but I was curious to see if it would float like an ordinary dry fly. I had not untied my leader, which was a 9-foot 3X, quite fine and hopelessly unsuited for such a large, heavy fly; but I didn't feel like changing leaders for the experiment and thought I could manage. I tied the fly on and in fact got it swinging well enough to cast it across the pool up in the corner where mill and dam met. It landed rather lopsidedly with a plop, but with the help of a couple of tugs, righted itself, sat up serenely on the water, and began drifting in an eddy. The dam exploded.

I tightened the line and could see its entire curve to a position two or three feet above the water, when it ended in the jaw of the largest brown trout I have ever seen in the East. He disappeared, came up again silhouetted against the mill wall, and in fisherman's time remained there in the half-light for many moons. He never again during this episode returned below the water but, seeming to forget his species, acted the rainbow with aerial work, balanced on his tail. At long last as I stood holding the bent rod, he went into a roll, spinning over and over under the waterfall across the dam to the deep near corner. With one lunge he went down, detached from me, his savage nose decorated with the Bergdorf Goodman Fly.

If this conveys an idea, I feel sure there is a fisherman around who can prove there's nothing new about it.

Chapter 5
GREEN DRAKE EYES

The tallest tale in fly-fishing is, as it should be, not about a fish but about a fly. Its name is the green drake. It is said to exist as an insect in nature, and so it does in the telling. The question, inescapable but never resolved, is whether the green drake is an imaginary being.

There is no ready approach to so ephemeral a subject. Allow me to begin again and say what may be safely said. The green drake is a name to conjure with in fly-fishing. I say *name* because, to avoid philosophic entanglement, I want to hold off a moment on what the name seems to stand for in insect life and artificial flies, and give a brief account of how the words "green drake" themselves have had a remarkable existence of their own in the angling universe.

We have been presented with three hundred years of talk about green drakes. As a reminder, I offer a small compilation of what has been said about the creature by some of our finest fishermen, from the river Dove in England in 1676 to Henry's Fork of the Snake in Idaho in 1971. These passages will establish the vision of the green drake in angling over time and on two continents.

The first recorded tribute to the green drake comes from Charles Cotton, our earliest known master of the art of the fly. His panegyric was given in the course of listing and describing sixty-five trout flies in the fifth (1676) edition of Walton's *The Compleat Angler*. "Of all these . . . very killing flies," he said, "none are fit to be compared with the [Green] Drake and the Stone Fly." Of the former, he said:

The [green] drake will mount steepleheight into the air, though he is to be found upon flags and grass too, and indeed everywhere high and low, near the river; there being so many of them in their season, as were they not a very inoffensive insect, would look like a plague; and these drakes . . . are taken by the fish to that incredible degree, that upon a calm day you shall see the still deeps continually all over circles by the fishes rising, who will gorge themselves with those flies, till they purge again out of their gills; and the trouts are at that time so lusty and strong, that one of eight, or ten inches long, will then more struggle, and tug, and more endanger your tackle, than one twice as big in winter. . . .

The green drake . . . is taken at all hours during his season, whilst there is any day upon the sky; and with a made fly, I once took, ten days after he was absolutely gone, in a cloudy day, after a shower, and in a whistling wind, five and thirty very great trouts and graylings betwixt five and eight of the clock in the evening, and had no less than five, or six flies with three good hairs apiece taken from me in despite of my heart, besides.

Step over a couple of centuries, during which the green drake thrived in Britain's and Ireland's waters and in the minds of fishermen, and open the book *An Angler's Hours* (published in 1905, but written some years earlier) by the editor-writer H. T. Sheringham. The title of Chapter 9 is "The Festival of the Green Drake." It begins:

To the angler who is modest in his desires the May-fly ["green drake" and "May fly" have now become synonymous in England] must ever be somewhat of a fearful joy. There is something uncanny about finding the trout in a well-fished stream, commonly epicurean of taste and cautious of habit, converted in the twinkling of an eye into omnivorous maniacs; and it is small wonder that the insect whose advent causes this remarkable change has sometimes been the object of invective as well as of panegyric, for there are many men who prefer a season of moderate (perhaps slight) sport to the "crowded hour of glorious life," which makes all after hours so dull and spiritless. And I am by no means sure that they are not right. . . . When small fly is plentiful enough to satisfy both angler and fish, a stream is sufficiently blessed and artificial excitements are not required.

But there is one aspect of the drake in which his value can hardly be overestimated. Many trout-streams in their lower reaches hold a quantity of coarse fish, whose influence on the trout is to make them large and few, and (for evil associations corrupt good manners) to render them indifferent to surface food. These waters in consequence become quite useless for legitimate fly-fishing except during the brief carnival of the May-fly. Then, and then only, has the angler a chance, for no trout, however large or addicted to minnows, can refrain from joining in the prevalent enthusiasm. And so you shall find a fish of five pounds feeding as eagerly as any troutling—ay, and catch him too if luck is with you, and then your happiness should be complete. Is not a great fish like that taken fairly with the fly worth a basket filled never so full with pounders? And are there not on the records of most streams inscribed the tales of trout taken with the May-fly of five, six, and even more, incredibly more, pounds?

In the United States in the 1930's, Preston Jennings (*A Book of Trout Flies*, 1935) wrote:

Very often the largest fish in the stream will surface-feed while the Green Drake is on the water in the daytime, and that is the reason why the Green Drake holds such an important place in the fly-fisher's list of flies, as these monsters, which every fly-fisher dreams of sometime catching, usually confine their activities to minnow chasing or feeding at night.

Art Flick (*Streamside Guide*, 1947):

On the Brodhead Creek in Pennsylvania, I am told by angling friends, it [the green drake] is by far the most important fly of the entire season, and when it is on the water all the really big fish in the stream come to life.

Ernest G. Schwiebert, Jr. (*Matching the Hatch*):

The almost unbelievable cloud of naturals, and the spectacular evening rises of Green Drake time, make some of the most exciting fishing of the year. And it is a time when the chunky old browns that rarely fall to anything but minnows or night crawlers can be deceived with the dry fly. No angler should miss this hatch.

Vince Marinaro (*A Modern Dry-Fly Code*) describes its effect upon anglers:

Near the end of May a great outcry is heard; it travels to all parts of the land by telephone, by mail, by telegraph, by word of mouth, and perhaps by mental telepathy, and it reaches every fly-fisherman. . . . By rail, by motor, by airplane, and on foot the great trek begins, from every hamlet and village, town and city, converging on the big northern limestone streams—Penn's Creek, Spring Creek, Spruce Creek, Fishing Creek—from all directions north, south, east, and west, drawn irresistibly by this Pied Piper of the insect world. Anything fabricated out of the imagination would not surpass the fantasy of Green Drake time.

QUILL GORDON

Doug Swisher and Carl Richards (*Selective Trout*, 1971) observed that among Eastern anglers, "Just the sight of one Green Drake struggling on the surface of a placid pool is enough to quicken the heartbeat and bring about a feeling of great anticipation." In their fine book they also mention a "Western Green Drake," a subject which they further develop in an article in *Fly Fisherman* magazine (July 1971):

Spring in the western mountains comes in June and with it comes the spectacular Green Drake hatch. This is the season when everything blooms, and the rivers are no exception. If there is a more exciting emergence than this large mayfly we have never fished it. . . . The hatch usually starts with a few flies coming sporadically from about 10:30 a.m. to 1:00 p.m. This phenomenon lasts from three to five days and fine fish are on the cruise for the occasional dun. Then suddenly the river erupts with drifting duns. This period of great activity is relatively short, lasting only three or four days, then tapers off suddenly and reverts to scattered flies in the morning for about a week. Even during the later period, surprisingly large fish seem to be on the lookout for the widely spaced emergers, taking the fly with a deep, loud slurp. However, the three or four days during the middle period are the dry fly fisherman's dream. Flies seem to cover every square foot of water and all the fish present will feed voraciously. Rainbows of two or three pounds are the average and eight-pounders are not unheard of.

This report set off a veritable gold rush to Henry's Fork of the Snake below Last Chance, Idaho, a clear-water stream mentioned by the authors as a prospect for the great hatch.

In sum these writers, whose enthusiasm for the subject is characteristic of most angling writers, maintain that the green drake is supreme among the insects of interest to trout and trout fishermen. In England in the seventeenth century this fly gave Cotton his best fishing; for Sheringham in the late nineteenth and early twentieth centuries the hatch was a "festival." In the United States on various streams in the twentieth century it is "the most important fly," "produces the most exciting fishing," and acts as a magnet on most anglers. All agree on its unique fatal attraction for very big fish which on other occasions seldom take an artificial fly modeled on an insect.

But that the green drake has remarkable powers is only the beginning of the story. There is, so to speak, even bigger game here; for not all the insects celebrated in the passages above as green drakes are the same insect. In all fairness let me say that the modern authorities I have cited are not unaware that there is more than one green drake. To my knowledge or according to my lights, however, they have not come to terms with

TROUT AND SALMON FLIES, OLD AND NEW

Two fine artists, John Atherton and John Langley Howard, painted the trout and salmon flies shown on these pages from models supplied by the author and the noted fisheries biologist and angler, Dwight Webster. The paintings, widely regarded as modern classics of angling, have been unavailable for a long time.

The models for Howard's paintings were developed conceptually from the original fifteenth-century text of *The Treatise of Fishing with an Angle*. Dwight Webster analyzed these texts, tied the flies, and collaborated with the author in writing the supporting text in Chapter 11. Howard himself studied the text of the *Treatise* carefully, especially with regard to the hooks, before picking up his paint brush. The result is the only painting of this earliest set of modern trout flies printed with an accompanying textual support.

John Atherton painted, fished, and wrote about fishing *(The Fly and the Fish)* with equal passion and precision, and the author was honored to be his friend, occasional fishing companion, and collaborator. He was a perfectionist in art and life. His personal style was crisp and yet warmly interactive. He was always a delight to be with at home and on the stream—generous, kind, and always surprising. He was as accurate and magical in his wit as in his painting. The flies from his brush are elegant in precision, hard-edged in color where the classic salmon flies and fancy trout flies demand it, and soft and subtle where the trout flies representative of nature invite it.

Atherton's models for the natural flies were caught by Dwight Webster in and near a stream in the woods around Ithaca, New York, and transported live by him to Atherton's house and studio on the Battenkill River in Vermont. The artificial trout flies that served as Atherton's models were tied at the author's request by some of the most noted flytiers of this century: Dan Bailey, Ray Bergman, Herman Christian, Reub Cross, Ken Cooper, Elsie Darbee, Harry Darbee, Walt Dette, Jim Deren, Elizabeth Greig, Don Martinez, Ed Sens, Roy Steenrod, and Paul Young. The author took the dressing for Gordon's Bubblepuppy—a sport—from the *Fishing Gazette* (London), where the editor, R. B. Marston, had described it in fine detail upon receiving it from Gordon in the spring of 1903. Elizabeth Greig had her guiding hand on the author's elbow when he tied it many years later. All together, the patterns here are fairly representative of the best-known trout flies in the United States.

Atherton's models for the salmon flies were collected by the author from numerous skilled amateurs and professionals in the United States, Canada, and England. They include all styles known at the time and one of the earliest dry flies for salmon, created by Gordon in 1903. These flies are discussed in Chapter 10.

THE BERNERS TROUT FLIES

Tied by Dwight A. Webster—Painted by John Langley Howard

DUN FLY (March)

First Choice

Alternative One

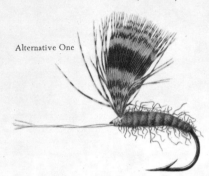

Alternative Two

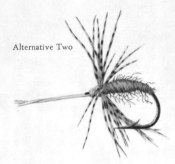

The donne flye the body of the donne woll & the wyngis of the pertryche

ANOTHER DUN FLY (March)

A nother doone flye. the body of blacke woll: the wynges of the blackyst drake: and the Jay und the wynge & under the tayle.

THE STONE FLY

(April)

The stone flye. the body of blacke wull: & yelowe under the wynge. and under the tayle & the wynges of the drake.

RUDDY FLY (May)

First Choice

Alternative One

Alternative Two

In the begynnynge of May a good flye. the body of roddyd wull and lappid abowte wyth blacke sylke: the wynges of the drake & of the redde capons hakyll.

THE YELLOW FLY (May)

Alternative One

First Choice

Alternative Two

The yelow flye. the body of yelow
wull: the wynges of the redde cocke
hakyll & of the drake lyttyd yelow.

THE BLACK LEAPER (May)

First Choice

Alternative

The blacke louper. the body of blacke wull & lappyd abowte wyth the
herle of y^e pecok tayle: & the wynges of y^e redde capon wt a blewe heed.

DUN CUT (June)

The donne cutte: the body of blacke wull &
a yelow lyste after eyther syde: the wynges
of the bosarde bounde on with barkyd hempe.

MAURE FLY (June)

The maure flye. the body of dolke wull the wynges of the blackest mayle of the wylde drake.

TANDY FLY (June)

The tandy flye at saynt Wylllyams daye. the body of tandy wull & the wynges contrary eyther ayenst other of the whitest mayle of ye wylde drake.

WASP FLY (July)

First Choice

Alternative (down wing)

The waspe flye. the body of blacke wull & lappid abowte wt yelow threde: the winges of the bosarde.

SHELL FLY (July)

First Choice

Alternative

The shell flye at saynt Thomas daye. the body of grene wull & lappyd abowte wyth the herle of the pecoks tayle: wynges of the bosarde.

DRAKE FLY (August)

The drake flye. the body of blacke wull & lappyd abowte wyth black sylke: wynges of the mayle of the blacke drake with a blacke heed.

Seth Green

Scarlet Ibis

Montreal

Rio Grande King

Parmachene Belle

Reub Wood

FANCY WET FLIES
• American and English

Established "fancy" flies, imitative of no particular species or group, but of the fly in general, tied by Elizabeth Greig, N.Y.C., First Lady of U.S. flytying.

Wickham's Fancy

Butcher

Silver Doctor

Professor

Grizzly King

Alexander

WESTERN FLIES

Many western U.S. flytiers defy tradition with new materials and bizarre forms, as in these typical gay innovations.

Buddy Mite,
Pott's Hair Fly

Bucktail Caddis,
Oregon Fly

Black Woolly-Worm
by Don Martinez,
W. Yellowstone, Mont.

Picket Pin (Bailey Version)
Originated by Jack Boehme,
Missoula, Mont.

Squirrel Tail Fly
Rocky Mountain Pattern

Joe's Hopper, by Dan Bailey,
Livingston, Mont.

Coachman—Wet
(American)

Leadwing
Coachman—Wet

Royal Coachman—Wet
(Split-Wing)

Coachman—Wet
(English)

California Coachman—Wet
(Split-Wing)

Variations on the COACHMAN

Most famous of all trout flies is the Coachman, originated by Tom Bosworth, who drove Queen Victoria's coach. The original and variations here are by the crack Montanan, Dan Bailey.

Royal Coachman—Dry
(Standard)

Daniel's
Coachman—Dry

Fan-Wing Royal
Coachman—Dry

Royal Wulff
Coachman

Bucktail Royal
Coachman

THE MAYFLY

Most delectable of the trout's natural foods, model of most artificial flies, it starts as an underwater nymph, hatches into a winged dun, dies a spinner.

Isonychia sadleri
Nympth (Mature)

Hexagenia recurvata
Male Dun

Hexagenia recurvata
Male Spinner

Isonychia sadleri
Female Dun

Isonychia sadleri
Female Spinner

Stenonema proximum
Female Dun

Stenonema proximum
Female Spinner

MAYFLIES
• Natural and Artificial

Artificial flies usually "imitate" natural species. But the treatment is impressionistic, as shown here by Reub Cross of Lew Beach, N.Y., dean of U.S. flytiers, and Walt Dette of Roscoe, N.Y., master of precision tying.

Ephemera guttulata
Female Spinner

Coffin Fly
by Reub Cross

Stenonema vicarium
Female Dun

March Brown
by Walt Dette

WET FLY AND DRY FLY

The difference in form between the wet fly (fished under the water) and the dry fly (fished on the surface) is shown here by Harry Darbee, superb flytier of Beaverkill, N.Y.

Iron Blue Dun—Wet

Iron Blue Dun—Dry

Cross Special
REUB CROSS
by Reub Cross

Quill Gordon
T. GORDON
by Reub Cross

Light Cahill
T. GORDON
by Walt Dette

Blue Dun
by Herman Christian
Neversink, N.Y.

Hendrickson (R. STEENROD)
by Roy Steenrod, Liberty, N.Y.

Pink Lady (G. LA BRANCHE)
by Ed Sens, N.Y.C.

IMITATION DRY FLIES

These are well-known American flies, by celebrated U.S. flytiers. The originators, when known, are in capitals.

Fifty Degrees
JIM DEREN
by Jim Deren, N.Y.C.

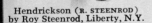

Black Gnat
by Mrs. Harry Darbee

Widdicombe No. 1
by Paul Young
Detroit, Mich.

Adams (L. HALLADAY)
by Ken Cooper
Detroit, Mich.

Lady Beaverkill
by Mrs. Walt Dette

R. B. Fox
by Ray Bergman
Nyack, N.Y.

STANDARD

The salmon flies on this page, with few exceptions, were observed by the author in actual use when he made a tour of the salmon rivers of eastern Canada. Each is popular on certain streams. Some are indigenous, but most of the standard patterns originated in the British Isles during the past century.

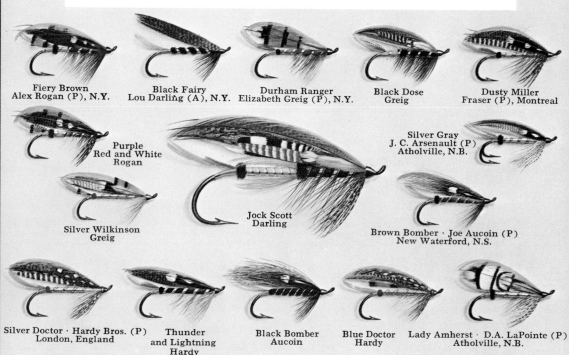

Fiery Brown
Alex Rogan (P), N.Y.

Black Fairy
Lou Darling (A), N.Y.

Durham Ranger
Elizabeth Greig (P), N.Y.

Black Dose
Greig

Dusty Miller
Fraser (P), Montreal

Purple
Red and White
Rogan

Silver Wilkinson
Greig

Jock Scott
Darling

Silver Gray
J. C. Arsenault (P)
Atholville, N.B.

Brown Bomber · Joe Aucoin (P)
New Waterford, N.S.

Silver Doctor · Hardy Bros. (P)
London, England

Thunder
and Lightning
Hardy

Black Bomber
Aucoin

Blue Doctor
Hardy

Lady Amherst · D.A. LaPointe (P)
Atholville, N.B.

HAIR

Celebrated by some, scorned by others, big, bushy salmon hair flies—derived from Rocky Mountain trout hair flies—have had a great vogue on the Restigouche River and, in sparser form, on the Margaree. The rivers where each is most popular are indicated in parentheses.

Silver Betsy (Restigouche)
Rogan

The Park (Margaree)
Dr. Edwards Park (A), Baltimore, Md.

Teagle Bee (Restigouche)
Rogan

The Rat (Canadian rivers)
Rogan

Red Abbey (Restigouche)
Rogan

Ross Special (Margaree)
Aucoin

Cosseboom (Canadian rivers)
John Cosseboom (A)

Nepisiquit Gray (Nepisiquit)
LaPointe

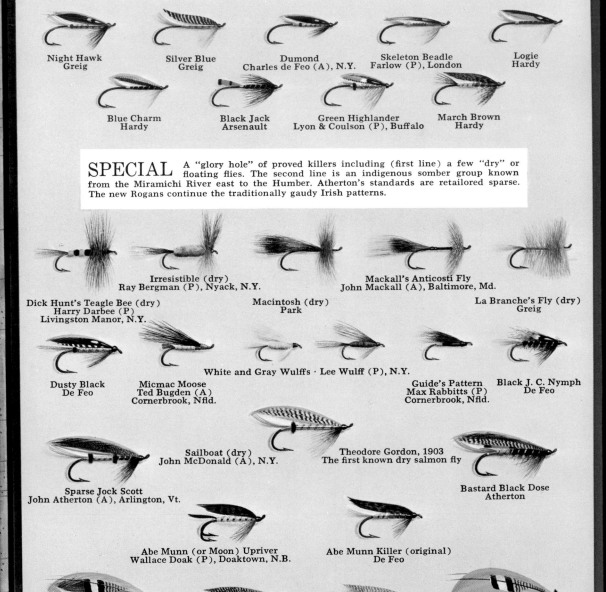

LOW WATER

A modern development in the game is the low-water, summer fly with an abbreviated dressing on a long, slender hook. It is often fished at or near the surface rather than sunk in traditional fashion—a new tactic thought by some to produce a more artful and interesting, though difficult, sport.

Night Hawk
Greig

Silver Blue
Greig

Dumond
Charles de Feo (A), N.Y.

Skeleton Beadle
Farlow (P), London

Logie
Hardy

Blue Charm
Hardy

Black Jack
Arsenault

Green Highlander
Lyon & Coulson (P), Buffalo

March Brown
Hardy

SPECIAL

A "glory hole" of proved killers including (first line) a few "dry" or floating flies. The second line is an indigenous somber group known from the Miramichi River east to the Humber. Atherton's standards are retailored sparse. The new Rogans continue the traditionally gaudy Irish patterns.

Irresistible (dry)
Ray Bergman (P), Nyack, N.Y.

Mackall's Anticosti Fly
John Mackall (A), Baltimore, Md.

Dick Hunt's Teagle Bee (dry)
Harry Darbee (P)
Livingston Manor, N.Y.

Macintosh (dry)
Park

La Branche's Fly (dry)
Greig

White and Gray Wulffs · Lee Wulff (P), N.Y.

Dusty Black
De Feo

Micmac Moose
Ted Bugden (A)
Cornerbrook, Nfld.

Guide's Pattern
Max Rabbitts (P)
Cornerbrook, Nfld.

Black J. C. Nymph
De Feo

Sailboat (dry)
John McDonald (A), N.Y.

Theodore Gordon, 1903
The first known dry salmon fly

Sparse Jock Scott
John Atherton (A), Arlington, Vt.

Bastard Black Dose
Atherton

Abe Munn (or Moon) Upriver
Wallace Doak (P), Doaktown, N.B.

Abe Munn Killer (original)
De Feo

Royal Rogan Gray Ghost
Rogan

Hollender's Scotch & Soda
De Feo

Oriole
Ira Gruber (A)

Golden Rogan
Rogan

this phenomenon. I shall try to set forth the main features of the mystery and to offer a possible resolution.

To clear a few things out of the way first, I must further deepen the mystery. In part we have here a phenomenon of words, so that all names must be clarified as well as they can be. In England the term *May fly* is reserved exclusively for the green drake, whereas in the United States it stands for all up-winged water-bred insects (grouped in science as Ephemeroptera). For simplicity of language I shall stick strictly to the American usage, except when quoting English writers. It is imperative also to take note of the four stages in the life of the May fly, which anglers have long recognized in their own language: the egg, which the female deposits in the water and which sinks to the bottom; the nymph, which hatches on the bottom and lives there for a year or so; the dark dun, which emerges from the water in the first stage of its winged life; and the bright spinner into which the dun is transformed a few hours to a day or so after it leaves the water.

In the passages quoted earlier, the question of these stages in the life of the green drake did not arise, and it is here that the mystery thickens a bit. When the green drake dun in due ephemeral time molts and becomes a spinner, further events of note take place. In England the female pales and becomes the grey drake, known all the way back to Cotton; the male, paling less, becomes the black drake. The great pioneer angler-entomologist, Alfred Ronalds (*The Fly Fisher's Entomology*), reported in 1836 that the English black drake was known also as the death drake, in the belief that it killed the female (grey drake). In the United States, both sexes of the spinner of the green drake likewise become very pale, and they are known as the coffin fly. The death drake and the coffin fly, with their common paleness, form another verbal bond between the green drakes of Britain-Ireland and the United States. But the (false) legend of the death drake has disappeared, and the sobriquet coffin fly is usually taken as referring to the ghostly hue of the green drake spinners (I am tempted to add: and to the intimation of their imminent end in a watery grave). All May flies in their spinner stage mate in the air in a "dance of death" and soon thereafter die in the water. The modern master of the early years of this century in England, G. E. M. Skues (*Silk, Fur and Feather*, 1950), describes this critical event: "After laying her eggs the female [green drake spinner] falls in the water in the throes of dissolution, usually in late evening. . . . In this stage she will at times bring out all the big old cannibal trout, which rarely take fly at any other time." So it is with the coffin fly in the United States. Thus the green drake is all one story even though, as I have said, there is more than one insect here. Indeed, as I shall now show, five different May flies are represented in the story of the green drake.

QUILL GORDON

For beauty of language, anglers are the insect-namers par excellence—especially in England, where they have traditionally chosen some visual aspect of an insect, such as blue-winged olive, yellow evening dun, pale watery spinner, or green drake, as the name both of the natural and its corresponding artificial. Although such designations are not precisely differentiating, they provide a link to the perception of the natural insect which is lost in the American custom of naming flies after their creators. American anglers consequently often work backwards from the dressing of an artificial fly to the natural insect it represents. But for system, precision, and universal nomenclature (allowing even in these matters for some degree of subjectivity), the best namers of insects are the entomologists. One must turn to them for help in unraveling the mystery of the green drake. If the reader can stand a brush with entomology—the relatively young discipline that deals with the class of animals, most numerous in the kingdom, called *Insecta*—I think I can demonstrate that the green drake is the subject of the tallest tale in fishing.

Anglers describe insects mainly by their color, size, and general shape—characteristics that are considered relatively superficial by entomologists, who classify by structural detail and other taxonomic features, such as the segments of the body and veins of the wing. Entomologists divide all insects into twenty-four orders. Even the casual fly-fisherman has no trouble recognizing which of these orders he is interested in, namely May flies (Ephemeroptera), stone flies (Plecoptera), caddis flies (Trichoptera), true flies, such as houseflies and midges (Diptera), alderflies (Neuroptera), and a few others such as beetles (Coleoptera) and grasshoppers (Orthoptera). The angler is chiefly concerned with the first three, all of which are water-bred, and of these the May fly is paramount. It accounts for a good deal of the trout's diet; it is the insect most often seen emerging from the water in the daytime; and it is the model for most artificial flies.

Entomologists divide each of their twenty-four orders of insects into subgroups called families, the families in turn into genera, and the genera into species—the ultimate entomological unit of insect life. Moreover, they have given internationally accepted Latin names to each category and unit in the system, which itself is constantly being enlarged and revised by new discoveries. It appears to be an established fact, however, that only forty-seven species of Ephemeroptera exist in Britain and Ireland. In North America, on the other hand, more than five hundred species have been identified, and field work on them is far from complete—which suggests that American fly-fishermen have vast prospects ahead for becoming better acquainted with their favorite order, the May fly, to which our subject, the green drake, belongs.

The green drakes described in this chapter include, in entomological terms, five distinct species belonging to two different genera and two different families. Why, out of hundreds of identified species of May flies (Ephemeroptera) belonging to many families and genera, have anglers singled out and given a common name to these five? Furthermore, why have these five different insects had the same remarkable effects upon both fish and fishermen? Have we here the elements of a fly-fishing myth? Do fishermen have green drake eyes?

It is time for an angler's description of a green drake. Because he launched the green drake on its fabulous career by celebrating it in the world's most popular fishing book, I turn back to Cotton:

> The green drake never discloses from his husk, till he be first there grown to full maturity, body, wings, and all, and then he creeps out of his cell, but with his wings so crimped, and ruffled, by being pressed together in that narrow room, that they are for some hours totally useless to him,[1] by which means he is compelled either to creep upon the flags, sedges, and blades of grass (if his first rising from the bottom of the water be near the banks of the river) till the air, and sun, stiffen and smooth them; or if his first appearance above water happen to be in the middle, he then lies upon the surface of the water like a ship at hull (for his feet are totally useless to him there, and he cannot creep upon the water as the stone fly can) until his wings have got stiffness to fly with, if by some trout or grayling he be not taken in the interim (which ten to one he is), and then his wings stand high, and closed exact upon his back, like the butterfly, and his motion in flying is the same. His body is in some of a paler, in others of a darker yellow (for they are not all exactly of a color) ribbed with rows of green, long, slender, and growing sharp towards the tail, at the end of which he has three long small whisks of a very dark color, almost black, and his tail turns up towards his back like a mallard, from whence, questionless, he has his name of the green drake. . . .
>
> I am now to tell you next, how to make an artificial fly, that will so perfectly resemble him, as to be taken in a rough windy day, when no flies can lie upon the water; nor are to be found about the banks and sides of the river, to a wonder, and with which you shall certainly kill the best trout and grayling in the river.
>
> The artificial Green Drake then is made upon a large hook, the dubbing, camel's hair, bright bear's hair, the soft down that is combed from a hog's bristles, and yellow camlet well mixed together, the body long, and ribbed about with green silk, or rather yellow waxed with green wax, the whisks of the tail of the long hairs of sables, or fitchet, and the wings of the white-grey feather of a mallard, dyed yellow.

1. Cotton seems to be in error here, unless May flies behaved differently in the seventeenth century. I know no other record of their taking *hours* to get into flight. The entomologist Justin W. Leonard observes (in a letter to the author) that May flies in the United States usually take a few seconds up to a maximum of a minute or so to start their wings functioning. Dragonflies, however, may need an hour or more.

That was Cotton's green drake dun, real and artificial, with a hint as to the origin of its name. Now for the transformation of this insect—indubitably the same one—into a spinner. Cotton says:

> I should now come next to the stone fly, but there is another gentleman in my way: that must of necessity come in between, and that is the gray drake, which in all shapes and dimensions is perfectly the same with the other, but quite almost of another color, being of a paler, and more livid yellow, and green, and ribbed with black quite down his body, with black shining wings, and so diaphanous and tender, cobweb-like, that they are of no manner of use for dapping; but come in, and are taken after the green drake, and in an artificial fly kill very well, which fly is thus made: the dubbing of the down of a hog's bristles, and black spaniel's fur mixed, and ribbed down the body with black silk, the whisks of the hairs of the beard of a black cat, and the wings of the black-grey feather of a mallard.

I shall make no effort to trace the course of the green drake through English history. Ronalds (1836) identifies the green drake as belonging to the genus *Ephemera* and the species *vulgata*, which would now be written in brief *E. vulgata*. Skip a century to the contemporary English angler-entomologist J. R. Harris (*An Angler's Entomology*, 1952) and you find that three species of green drake, *E. vulgata*, *E. lineata*, and *E. danica*, have been sorted out. These are the only species of *Ephemera* in Britain and Ireland. The most common today is *E. danica*.[2]

Harris describes the female dun of this species ("male very similar but smaller and usually duller in color"):

> *Wings:* Variable but usually faintly green or yellowish-green; several brown marks near the middle of the wing; veins blackish.
> *Thorax:* Dorsum, brownish-black; venter and sides, olive varied with brown.
> *Legs:* Dark yellowish-olive.
> *Abdomen:* Faintly yellowish, cream or oliveaceous with a series of brown markings which become predominant on the dorsal surface of the posterior 3 or 4 segments.
> *Tails:* Black.
> *Transmitted light:* Wings faintly yellowish-green; body pale yellowish becoming brownish in the last 2 segments; tails brown-black.
> *General appearance:* A very large yellowish-bodied fly with grey-

2. Leonard in his letter also identifies Cotton's green drake as *E. danica*. Neither "green drake" nor "May fly" appears in the language of the fifteenth-century *Treatise of Fishing with an Angle*. However, conjectures on the presence of *E. danica* among the *treatise* flies will be found in Chapter 11.

green or faintly yellowish-green wings lightly mottled with brownish; three tails.

This *E. danica* green drake is "slightly paler and perhaps more greenish coloured in the wing than *E. vulgata,*" says Harris, and is also distinguished by the abdomen, which has a different color and different markings. Of the rare *E. lineata,* Harris remarks only that it "closely resembles" the *E. vulgata* in color and size. All of them are relatively large May flies (Ephemeroptera).

Harris gives some curious information about the English green drake. Where pollution has not destroyed it, he says, it is "conducive to some of the best fishing of the year"; but it is not the most common of the Ephemeroptera in England. That distinction appears to belong to the large dark olive (*Baetis rhodani*) or the blue-winged olive (*Ephemerella ignita*). Nevertheless, the long-standing reputation of the green drake is operational among flytiers. In the number of available patterns, the artificial Green Drake has a claim on being No. 1 in England.

How the green drake crossed the Atlantic and became still another species in the eastern part of the United States, I do not know. J. J. Brown (*The American Angler's Guide*) described an artificial Green Drake, probably of English origin, in 1845, and said that the natural appeared on the water in May and June "in such vast numbers that the trout become glutted with them, and grow fat upon their good living." Henry William Herbert (*Supplement to Frank Forester's Fish and Fishing of the United States,* 1850) was familiar with the reputation of the green drake in England and Ireland. He writes of a "green drake month" there during which the trout reject every other kind of insect. He says, "At no period of the Trout season are the fish so powerful, vigorous, and fine flavored." But according to him, the green drake is not an American insect. He was puzzled that the English artificial was a killing fly in the United States, and concluded that the opponents of imitation-fly theory might be right.

When I first fished fly in the 1930's, the green drake in the eastern part of the United States had been identified as *Ephemera guttulata* (family Ephemeridae), and its reputation—equaling that of the English species—had been established. It was widely known as the most sensational hatch of all known May flies.

I have been in doubt about which of the many American authorities to call upon for a description of *Ephemera guttulata,* and I choose Swisher and Richards (*Selective Trout,* 1971) because theirs is the most recent and suitably cryptic for the occasion (washing out, among other things, distinctions between male and female), and because these authors loom large in the story ahead. First the dun. They describe the body as "creamy yellow with brownish markings"; the wings, "light gray with distinct olive cast and

57

brown mottlings"; the tails, "3, dark brownish-olive"; and the legs, "creamish with brownish markings." The spinner: body, "light cream, brown markings on thorax"; wings, "hyaline, heavily mottled with dark brown markings"; tails, "3, brown"; legs, "yellowish, forelegs brown." (This description does not correspond in all particulars with Jennings's, but Marinaro has pointed out that "there is a marked difference in the color of specimens [of green drakes] from different streams.")

Since English and American green drakes have apparent similarities and are all of the same genus, one might be inclined to make out the case that the genus *Ephemera* explains the green drake phenomenon. Several objections preclude this thesis, but it is plausible at first sight. A few of the most striking differences between May flies are evident in the nymphs: some burrow and some do not, and they have different body structures that determine such different ways of life on the bottom of the stream. The genus *Ephemera*, for example, is a burrower, with strong forelegs and a couple of tusklike instruments for digging. This characteristic has much to do with the kind of water the *Ephemera* inhabit: they need the soft yet firm mud of lakes or slow-flowing streams. The features of the winged stage of the *Ephemera* are also distinctive. J. W. and F. A. Leonard, in one of the most beautiful and instructive little books ever produced on angling entomology, a model for regional work (*Mayflies of Michigan Trout Streams*, 1962), give a professional summary of this genus: "Moderate to large in size. . . . Both subimago and imago have prominently spotted wings. . . . This heavy spotting serves to separate adults of the genus *Ephemera* from [other genera]. . . . A middle tail as long as the outer tails separates adults of *Ephemera* from those of [others]."

It could be that the middle tail is what gets the trout, but the more obvious attractive feature is size. Anglers, as we have seen, associate the large size of the green drake with the large fish it brings up. But here the trouble begins. At least two other species of the genus *Ephemera* do not produce such notable effects and are not called green drakes. The Leonards found no green drakes in Michigan, but they did find two species of *Ephemera*, one of which, *Ephemera simulans* (called the brown drake by anglers), inhabits trout streams (the other, *Ephemera varia,* is found in other waters). The brown drake dun has the now familiar appearance: "Wings olive, heavily spotted with dark brown; body chiefly dark brown, suffused with olive." But only modest angling claims are made for this delectation: it merely "whets the appetite of the larger fish for the 'caddis hatch' to come."

This observation introduces an even more formidable difficulty into the *Ephemera* thesis. For the *Ephemera,* to which our four present green drakes belong, is not the largest of the May flies. "Caddis hatch" is a misnomer (apparently confined to Michigan) for the May fly *Hexagenia limbata,* a much larger insect than the brown drake and by far the most sensational May fly in Michigan. Indeed, according to the distinguished American entomologist-angler of a generation ago, Paul R. Needham (*Trout Streams,* 1940), the whole genus *Hexagenia* is larger than the genus *Ephemera.*

Let us say, nevertheless, that in the genus *Ephemera* a thread of connection has been established between the idea and the observed reality of the green drake. How then is one to accommodate the Western green drake in this Platonic ideal? The issue cannot be avoided. Swisher and Richards report: "If there is a more exciting emergence than this large mayfly we have never fished it." Here then in the chronicles of angling is the supreme insect, the archetype of all green drakes. Certainly, too, it is the greenest of all green drakes. The authors describe it:

> Freshly hatched duns have bright green bodies with light yellow-olive rings and slight, dark brownish-green markings on the back. The bodies very quickly change color, darkening greatly. Only a few minutes later they acquire a dark brown appearance with slightly lighter rings. The fish, of course, prefer the color of the freshly hatched subimago. Legs are light olive-yellow with a few darker bands, and wings are very dark slate. Tails are light olive with dark bands, and rather short.

They identify it: *Ephemerella grandis.*

The thread, for whatever it was worth, is gone. Here is not only a different species but also a different genus and a different family.[3] The only thing the Western green drake has in common entomologically with the others is their insect order, Ephemeroptera (May flies). Altogether we now have five distinct species, two genera, and two families united by the name green drake and, above all, by the close similarity in the stories told about them by anglers.

Assume it is significant that green drakes are relatively large May flies, presenting large morsels for large fish. But we have already seen that

---

3. The family is the Ephemerellidae. Schwiebert identified an *Ephemerella grandis* on Western streams in the 1950's, ranking it as "perhaps the most important insect of the season" on many of them. But the description is not the same as that given by Swisher and Richards, and their hatching calendars differ. The *Ephemerella grandis* of Swisher and Richards appears only in May and June (varying by region, weather, and altitude). Schwiebert's appears only in July, August, and early September (likewise varying by region, weather, and altitude). Schwiebert places his in the "family Baetidae," in accordance with the then prevailing practice of taxonomy. When Schwiebert was writing, most authorities placed the Ephemerellidae as a subfamily of Baetidae. The Ephemerellidae have since been given full family status. Schwiebert does not call it a green drake or give any common name; he says, "The Dark Great Red Quill imitates the male dun in a size 10. The Great Red Quill imitates the females in the same size." Swisher and Richards recommend an artificial "Paradrake" of their own pattern.

this will not resolve the question, as there are even larger May flies which anglers do not include among the green drakes. This difficulty can now be quantified. Swisher and Richards give the size of the Western green drake as 14 to 16 mm. They give the size of the Eastern green drake (*E. guttalata*) as 18 to 22 mm. The Leonards give the size of the *Hexagenia limbata* of Michigan as 18 to 30 mm. Thus the largest Western green drake is smaller than the smallest *H. limbata;* the largest *H. limbata* is about twice the size of the largest Western green drake, and the Eastern green drake falls in between. If we try the tack, adopted by many anglers, that the name "drake" belongs to all fairly large artificial May flies, we are still far from a solution, for drake is not *green* drake. And if we try uniting all green drakes by their shade of green, we are up against the difficulty that the duns of other species, and especially many of the genus *Stenonema* (family Heptageniidae) are also characteristically green, and none of them are green drakes. As a last resort, it might be asserted that green drakes are the large May flies that are *widely* taken by the trout. But that begs the question; we are back where we started.

Since fly-fishing is a fairly precise affair, one might think that all this should be set straight by having official bodies stabilize the common names of trout-stream insects, as they have those of fishes. But no. The linguistic tendencies of fishermen would happily outwit any formal lexicography, and it would also miss the point.

Until a more satisfactory solution is offered, consider the green drake as the angler's myth. Grant that a few anglers have not fished within the myth. In England about the middle of the nineteenth century, W. C. Stewart, who made the case for upstream fishing, wrote:

> We think it just possible that when a large fly, such as the green drake, remains a long time on the water, trout may recognize it, and when the waters are dark coloured and there is a strong breeze of wind, take an imitation of it more readily than any other. But in our own experience we have never found this to be the case; and though we have frequently tried this fly—so celebrated on English streams—we have never found it nearly so deadly as our usual flies, even when the water was coloured; and in clear water it failed entirely, as all large flies will, for the obvious reason that their size enables the trout to detect their artificial character.

Among Americans, I find no mention of the green drake by Theodore Gordon (an observation that may be corrected by a more perceptive reader). Sparse Grey Hackle writes (in a letter to the author): "I've never bothered about the Green Drake [*E. guttulata*] because it hatches a few at a time all day long, and particularly on limestone streams there aren't enough of them on the surface any time to start a good rise." Marinaro was bemused enough by it to participate in projects to transplant green drakes (*E. guttulata*) from one stream to another. Consequently he witnessed many hatches of the insect, whose powers he respected: "And I was always ready to fish as well as collect; and I am struck, upon reflection, with the realization that the fishing has been exceedingly poor with this insect."[4]

But a myth is not shattered by a few skeptics. Nor is it upset by realities. I do not doubt the direct observation of Cotton (except in the one detail noted) and the other authorities cited here. The issue lies in the connection made between their observations. Myths contain meaning, and the repository of the meaning of the green drake is the *words* green drake.

I leave the linguistic interpretation of these magical words to others and pursue a different route to the same end. If the green drake cannot be fitted into the categories of entomology, if not all anglers have seen the dream come true, the attraction of its myth still endures. Fly-fishermen on inland waters have chosen a closed sphere of beautiful objects: stream, woods, the dainty trout, and the winged May fly—fragile, ephemeral, with curved segmented body, translucent wings held upright, arched forelegs held out forward, slender legs, either two or three tails sweeping upward, all in combinations of subtle colors. Fishing fly is a delicate sport. An insect is seen emerging from the water or returning to it. The fish are rising. The fly is chosen—the game begins. The cast. Uncertainty. Suspense. Difficulty. The trout too is wary and selective. In nature, several species of May fly emerge. Which one is the trout taking? Should I match the hatch or oppose it? Decision. At last, perhaps, a rise to the fly. But now and then the scene is different. The trout go mad. Or are remembered as going mad, or are imagined. . . . Why? There must be out there among all the May flies one that makes the trout go mad. The fisherman goes mad and sees "green drakes."

I have seen green drakes. I saw them once. It was in June 1937, when I had fly-fished for only a couple of years. I wrote about them then and later published the story (*Town and Country*, May 1939). Here is what I wrote:

For a few months last season, I lived beside a small trout stream in the woods near Accord, New York, and for a few hours each day stalked a mile upstream or a mile down, until I knew every rock and pool and streamy spot where trout were hidden. It was a difficult stream to fish, narrow, strewn with protruding and submerged rocks and deep holes, and overhung with low foliage and interlocking trees, a "pocket stream" that would discourage the angler accustomed to the broad, clear reaches of the Neversink or the Beaverkill. The footing was always a little slippery, and not until well in training did I cease to mind cracking hip and shinbones in occasional

4. There is also an opposite school of anglers transfixed by the Caenidae family of May flies because of their exceptionally *small* size.

plunges. But the mountain water was bracing and the fishing was good. Two hours almost always yielded four or five pan-size browns and at least one over 12 inches.

But many of the larger ones never gave me the chance to release them— voluntarily. Big ones, or what are considered big ones in the East, were difficult to take. They ran under rocks and sawed off leaders, or threatened ruin by charging downstream through rapids and under logs faster than man could follow. One of the largest and smartest of them once described four loops in the air, winding the leader around an overhanging bough, and deliberately snapped off its tip.

Although at the end of five weeks I had taken nothing over 15 inches, I had come to know some extraordinarily good trout. I had either seen or had a strike from 16- or 17-inch fish in several pools, and had always given them patient attention. But they seldom came up for dry flies. Then one day at the end of the first week in June I noticed the dark membranous net-veined wings of the green drake struggling on and fluttering over the stream. Long hours of waiting brought no signs of the hatch. Somehow they had come out while I was on the stream without my seeing them.

The following evening I went into the woods late and cut into the stream a little below the largest pool. White and pink laurel along the water's edge were toning down their brilliance in the early twilight of the valley. The sunless air was still warm, saturated with the smell of dank vegetation. Insects droned under the high-pitched whippoorwill, and the mosquitoes bit through the reeking citronella.

For some reason there were only three flies in my box, a White Wulff (wing and tail of white bucktail, hackle tan with black center, cream body), a Bailey Grizzly (brown grizzly hackle wings, yellow latex body), and a regulation March Brown, all No. 12 dry.

Several flies were playing over the stream as I dropped the Grizzly 30 feet away in fast water and watched it ride the miniature whitecaps. It went only a few feet when a little fountain sprayed up and the line streaked past into the pool below. He showed his colors in several leaps before freeing his 12 or 13 inches of startling beauty.

Moving slowly upstream I was astonished at the number of rises that followed. In an hour a half-dozen medium browns had bent the rod and sparkled against the dark rocks. The time taken up with washing and drying the fly led me to strike back only at the heavier rises, and in the excitement I had not noticed the growing predominance of gray insects. They were floating thickly, though not swarming around my head. It came to me with a start that they were coffin flies, and that they must be swarming somewhere nearby. I stopped fishing and stumbled rapidly upstream. The flies grew thicker and I decided to make for the big pool and the biggest trout.

The big pool was formed by an elbow in the stream at a point where the fast-running water had veered from its normal course and run headlong into the valley wall. The pool was approachable only from two sides, the right angle where the water ran in and ran out, the other two sides being sharply cut off by steep wooded slopes. The high rimming trees permitted the sun to strike directly into it only during the early afternoon. I had caught many trout in that pool and often had lain on a rock watching the large trout playing in it.

Slowing down to what goes for tiptoeing in boots and fast water, I crept toward the lower end of the pool. When I raised my head over the cascading torrent and looked into the pool in the deepened twilight, I saw the treasured secret. Like a fog rising above the water, a seething cloud of gray flies filled the enclosure. It was snowing coffin flies. And the surface of the pool was alive with dancing trout, some of them leaping high toward the cloud of flies, some of them slashing at the gray flakes alighting on the surface; others, leaving the water at a low angle, shot across the pool, spraying white water before their half-submerged noses. They were all out, from the smallest to the largest, electric in their energy, seemingly divided in their desires between voracious eating and acrobatic clowning. It was the tail end of the great hatch, and the flies were in their dance of death, mating, dropping eggs, and dying.

Hugging a rock, the water tumbling into my boots, I was held by the weird celebration. I thought of putting a fly into the center of things, but the obvious ease with which any number of trout could be caught made it seem superfluous. At the moment that I was taken with such fine thoughts, one of the largest trout I have ever seen rise in a small stream came out in a beautiful twisting arc and rolled waves away from him as he lit flat with the resounding smack of a plank being dropped on the water. I raised my rod nervously and hung the Grizzly high in the trees behind me. There was no getting it out in a hurry; so I broke it off and quickly tied on the White Wulff.

With more care I placed it above the spot where the big one had risen, hoping to float it over him. But it had scarcely settled when what seemed to be three fish hit it at the same time. I struck and one of them was on. He was small and I sent him back to the games. The next cast was better placed, but the luck was worse. The belly-smasher came up like a bull. I struck, and it was all over. Bull and fly disappeared in rolling waves. I was really rank. But blunders and cursing failed to disturb either the milling flies or the inebriate trout.

I tied on my third and last fly, the March Brown—hardly to be recommended when coffin flies are out. But for whatever it is worth to the chronicles of fly-fishing, I have to record that it made no difference. It was snatched out of the air as it floated down through the cloud of May flies. But the riser was only another small one.

It was then deep twilight, although through the trees the sky above was still light. I stopped for a moment and waited for another big rise. One came, nothing like the belly-smasher, but a good one, about 60 feet away. A few moments later the March Brown floated over him. It was clockwork. He struck in a spray and I came back firm. After two great leaps he sank sullenly to the bottom near the center of the pool. The others seemed hardly disturbed and went on frivolously jumping. I tugged slightly and he cruised slowly toward the lower end of the pool. I stood up and waded toward him. He darted away powerfully. Then he began the rounds, circling slowly and endlessly. The evening grew darker. He pulled hard. There was a flash of light and a splash as he leapt in the darkness. Twice again he flashed and then came in.

Out West he would not be large. And there are fishermen in the East who would not regard his 18 inches as a trophy. But he was a large trout for any Eastern stream. As I looked down at him, his dotted colors gleaming under matchlight, I felt that it had taken the great hatch to give this tyro his greatest fishing experience and as large a trout as he ever hoped to take.

Suddenly it was night. The coffin flies disappeared. The trout subsided and the water calmed. The pool was a black disc.

Chapter 6

YELLOWSTONE WATERS

The temple of fly-fishing in the United States is reached by the logic that guided Lewis and Clark: follow the waters upstream to what the Indians called the summit of the world, which is indeed the summit of the United States—Yellowstone National Park. There in the northwest corner of Wyoming, wedged into Idaho and Montana, a 2,200,000-acre group of plateaus surrounds the crest of the continental divide and impounds rain and snow to form the source of two basic river systems, the Snake and the Missouri. Steadily in every direction out of this singular eminence of American topography pour tons of that increasingly prized national treasure: cold, pure, bubbling water, the natural habitat of trout, saved from the ravages of industrialization by the farseeing environmentalists of the nineteenth century.

Draw a circle around the park with a radius of 100 miles or more and look at the streams that flow out through national forests and ranch land to form the big river systems lower down. Here is trout water of all kinds, from rivulet to river, fast and slow, running through steep canyons and broad valleys, roaring in cascades and falls, purling in sunny meadows and along shady forest banks, following main roads and byroads and slipping through wilderness. In parts of it even children can fish and catch fish, but there are other parts that fishermen have seldom reached.

And the fish: The native Western cutthroat, a red gash between gill and mouth, known in some quarters as black-spotted trout, a hard hitter and an underwater runner; the aerial rainbow; the imported brown (or Loch Leven), which is sometimes colored bright yellow and which becomes

65

increasingly difficult to catch as it grows older and bigger; the brook, as colorful a trifler in the West as in its native East; and the big lakers of the depths. Here too, rising among the trout, are the Rocky Mountain white-fish and occasionally the delicate grayling.

Angling in the big streams is usually easier and more rewarding than in New York's hard-fished Beaverkill, say (if one does not count the hatchery trout planted in the Beaverkill every spring). But fishing can be difficult and sometimes impossible in Western rivers, even for the good fisherman; and in the Western spring creeks, the trout are as elusive as those in the limestone creeks of Pennsylvania. In the West, as everywhere, a small minority of the skillful catch many more trout than others do. Thus the expectations are good enough to make the angler's journey worthwhile, but not good enough to assure him of sport without effort. He will have to bring along all his angling skill and intelligence, and the strength to master the rugged terrain and heavy waters.

Because fishermen throughout the United States have been pushed farther and farther upstream in this century, and because their total numbers are increasing, there is the possibility that they will overrun even this great area. Yellowstone Park itself attracts so many tourists that its roads are jammed bumper to bumper in the summer, and park pollution has become a problem. Outside the park along the great rivers there is less isolation for a fisherman than there was a decade or two ago. Threats to destroy the river valleys by damming have been successfully resisted, however. Since the Second World War, fishing in the Yellowstone River has actually improved. The diversion of water for agriculture has not increased, the number and size of fish have not diminished despite increased fishing, and pollution from mining and the sewage of the towns of Livingston and Big Timber has been reduced. The only real question is whether the area can survive its increasing popularity and the impending resort developments.

One late afternoon in the early fifties I stood on a bank, looked at one of the many pools on one of the many streams of this region, and saw dimples of feeding trout like rain on the water, as Theodore Gordon saw them on Eastern waters in the nineteenth century; and the scene is still not uncommon today. The good fisherman on a very good day still may take and release thirty or forty trout—one, two, or three of which may run 2 to 7 or more pounds. Even on the worst days there is suspense in every cast.

The relative abundance and large size of trout in Western waters are largely due to the multitudes of water and land insects. The winds blow meaty winged food from the hills and wide-open spaces into the water. These heavy insects account too for an occasional unwariness in Western trout; it is more difficult for them to make a fine calculation concerning the plop of a grasshopper than it is for an Eastern trout to judge the delicate egg dipping of the May fly. The variety of Western insects has brought about the use of a wider variety of trout flies (including some garish specimens) than is found in the East. From this has come the notion that Western fly-fishing is occupied not only with wild trout but with crude methods. There is some truth in the notion, but it is exaggerated and conceals a fallacy regarding the nature of fly-fishing.

Most of the best-known artificial trout flies were originated in England and (much later) on the Eastern Seaboard of the United States, where the May fly predominates. The central position of this fly in the sport has made it the model of most trout flies since the fifteenth century. Many new May fly species in new colors have been found on the American continent, and in the late nineteenth and early twentieth century American flytiers developed the appropriate artificial flies: Quill Gordons, Cahills, Hendricksons, and the like.

Farther west, fly-fishermen discovered the grasshopper, and not being traditionalists at the expense of good fishing, they made or adopted a basic new fly, the Hopper (once called the Michigan Hopper, now usually Joe's Hopper), not bad looking but no May fly. They also created the Wooly Worm, the Muddler, the Goofus Bug, the Mizzoulian Spook, and a whole menagerie of other artificials described recently by the flytiers of the Inland Empire Fly Fishing Club of Spokane, Washington (*Flies of the Northwest*, 1970). The sight of some of them scares Easterners, but in fact most are true trout flies.

The Wooly Worm is the lowest in the order of artificial flies, with its simple caterpillar body made of chenille, the Plymouth Rock hackle wound around palmer-style, sometimes with a little tinsel. Yet on this rudimentary base, flytiers have created over fifty variations. Possibly the Wooly Worm is of ancient origin: English anglers in the seventeenth century fished with caterpillars "rough and wooly on the outward parts, hence by some called Wool-beds." (James Chetham, *The Angler's Vade Mecum*, 1689)

The basic Joe's Hopper, from which come dozens of variations, has wings of brown mottled turkey feather cupped around a body of pale yellow wool; the body is also wound with furnace hackle, palmer-tied and clipped short; the hackle is brown rooster and grizzly; the tail, a red feather. It is a rugged fly which can be fished wet or dry in rough water. Its style marks the region.

So does the Muddler's, with its deer-hair hackle, turkey-feather wing, underwing of a day-old calf's tail hair, and gold tinsel in the body—though the low luring purpose of this fly is stated candidly in the usual appendage to its name: Minnow. David Coln-Pickering has linked the Muddler to an almost identical fly, the Replica Minnow, created by Ludwig Moedler in about 1886; his surmise that Moedler's Minnow over time may have become our Muddler Minnow is made even more plausible by the fact that Amer-

67

ican flies are so often named for their creators. To my eye, however, the Muddler also often looks like a grasshopper plopping on the water; such a dual representation may account for its considerable success in Western waters.

The Goofus Bug is a fly of a different order. It is classic enough in the Western sense, with deer-hair divided wings and tail (like a Wulff), but with the hair pulled up over the back into a hump (hence its name, Humpy, in Wyoming), the underbody of yellow (or black or red) silk floss, and brown Plymouth Rock grizzly hackle. Some say Pat Barnes of West Yellowstone named it. Some say it is modeled on the Goofus Bird (occasionally called the Filaloo Bird) which Jorge Louis Borges (*The Book of Imaginary Beings*) places among the fauna of the United States: It "builds its nest upside down and flies backward, not caring where it's going, only where it's been." The Mizzoulian Spook is merely a Western version of Theodore Gordon's fancy-built Bumblepuppy.

If the variety of Western fly materials seems esoteric, consider Chetham's list of English fly materials in 1689: bear's hair, camel's hair, badger's hair, spaniel's hair, dog's hair, hog's down, the white hog's down dyed in any color, sheep's wool, mohairs, cow's hair, "camlets" (fabrics of the hair of the Angora goat), abortive colt's and calf's hair, furs, feathers, "cadows" (varieties of woolen coverings), blankets, silks, wire, and thread.

In sum, contemporary Westerners employ a wide variety of flies—but not so much wider than tradition decrees—commonly extending in its full range from the Hopper, size 8, to a Quill Gordon, size 20 (the size of a mosquito), on a 14-foot leader tapered to 6X, which is so fine that many fishermen use a magnifying glass as an aid in knotting a fly to it.

Fishing fine is the usual way of fishing Montana spring creeks (see Chapter 7), as it is the chalk streams of England and the limestone creeks of Pennsylvania. But the newcomer to the West should not be surprised to see even Light Cahills and Adamses and some beautiful Western May fly creations in these small sizes floating down great rivers such as the Big Hole, the Madison, the Gallatin, and the Yellowstone. I remember that one year the trout, including big ones, disdained anything else throughout the season. Thus there is subtlety in these waters; there are many kinds of fishing and many conditions, creating all the old problems and some new ones.

The seasons for Western trout are determined by the runoff of snow water as well as by regulation. The Yellowstone River is open year-round. I have had good days on it during sunny interludes in January, dry-fly-fishing from banks of ice. Nature limits the fishing, especially fly-fishing, on the Yellowstone, from the beginning of May to the middle of July, with relatively high and murky water. But there is always fishing somewhere in the spring creeks or rivers. The great stone-fly hatch takes place on the

Madison, Big Hole, and Yellowstone Rivers in late June and early July. Up in the plateaus of the Park the waters are good early, and fishing on most of them begins in late May. As the season proceeds the easily accessible Park waters—those along the road—become less good, perhaps because of excessive fishing, while the waters downstream and out of the park improve as the water level falls. The best season for most of the great rivers is usually from the middle of August to the end of October.

The fly-fisherman can choose a river to suit his taste. For example, the most prized stream in the Park is the Firehole, which originates in the geyser country around Old Faithful and glides north along the Park's west side, drops over falls, and joins the Gibbon coming down from the north to form the upper Madison. The Firehole makes a smooth run through a slightly graded plateau, causing it to be a favorite of dry-fly-fishermen. The same is true of the upper Madison, winding westward through woods and meadows to Hebgen Lake just outside the Park. The Madison here flows slick and bears no resemblance to its turbulent waters below the lake. It is water for the long leader and the small fly, and it is best early in the season.

In the northeast corner of the Park rises the pretty Gallatin; in the south, the Lewis and the Snake. The Yellowstone rises outside the Park and runs into Yellowstone Lake—the largest lake at its altitude in the world, and alive with cutthroat trout. Below the lake the Yellowstone begins its long great run, at the north end of the Park picking up the Lamar and the Gardiner, both good fishing streams. But the best fishing, and most of the fishing in the area, is outside the Park. On the north, in Montana alone, and well within the 100-mile radius, there follow in succession from east to west, about 25 miles apart and separated by mountain ranges, Clark's Fork of the Yellowstone, the Stillwater, the Boulder and West Boulder, the Yellowstone (on its northward run), the Gallatin, the Madison, the Jefferson, and the Big Hole—a concentration of the greatest trout rivers in the United States, and a natural bastion for anglers of the nation to defend.

Although these rivers have been fished with one kind of tackle or another for many years (in particular those to the east, close to the populous center of Billings, are heavily fished), they will not be tamed, short of damming or complete drain-off for irrigation. They rise in permanent mountain wilderness and have in their nature the quality of wild water. This quality is inherent in Western fishing, distinguishing it from the domesticated East and from England, which have been most often described in five centuries of trout-fishing literature. Eastern fishing takes much of its inward, intimate charm from its connections with the past. The West cannot now and perhaps never will satisfy this taste and the traditional fishing dogma that goes with it. Fly-fishing in the West is a relatively new sport. The late Western writer John Hodgdon Bradley, who may have fished more Western

QUILL GORDON

waters than anyone in his time, wrote that in 1920, when he first went out there, he saw no dry flies and few flies of any kind for sale or in use in Wyoming or Montana. Despite the widespread adoption of traditional fly-fishing techniques since then, the West remains incorrigibly wild, a country of great shapes and spaces and constant transformations. The Western fisherman carries a bit of tradition in his fly box, and by this thread alone is tied to the past.

Chapter 7

ARMSTRONG'S CREEK

There are two classes of water which make the highest appeal to the imagination and the emotion. There are those which are unknown and unfished, whose mysterious depths may contain anything, and which you are the first to explore. Everyone who has fished such knows with what expectation and awe you draw near. But an emotion equally strong, though different, is given by fishing a river which has been fished for centuries. As I walk its banks I like to think of those who walked before me.

JOHN WALLER HILLS in *A Summer on the Test*

The first time I came upon Armstrong's Creek in the Montana valley called Paradise, I was startled by what I saw and did not understand it. To the west lay the foothills of the Gallatin Range; to the east, rising sharply to an 11,000-foot peak, the Absarokas, "Land of the Raven," named for an ancient race of hunters and fishermen, the Crow Indians. My friend Dan Bailey and I were looking for ducks. It was December, and though the sun was shining the air was cold—early that morning it had been 23° below zero. On our way across a plain of snow we came on the creek cutting its clear green way through banks of ice. As we stood there, guns under arms, gazing at this wonder, a trout rose and slashed the water with his tail as he turned down. Then another and another, and the water twinkled with them. I never saw the hatch; it was Bailey who told me about the snow fly, a tiny member of the Diptera order that hatches in the winter and is named not for its own color but for that of the landscape into which it usually emerges. The snow fly is gray to near-black and may be represented by the Black Quill or Mosquito No. 18 (or No. 16 with a short-shank hook). What I did not realize then was that I had just seen why this creek is one of the finest and "oldest" trout streams in the United States, and a creek upon which nature and custom have imposed the most rigorous conditions of fly-fishing and conservation.

It was several years before I saw the creek again and then it was summer, and paradise. From the meadow through which it flows, I could see the permanent pockets of snow in the high crevasses of the Absarokas. Beyond was the wilderness, whose proximity one never forgets. Round about lay the great green-yellow, half-irrigated, half-prairielike valley, Western in its vastness—15 miles wide, 40 long—through the center of which winds the stateliest of Western rivers, the Yellowstone. Overhead, phantom storms gather, blacken, blow, and vanish. The creek, a tributary of the Yellowstone, is a couple of miles or more long—depending on how you measure it— and runs more or less parallel to the big river before they meet. It starts from the ground in gushes and flows gently, steadily, constantly, and firmly, at most 200 feet wide, knee-to-waist-deep, on its brief course to the river.

Thickets of tall grass, shrubs, river willows, and wild roses hedge its banks. Hereford cattle of the Armstrong Ranch grunt pleasurably as they graze in the meadow or stumble across the fords and into the cottonwoods. Here and there are mallards, blue heron, porcupines, families of pretty skunks; innumerable small birds streak from cover to cover. There is shade for retreat from the hot afternoon sun. In the still evening, the watery clump of the otter, the slap of the beaver, the slow glide of the muskrat— a river-jungle oasis in a subarid air, and an angler's pastoral.

Spring creeks are a peculiar kind of water owing to their stability: their mean temperature favors year-round growth in the life within them, and neither ice nor flood scours their bottom. Thus they are unusually productive, yielding hatches of flies even in very cold weather—though I can't imagine how the flies take it after they emerge. Armstrong's flows into a great river, yet its trout—wild trout living on May flies—are on the average larger and relatively more numerous than those of the river. A test of the trout population in the creek, made by the state's department of fish and game in September 1970, came up with the astounding figure of 5,700 catchable trout per mile, the largest number recorded for any stream in the area. The fast-flowing Madison River, a far larger body of water, ranked second at a point near Norris with 3,750 trout per mile, and the Yellowstone River, with its long, wide, deep pools, ranked third at a point near Carter's Bridge with 2,675 trout per mile. Recordings made in other good fishing waters ranged down to 400 per mile. Most of the trout in Armstrong's Creek are browns, some are rainbows, and a very few are cutthroats—a phenomenon certainly of this century, since the cutthroats are natives of the West, and the browns are late-nineteenth-century immigrants to the United States. To habitués of the creek, the trout today seem more numerous than they were, say, ten years ago, but smaller in average size. "Smaller" means that there are now a lot of trout to be measured in inches, and quite a few two- and three-pounders; the few very big ones sighted have been spawners.

The fly-fisher in this creek wades through beds of watercress, scooping up handfuls to eat as he moves along. In the center of the stream the grass grows long and thick and supports pads of moss on the surface. It is a dry-fly creek par excellence (and also attracts the nymph- and wet-fly-fisherman). Across any 40 feet of line many currents of different widths and speeds twist the fly from its natural course and put down a rising trout. A thousand tiny whorls agitate the surface, some made by convoluting currents, some—easily distinguishable—by the unseen turning motion of rising trout. At times, as when I first saw the creek, they splash. So silent is the gliding water that one can hear the sip and suck of the trout when the hatch is on, as it is most likely to be between 10 in the morning and 2 in the afternoon; and from the size of the rise, typically smaller than a small tulip, there is no way to tell whether the trout is a ten-incher or a four-pounder.

For reasons I do not know, the duns that emerge, flutter over, and sail down this water in fleets of hundreds of thousands are small—and the smaller they are the better the trout like them. "Sail" is a common fly-fisher's metaphor for the May fly's upwings. In a good wind they tilt to one side or the other or may be blown across the water; in the absence of wind they flutter or sit still, when floating, and are carried along by the currents. Float a moderately small (No. 14) Light Cahill on Armstrong's Creek. You will see it riding nicely between stretches of moss, say in the direction of a ring where natural flies are steadily disappearing. Though it passes directly over the rise, it will float on untouched, and you will see no more sign of the trout until he recovers from fright. Fly-fishers used to think No. 16 most useful, as it is fairly attractive and large enough to take a leader with the strength to hold the fish. The trout have always preferred the tiny No. 18, or something even smaller. They go off with it into the grass and often make short work of the 5 or 6X leader required of so small a fly. But many good fly-fishers prefer the action, and for them No. 18 is standard for this creek. Some go to No. 20, and an occasional esoteric fisherman works with even more microscopic attractions. Although the trout of the creek are extremely shy of leader and drag, they are almost indifferent to the angler when the hatch is on. Drag is the overriding consideration in the angler's performance. It calls for a short float and intensive casting.

The water flies of the creek are mainly May flies, of which one species, a pale yellow dun represented by the Light Cahill, is the insect most often seen on the water. But many species are there, in a wide range of colors from dark olives to white—pale shades in the summer, darker in the fall. The dark duns may often be fairly well represented by the Quill Gordon and the Adams. In November a Blue Dun is often best. On occasion there is a very pale, almost white, fly on the water. Gil Meloche, a passionate angler who once frequented the region, one day saw a big trout taking this fly and refusing all the artificials he put up. Having nothing like it in his fly box, he took off his hat, caught one of the naturals in it, and rushed

73

back about seven miles to the Fly Shop in Livingston. When he opened up the hat, the little May fly flew away in the store. Meloche described the insect to Dan Bailey, who sat down and tied an artificial accordingly—an all-pale cream-colored fly: cream hackle, tails, hackle point wing, and fur body. Meloche rushed back to the creek with the fly and cast it over the still-rising trout. A half hour later he walked into the Fly Shop carrying a 4½-pound brown. That was in 1938. The ink tracing of his trout was the first to go up on the shop's famous wall, and the artificial fly is called the Meloche—a fly to remember.

It is to the rise that the angler must usually fish on Armstrong's Creek. But there is no one best way to approach the trout. I have seen Paul Stroud of Marshall Field stride down the center of the creek, careless of movement and splash, and cast his fly quickly to one bank and then to the other, to the rise or to a likely place, and the trout tumble over themselves to get on his hook. And I have seen the methodical retired Minnesota sportsman Phil Fjellman, who returns to the creek every year, work the water slowly, carefully, and thoroughly and bring the big ones to his fly. It is hardly surprising that many noted angling writers have made a pilgrimage to this remarkable creek. Ernest Schwiebert (*Matching the Hatch*, 1955) has studied its natural flies, and so have Doug Swisher and Carl Richards (*Selective Trout*, 1971); Lee Wulff has made fly-fishing motion pictures there; the late Paul Young tried out some of his own fine rods on the creek; Al McClane, who compiled the great *McClane's Standard Fishing Encyclopedia and International Angling Guide* (1965), got some of his learning while fishing there; a cluster of wondrous fly-fishing wordsmiths, the poet Jim Harrison and the novelists William Hjortsberg and Tom McGuane, have settled nearby. Joe Brooks, Tom McNally, Ted Trueblood, Ed Zern, and numerous other scribes have been seen passing through town on their way to the creek.

The interest of fishermen in this creek is not new. It was named for Paul Armstrong, the late owner of the ranch through which it flows. A friend of fishermen and a fisherman himself, he was a tall, weathered, gentle, statesmanlike rancher who changed to clean overalls in the evening. He was born on the ranch and lived in a modest ranch house above and within sound of the biggest of the springs that feed the creek. One day he told me what he remembered or remembered hearing about the creek.

Long ago, when the Sioux Indians were driven west, they drove the Crow before them, until both came near the mountains. In the summertime the Sioux around what is now Miles City, Montana, went further up the Yellowstone, as far as what is now Livingston. There the retreating Crow took a trail that today is Route 89 to the south through a canyon into Paradise Valley. The valley lies just north of Yellowstone Park, whose geysers the Sioux regarded as evil spirits. Hence the Sioux would go no farther than

Livingston, and the Crow, who were less afraid of the spirits than of the Sioux, or who perhaps held different beliefs, found the valley a summer haven. They pitched their tepees not far from the spring creek and fished there for the big blue suckers that lined the bottom, as well as for the trout in the grassy pools.

Two of the first white settlers in the valley, Fred Boettler and his brother, learned of the Indians' interest in the fishing when they came through in a wagon in the year 1869. The two men camped at the head of the creek and concluded that this was one of the things they had gone West for. As they set up camp, however, they saw the Crow gathering for a powwow on a nearby ridge—an unfriendly sign from the usually friendly tribe, which was disturbed by the threat to its fishing rights. Since the Boettlers aimed to live in peace near the Crow, the Crow kept the creek and the two brothers went up the valley and settled below Emigrant Peak. To orient you, the year 1869 was the year the first cattle arrived in Montana from Texas; it was twenty years before Montana became a state of the union; it was two years after John M. Bozeman, who built a gold-rush road through the Gallatins, was killed by the Piegans on Mission Creek east of where Livingston was founded; and it was seven years before Custer's Last Stand against the Sioux to the southeast on the Little Big Horn.

There is a hiatus in the story here which contains events that form a moral impasse in U.S. history. One summer the Crow did not return to the valley but settled elsewhere, on a reservation. In the late 1870's a Major Pease stationed at Fort Ellis (Bozeman) came over the mountain and squatted at the head of the creek. Not long afterward, a General Brisbin bought out Pease and, what with homesteading and desert-land claims, set up a 1,100-acre ranch. Many fish were caught in the creek and taken over the mountain to Fort Ellis in the Gallatin Valley. In 1886 two sportsmen, James and Win H. H. (Doc) King of Jacksonville, Illinois, bought the ranch for a hunting and fishing lodge. James was a merchant, Doc was a surgeon. A rancher, O. T. Armstrong, who had come from Missouri in 1878, rented the ranch from the King brothers and worked it while the sportsmen brought hunting and fishing parties out from the East. In the 1890's Armstrong bought out the King brothers, put their land together with his own 400 acres, and made a 1,500-acre ranch. O. T.'s son Paul grew up fishing the creek.

Until he died in 1969, Paul Armstrong welcomed fishermen to the creek. He set no formal rules, but the sportsmen responded with remarkable decorum. It is, as noted, primarily a dry-fly creek, difficult to fish, and it attracted anglers—resident and nonresident—with a feeling for the relationship of the sport to conservation. Their conduct has been consistent with the code of behavior laid down in the fifteenth-century *Treatise of Fishing*. They shut the gates they opened, released most of the fish they caught, and

75

took their pieces of paper and empty tin cans away with them. Somehow ideally inspired, most men and women for once, in this one place, became a natural part of nature.

Allyn O'Hair, Paul Armstrong's son-in-law who in recent years has operated and expanded the ranch, sustained the same tradition of open fishing. But other creeks, including an extension of Armstrong's through the ranch below, began to be rented and closed for private fishing. In fairness to O'Hair, a number of the local fishermen who made up the Yellowstone River chapter of Trout Unlimited, led by Dan Bailey, entered into a most unusual cooperative leasing arrangement: They got together with several individuals and tackle companies, raised a fund to lease the creek, and then declared it open to the public as before. They made their own rules, which were a codification of the dominant past practices on the creek: fly-fishing only, a keeping limit of two trout, and so on. Thus the creek in the seventies serves to suggest what, in these circumstances, can be done voluntarily to keep good fishing water open and yet conserve it.

Chapter 8

ALL THE BIG ONES GOT AWAY

Every day I see the head of the largest trout I ever hooked, but did not land.

THEODORE GORDON

Of course all the big ones got away, and we all know why. Lies, delusions. And, in violation of the law of sufficient reason, it's plausible. That's how the big ones got big. But see how the old story goes when you try to put it down chapter and verse.

To start, you have to untangle the question: What's a big fish? Every angler has his private scale. On mine, thinking of good, not big, fish which I have actually caught, I can say roughly that a 14-inch trout in a Catskill creek equals a 2-pounder on the Yellowstone River equals a 17-pound salmon on the Restigouche. On the same scale, a 2-pounder in a stream equals a much larger one in a lake; and a 2-pounder caught on a fly representing an insect equals a much larger one caught on a streamer fly representing a minnow—all quite arbitrary according to one's own game rules and values. *Big* before fish is a peculiar word, suggesting, I imagine, for many anglers something outlandish in relation to the circumstances. I have seen Lee Wulff, who has taken the biggest fish in the world on the lightest tackle, catch a 10-inch trout on the Battenkill with sewing thread, to his evident pleasure. Joan Miller, who once caught a 900-pound swordfish off Cape Cod with spear and barrel, yelled "Oh my God!" when she hooked her first trout later in the Yellowstone—a 9-incher on a tiny Gray Wulff dry.

When I say that all the big ones got away, however, I have in mind for the occasion a formidable minimum on an objective scale: a 4-pound trout caught on fly in a stream. The scale was set by Dan Bailey for the walls of his Fly Shop in Livingston, Montana. You can put a tracing of

77

the outline of your trout on the wall if it meets these conditions, and few anglers who have qualified have disdained the invitation. Bailey set the scale remarkably well for that country, whose streams yield an extraordinary number of trout below 4 pounds and relatively few above, so that a 4-pounder or better is an event to bring everyone running. Some anglers around there have caught numerous wall fish, and since so many are on the wall now, the rule is that a fisherman can add a new one only if it is larger that the one he has already put up, in which case the old one must come down. This rule can give the angler a tough choice: Does he want to take down his 5-pounder caught on a big streamer fly and put up a 4-pounder caught on a No. 16 Quill Gordon? I have not had to face such problems; after more than twenty years of visiting the Fly Shop and fishing the Boulder, Yellowstone, Gallatin, Madison, Big Hole, and many other rivers, streams, brooks, spring creeks, and ditches of Montana, I am not on that wall.

I regret the omission for all the obvious reasons, and for another more obscure personal one. When Bailey and I shared a cabin beside a creek in the Catskills in the 1930's, we casually put our larger trout on the cabin wall. We traced the shape of the trout on a piece of paper and took it off in a line drawing in ink on the old faded wallpaper, writing in the name of the one who had caught it and the date, and attaching the fly to the nose of the outlined trout. Bailey put up the first one on July 14, 1935, a 15-inch brown which really looked impressive coming out of that creek; and we made a rule that the next one would have to be larger. It was two years before another went up, a 16-incher of mine, and thanks to Bailey's emigration to Montana, I had the honor of putting up the rest. There were only four in all—the largest one 18 inches—when I abandoned the cabin in 1941, carved the whole thing out of the wall, and took it to New York to be framed.

That I never put a trout on the wall in Montana was not for lack of expert teachers. I have fished under the aegis of some of the best and most dedicated fishermen since Gordon. I have seen Bailey catch wall fish without particularly trying, that is, while fishing wet or dry, with tiny delicate flies or large Muddlers. Phil Fjellman, a habitué of the Yellowstone with whom I often fished, put fifteen trout on the wall while I went blank. Joe Brooks (*Trout Fishing*, 1972) a fabulous fisherman in all styles and a specialist in power fishing, a style he popularized for catching big fish in Montana, said to me one day in the Fly Shop, "I think you ought to be on the wall. Come with me."

Power fishing, or perhaps more correctly, power casting, is a mode of fishing that grew out of tournament techniques for casting long distances. It is widely practiced in San Francisco and around Miami. Some tournament casters never actually go fishing, but many do. Their techniques are now standard practice in steelhead fishing and saltwater fly-fishing. Visiting fishermen brought the techniques to Montana, and Joe Brooks had a lot to do with demonstrating that they paid off in big fish. Since then the style has become a vogue with a number of good Montana fishermen.

Power fishermen discard the old casting styles, familiar to Easterners, of holding the arm to the side. The key to the power style is the "double haul." If you are right-handed, you work your line with your left hand, giving it impetus with a sharp stripping motion when picking the fly off the water and again in the forward cast. The equipment includes the "shooting" or "torpedo" line, which weighs more near the forward end. When you go over to power fishing, you have to give up the versatility of traditional delicate styles for working varieties of water with small flies. And if you fish in the traditional style, you have to give up a lot of big fish, which you will see others taking in the big-fish season (September and October in Montana) with rods that are 8½ feet, 5½ ounces or larger.

On the rivers I have fished, power fishing appears to be almost exclusively a man's sport. Yet this kind of casting does not take unusual strength with a floating line, and tournament-casting women—Joan Wulff, for one—get considerable distance. Perhaps one difficulty is the strength needed to stay at it with streamer flies for hours on end. Another is the real power it takes to drag a long sinking line out of the water.

In any case, this circumstance has not worked altogether to the disadvantage of women. Their mastery of the dry fly followed on its invention. And although far fewer women than men fish fly, six have put stream trout on the Fly Shop wall since 1958. Debie Waterman, of the fishing team of Debie and Charles Waterman of De Land, Florida, is represented with a 7-pound brown from the Missouri, caught on a Silver Outcast or Renegade (an outcast from the Silver Doctor Salmon fly), and a 4-pound, 1-ounce brown from the Yellowstone, caught on a Muddler. As she had to choose one to stay up, I asked her which it would be. She replied without hesitation, "The four-pounder. The Yellowstone is more of a challenge." This preference reflects the impression that big browns are comparatively easy to find and catch in the rich trout grounds at the confluence of the Missouri and Beaver Creek near Helena, where they come down from the lakes to spawn. Consider also a further complexity in fishing values. Debie Waterman says, "I come to Montana to fish dry fly. The greatest catch of my life in salt or fresh water was a three-and-a-half-pound brown on Nelson's Spring Creek [a tributary of the Yellowstone] with a No. 16 [fairly small] Cahill on a 6X [extremely fine] tippet."

Mary Brooks, of the far-ranging fishing team of Mary and Joe Brooks of Richmond, Virginia, is on the wall with a 4-pound, 14-ounce brown from the Yellowstone, caught on a Muddler. Sue McCarthy of Daytona, Florida, displays a 5-pound, 4-ounce brown from the Missouri, caught on

79

a Muddler. Ann Prickett has a 5-pound, 13-ounce brown from the Yellowstone, caught on a Muddler. Mrs. Winston Dine-Brown is represented by a 4-pound, 12-ounce brown from the Yellowstone, caught on a Dark Spruce streamer. And Patricia O'Neill has hung a 6-pound, 1-ounce brown from the Madison, caught on a Salmon fly (mysteriously named, as it represents rather realistically a large natural stone fly). Perhaps someone can figure out why four of the six caught their trophy trout on a Muddler (a fly discussed in Chapter 6). Although it is a big-fish fly, on one wall panel displaying sixty-three 4- and 5-pounders caught by men and women, only twelve were caught on a Muddler; on another panel containing 6-pounders and better, very few were taken on a Muddler.

Joe Brooks and I went out together on a great pool of the Yellowstone, once called Paine's Pool—the only time I recall going out especially to try for a big trout. Joe lent me a powerful rod, a shooting line, and some large, bright-blue streamer flies from the Argentine, along with a couple of dark-brown patterns. A master of casting who has written authoritative books on the subject, he showed me how to get the wind-resisting streamers out to the edge of the fast water on the far side of the pool, where big trout often lie. I didn't catch anything worth talking about, but Joe, illustrating his teaching, brought in and released a great trout which he denied would go 4 pounds, though I knew better. The kick in this kind of fishing is in the great expectations and the suspense. But I had to say that I found it too repetitive, and Joe agreed with that. He is a generous and versatile fisherman who likes to work the water.

Certainly fishing in traditional ways excuses no one for failing to catch big trout; anyone who fishes long enough should get at least a few. But as it was, I amassed a record collection of ways to lose the big ones. Of course there are the routine ways of striking too soon or too late (these account for a normal number of my losses), inattention to damaged tackle (quite a few), entanglements in moss and other flora of the watery depths (quite a few), buck fever while casting to a big rise (a few), and the like. Altogether these mount up, but come to no more than most fishermen have experienced. Indeed, there is no normal way for me to account for all the big ones getting away. I like to think that I am absolved because the really big ones got away by being inspired and superbrilliant tacticians. I give just three examples, from the Madison River.

Here I was in the Bear Trap stretch of the Madison, a wilderness area where the great river narrows and the water crashes through a gorge—unfishable except in side pockets and eddies. I hooked a trout on a No. 10 Bailey Grizzly in a large pocket and saw him only in the shape of the swirls he made before he plunged recklessly into the gorge and—upstream! It made as much sense for a fish to go upstream in that water as it would for one to climb Niagara Falls. However, the maneuver gave me the advantage of holding for a moment. He then turned and raced down 20 yards or so with the torrent and should have kept on going. But he didn't seem to want to leave the neighborhood. Against the laws of nature, he turned again and streaked upstream through the middle of the gorge. Then this old Greek fish-god settled to the bottom under a great rock in front of me. I sat there above him for a long time before I concluded that he would outwait me. I then broke him off and went on my way looking for more natural fish.

Doubt unsettled me. How can one have an experience with nature contrary to its laws? Could the fish have been a phantom of my imagination? Did the swirls of its rise actually belong to a whirlpool in the pocket? Were line and fly dragged by an unseen current into the maelstrom, where one or the other caught on a rock at the bottom? Was the dash upstream my own doing as I raised the rod to get a tight line, and the dash down a result of my yielding to the pressure of the heavy rushing water? Was the return to the rock my return to a tight line? Descartes' aphorism, "I think therefore I am," ran through my head, and I wondered whether my doubt about the existence of the Bear Trap trout did not attest to *my* existence—a consolation of angling that I believe has heretofore gone unnoticed.

Again, I stood in late afternoon on the east bank of the Cameron stretch of the Madison—several miles of flat prairielike rocks and sagebrush cut through with winding roads, near the town of Cameron. I left my companions and went downstream, casting from the bank into the swift runs that pushed up and around protruding rocks close by. I caught several 10- and 12-inch rainbows on a small, slender wet fly, which suggested that the fishing might be very good. The Madison here is wide, straight, and powerful, strewn with open and slightly submerged rocks. A fisherman in these parts usually keeps restlessly moving down or up, and on occasion across, if the opportunity appears. But crossing the Madison is a considerable undertaking when its depth ranges from knee to waist. Only in a few spots can it be done at all, and the angler can never be sure of making it all the way. I began to have eyes for better water on the other side, however, and looked for a possible crossing. Presently I found one that seemed feasible. Holding the rod high, I fished across inch by inch, the pressure of the current just short of carrying me away.

For this heavy water I had put on a No. 10 Trude (a down-wing hair fly looking rather like a wet Royal Coachman), which tended to float a little before sinking. Three good strikes came, and though none held, I concluded that I had the right fly (no insect hatch was visible). When I reached the other side, I fished down again through some long streamy runs, and the fishing was beautiful. Cutthroats. Good ones, never jumping (they almost never do), but fast, hard runners. I lost track of time and distance, until the water turned black and its whitecaps crystal in the twilight. I looked for a ford, found none, turned back, and tried to remember the landmarks

81

of the crossing: a fallen aspen on my side, a clump of willows standing alone on the other. Here they were. I relaxed and started carefully fishing across.

About a third of the way, balanced on my left foot against the force of the water and casting straight ahead, I let the Trude fall over the bulge of a submerged boulder, lifted the rod, and—it stopped. It seemed that a full minute passed, during which the powerful water rushed on while the fly stood still below the bulge. Then it started moving away from me at a right angle to the current, toward the other bank. I held the rod high with the line running and edged forward while I tried to find footing. But it wasn't necessary to follow, for the trout changed course in a sweeping, arc-shaped run downstream and back toward the middle of the river. At the end of the run he came out high and twisting, a great rainbow, I judged, from the way he danced on his tail. I stood still as he went under, moved slowly up against the current, leaped again and again, and rolled away, tearing the river into swirling black and white designs.

He was one of those trout over whom the fisher has at this stage no control whatever—every move an awesome phenomenon. He held again, and neither trout nor angler moved in the deep dusk, all but night. It was a long hold, giving me time to ponder a question. This was a very big fish—pounds greater, I imagine, than the wall's minimum (I say that now, though the wall was not in my head then). It was the kind of fish I would stay there all night with. If luck favored me I would eventually catch him somewhere downstream along the bank I had come from. But if I did that, I would be marooned in darkness on the west bank, with several square miles of rangeland around me. My companions would be at the car on the east bank, waiting, knowing nothing of this adventure. If only I had carried a flare! (The thought of carrying a flare had never occurred to me before that moment.)

I came to understand that I had no choice; I had to cross. I began a maneuver to get below him, but when I moved down, so did he, maintaining the same angle. We must have been together about a half hour when I took the only way out. I started moving across upstream from him, the worst position for an angler; but as long as I was on either side of him, I could go with him and turn him so that he couldn't break away. The critical point would come when I passed directly over him. I hated to reach that point; I felt like an astrologer before an eclipse. Would he know what I knew?

He knew. As the line came parallel to the main current straight above him, he rose, not 40 feet away, carrying the entire line into the air. Against the white water I saw him full and entire, the biggest thing imaginable in the whole river. Wise old trout, like all my big friends and antagonists in the water, he came down, a launched torpedo, and shot straight downstream.

82

I let the line run freely into the backing, knowing he was gone before he was off. As the line ran out, I pointed the rod down and straight after him, in a sign of resignation, for the snap which came in due course. So I wound up with the story and without the fish, and did the talking at supper that night.

It is twenty years since I first met the king of the Madison trout, a brown, at Papoose Creek—the best-known big fish not on the wall at the Fly Shop. It was a clear August morning, too clear to be promising, and the salmon-fly hatch for which the Madison is celebrated—its great stone fly that brings up the big fish—was long past, when Pat Barnes, Dorothy McDonald, and I set out to float the river. The practice of floating the Madison has been criticized because thoughtless boatmen pass through water being fished by wading or bank anglers, and some of them are fish hogs. We felt innocent enough, since Pat is a scrupulously courteous as well as skillful boatman (and angler), and we were not out to kill many fish. Pat grew up fishing the Madison, taught school until recently in Helena, and spends all his summers in West Yellowstone, tying flies and running an elegant fishing shop with his wife Sig, and guiding, not to speak of fishing. He knows the Madison the way a deer knows its woods.

We launched the boat about 30 miles downstream from the river's start in Hebgen Lake. It was a McKenzie River boat made to run rough water, with 8½-foot oars for control among rocks. In the bow was a sort of pulpit against which one could lean and cast without losing balance. These features were a necessity, as we were soon running through rapids and around submerged rocks.

Of the hundred or so flies in my fly box I picked out a No. 12 Royal Wulff dry, a variation on the classic Royal Coachman. Theodore Gordon never liked the Royal Coachman; indeed, he was positively irked by it. He knew of it as a renowned killer, but he considered it a lure and could not understand what its attraction could be when fished dry. His best guesses were that it resembled a "glorified ant" or that its colors aroused the trout's curiosity. "One thing sure," he conceded, "the trout can scarcely fail to see it." He had in mind the quieter waters of the East, where this fly might be seen too well. I have often found it an effective dry fly in fast, splashy water, where it throws off distinct glints of light—not, I imagine, with the effect of a lure but with that of some brilliant spinner.[1] Fishing dry in the absence of a hatch, especially on Western waters, I sometimes begin the day by experimenting with the light effects of fancy flies.

1. The legitimacy of this fly has been championed by Preston Jennings (*A Book of Trout Flies,* 1935) and by Arnold Gingrich (*The Well-Tempered Angler,* 1966). "There IS a Royal Coachman," Gingrich prodded Jennings into revealing in the July 1956 issue of *Esquire.* It's a group of May flies, said Jennings, called *Isonychia bicolor,* or *albomanicata,* with species to be found East and West.

QUILL GORDON

As it turned out, the Royal Wulff was the only pattern I needed to use all day. Standing in the bow, I cast to one side or the other, 20 to 50 feet and slightly ahead of the boat. All day I saw that sparkling fly bobbing or gliding through marvelous waters. Floating the Madison introduces one to every conceivable kind of fishing water. It was a much better day than we had expected, and we began catching and releasing quite a few fish— Dorothy and I alternating with the rod. After awhile we approached the little tributary, Papoose Creek, which comes down from the east out of the Madison Range.

We left the main current for a channel between an island and the east bank, and with Pat braking the boat, I dropped the fly into a deep, slow run along the bank. At the confluence with Papoose Creek I saw a shallows, and beyond it the incoming flow of the creek. I dropped the fly just inside the flow, with some slack leader curled behind it. The fly moved naturally with the flow; and disappeared. I drew up and the line tightened. Pat held the boat. The king came straight up, clear of the water, framed against the bushes on the other side of the creek: a yellowing brown trout of enormous dimensions. We had a long time to look at him as he hung, seemingly weightless, at the peak of his jump. He fell back with a great splash and circled around the same point several times, while Pat maneuvered the boat backward and toward the bank. Then he came up again, giving us another full view as he turned completely over and dived nose first, with only a swish, into the water. I was so spellbound that, although I automatically held the line tight, I forgot I was fishing.

Two things then happened almost at once. Pat, who had kept his head, jumped into the deep water, clothes and all, to drag the boat to shore. Had I not been distracted, I should have followed him. In the next instant the king rose again sidewise, throwing himself out into the river. I came to, and saw I had to make a choice. Pat had assumed that I would play the fish from the shore, which would have been a sound move if I had left the boat when Pat did. But now the fish was off and running downstream, and in the split second of decision I yelled to Pat to come back in. The old king had benefited by the spell he had cast which put Pat in the water and left me in the boat. Pat was back in the boat in another moment and we were soon after him, but he had taken a lot of line. He was fairly far out and going swiftly downstream before we were moving with him and I was taking in line. Some 300 yards downstream were two boulders, the larger one about 100 feet offshore. But for those boulders the course of my angling life would be quite different—I should not be writing this story. The king knew his territory well. I had recovered a good deal of line when he went outside the big boulder and circled it. We couldn't make it quickly enough, and as we circled it the line slacked. When I reeled in, the fly was still on and the hook was bent straight.

We crossed to the other side. I listlessly dropped a new fly along the edge of a wide pocket. It disappeared and I drew up. A trout came out into the river; about five minutes later I lifted him out of the water and, deciding to keep him along with a couple of others, knocked him on the head and tossed him into the boat. That evening when we beached the boat 17 miles downstream from where we had started, I laid our fish on the bank. Dorothy looked at them and said, "That last one was pretty good." I took out a pocket scale and weighed him: 3¾ pounds. With the Papoose measure in my mind, I hadn't thought much of him for size. Yet he was the largest trout I have ever caught.

The next day when I came into the Fly Shop, I looked at the wall for the largest stream trout caught on dry fly. There it was—a rainbow, 10 pounds, 3 ounces, caught by a Livingston fisherman, Roy Williams, on a Grey Hackle Yellow dry fly in the Yellowstone River in October 1950 (a record that still stood in the spring of 1972). I studied this fish and compared him in my mind's eye with the lost king. Needless to say . . .

During the next two years, I went back to Papoose Creek several times with different companions. On one occasion Dan Bailey went along, only because he was willing to humor me. We got into the water a couple of hundred feet above the confluence of creek and river and waded out to the shallows. Dan started fooling around a boulder below the island, waiting while I waded down the shallows and fished back in toward the bank until I came to Papoose. When I reached the creek, I heard a shout from Dan that told me he had a strike. I found him a few minutes later, aghast. "The waters parted," he said, holding his arms wide and laughing, "I was catching some little fish on a small Grizzly Wulff and this fine leader, not expecting anything else, when he rose beside that rock. All around, the river went dry behind his rise. He went straight across to the end of my line and never stopped."

Chapter 9
CANYON FISHING FOR STEELHEAD

You won't get your steelhead on fly in the Salmon River, they said. In the Snake or the Clearwater or somewhere else, but not the Salmon. The Salmon River is for bait and spinning. They said it in Montana and California. They even said it in Idaho, where the great river, running through mile-deep canyons, deeper than the Grand Canyon, cleaves the state in two. You once fished bait or lure and liked it, they said. Fish them in the Salmon and you will get your steelhead. They said *get your steelhead* the way they say get your deer or elk. It's an event.

That's a shame, I said. The greatest steelhead river not for fly. For thirty-five years I have fished fly and it catches more fish. I will fish fly in the Salmon River and get my first steelhead or find out what's the matter with that river or that fish.

Arrogance becomes the angler, and gets him into deep water. I had never fished for steelhead and couldn't even remember my booklearning about it.

Only two decades ago, flying into the 80-mile wilderness stretch of the Salmon River canyon, from the road's end near North Fork, Idaho, to the road's end near Riggins in the west, was as much of an adventure as the first trials by boat in the nineteenth century. It was these that gave the stretch its legendary name, The River of No Return. It still seemed an adventure to me (though it is now usually routine to experienced mountain fliers) when at three o'clock on a wintry afternoon at the end of October 1971, I sat next to the retired TAC and sometime U-2 pilot Paul Hungerford, a large, calm, comfortable man, in a little two-engine Cessna. We were flying between blowing snow clouds in eastern Idaho just west of the continental divide. He was looking for a clear way to turn north to the mouth of the canyon. I looked down at the earth map in my lap and out at the heavenly scenery and tried to connect them.

Paul made his turn, which I identified as up Interstate 93, and came through the 4,000-foot-high valley. To the right above us rose the cloud-covered peaks of the Beaverhead Range; to the left was the blurred sky-line of the Salmon River Mountains; below we could see the main course of the river. We passed over the town of Salmon and Paul made a far right sweep, peering northwest across the widened, saucer-shaped valley. He was examining the point at which the main river joins its North Fork near the town of that name, turns sharply left, and disappears into the mountains. At that point a narrow shaft of light showed between banks of clouds rolling eastward over the peaks on either side, dark to the north, gray to the south.

We were conversational. We've got changeable weather and uncertain-ties but let's try it, he said, banking left and floating into the light between the canyon walls. Approaching a leftward bend he took to the right again, near the evergreens starkly traced against the steep white slope of the mountainside. He peered into the further reaches of the canyon. Not predictable, eh? I said. In that case, how do you do this thing? You feel your way, he said. If we can't get through we've got room to turn.

Thirty miles further into the curving gorge, a black wall of falling snow loomed ahead. Snow is black when it eclipses the sun. In position to turn, Paul turned and put his esoteric talents to work as a bush pilot with a problem. The place to go was up, through a cluster of peaks, in a cork-screw climb. Soon we were on instruments and reading maps. No peaks nearby over 10,000 feet, Paul observed, and the Cessna was good for more than 13,000, with ice-free wings. It looks like the steelhead are safe, I said. Are we going to Boise? Paul studied instruments and map and said reluctantly, perhaps. But we'll pass over the ranch and maybe there'll be a hole. There is a saying, I said, faithful to his mission-bound intrepidity, that fishing is best in bad weather except when the east wind blows.

To look over and beyond them for light, we visited some high ridges in the mists and saw little but shrouds. It's Paul's pastoral, I said to myself. Then he sighted the hole, pointed the ship down through it to the band of clear air under the cloud cover, and eased into the canyon. Presently he skimmed the water and dropped like a dry Royal Coachman onto what looked like a potato patch beside the dark green river. A few minutes later I was bouncing swiftly downstream in a flat-bottomed jet boat driven by its designer and builder, the Mackay Bar guide Ben Flaunce. He stared straight ahead, intent upon picking his way through the channels in the rapids. We had only an hour of daylight left to fish.

QUILL GORDON

Ben put me on a rock a couple of miles downstream and I cast a Dark Gordon, a classic-looking steelhead fly with a dull red body—very like an Atlantic salmon fly in that it is dressed to the length of the hook. I cast it straight out across the currents and began stripping line, as one does when fishing large wet flies for trout in the big Western rivers east of the continental divide. In my pocket were a Skunk, which looks like a Wooly Worm, a luminous red Skyomish Sunrise, and a Red Ant with muted red body and spotted tail, all steelhead flies tested elsewhere on Idaho and Oregon waters, and given to me by a flytying friend.

Ben sat on the boat skeptically observing my activity. They're on the bottom, he said. I have a sinking line at the forward end, I said. It's a slow-sinking line, but it gets down a little. Not enough, he said. Won't they come up at all? He shook his head. Until the hour was up I went on casting, now with the Skyomish Sunrise, and raised no fish.

Back at the ranch I met Norman Close, the chief guide. You want to fish fly he said, bringing out his own fly-fishing tackle. The most significant element I saw was a small piece of fine lead wire which he had coiled around his leader for a half inch. I had heard of lead on the leader for lake fishing, but had never had occasion even to think of employing it. It will get you to the bottom, he said, and that's the only place you'll find them.

I must say the lead-wire coil gave me a twinge, and I suddenly understood why the Salmon River had a no-fly reputation. How you choose to fish is quite arbitrary within nature's limits. Ever since writing on angling began in the fifteenth century the great teachers of the sport have instructed us to divide fishing into three kinds: bottom, middle, and top. And so we have done, with a variety of weights providing the control. Fly-fishing in this scheme is fishing at the top. It is generally nature's rule: trout rise to the top for emerging water-bred insects. It has also become doctrine, any significant departure from which is heresy. Hence the twinge at the thought of a sinker on a fly leader.

There's no choice, said Norm. This can be a fly-fishing river if you understand it. The steelhead are down deep on the bottom. *Deep*. That explained another thing. The floating line is the standard of fly-fishing because it keeps the fly at or near the top. Legitimacy has been claimed for the sinking line because, as one ordinarily fishes, it is still not far from the top. Fly-fishermen use it to catch big trout with streamers in the pools of the Yellowstone and Missouri. I had heard that fly-fishermen also use it for steelhead on or near the bottom of the relatively shallow riffles of the Clearwater River, not far north of the Salmon. But here, *the steelhead are on the bottom and the water is deep*, and so I understood why fishermen on the Salmon River normally spin for their steelhead with sunken lures.

My dreams that night were out of Roderick Haig-Brown's moody classic of the Northwest, *The River Never Sleeps*, which I had read when it came out twenty-five years earlier: his first steelhead which wasn't a steelhead and then the one that was.

In the morning I had two hours to fish before flying out. I had to make a decision: Fly-fishing on the bottom? Or the alternative, some forlorn classic casting? I decided to revise my assertion that fly catches more fish to a more precise dictum, namely, that with a little heresy the fly may do anything.

Norm lent me his fly tackle and I went downriver again with Ben. We passed a solitary spin fisherman here and there along the banks. Ben drove the boat up a patch of beach above an attractive curl of water that ran around a large rock. I jumped out onto the glistening quartz and agate pebbles of the Gem State and chose a fly—one of Norm's Wickerbills, as they call all their otherwise unnamed patterns. It was a fairly large streamer, an effective type of fly, standard equipment of fly-fishermen in many waters, but not my ideal. It was a nice-looking fly, rather sparsely tied, with a black chenille body wrapped with gold tinsel, some strands of red and white bucktail streaming beyond the bend of the hook, and—its special feature—some short hackle of orange-dyed polar-bear hair.

I tried a few false casts to get the hang of holding the leaded leader in the air. Then I laid out the line crossways to the current, let it sink a moment, and began stripping. There is a lot of roulette in this style of fishing, which is common on Atlantic salmon and big trout rivers, but it's not a hundred percent luck. I realized this when I heard Ben sigh. If they will take a fly, he said, they'll take it just before it straightens out. Then you strip slowly. The motion is slow. I obeyed. After awhile we moved farther downriver to a flat below high crags. Still no action. We moved again, down into the longest pool I have ever seen. I could hardly sight the end of it. Manns Creek Hole, Ben said. Hole? Pools here are holes, he said.

He set the boat moving slightly faster than the slow current, 50 or 60 feet out from the north side. I sent the fly to the edge against the almost black perpendicular wall, let it drift freely, and as it came around started slowly stripping. We moved on slowly, and I went on casting in more or less the same way into the slicks along the canyon wall. I don't know just what my level of confidence was concerning an actual strike—no one would be fishing without expectation—but I thought the water, sliding along in weavy bands of currents, looked fishy. The line was near the end of its arc. I started a slow strip and came up locked. Hey, I said. The fish rose in a swirl and barely cleared the water—enough to see steelhead whole. I stripped fast as he came toward the boat, yellow and red in the dark gray-green water. He turned away, taking back the coils of stripped line, and came on the reel to run hard across the pool against a stiff drag. He stayed far out there awhile—never again breaking water, which surprised me, for I had heard that the steelhead jumps high and often—and after several rushes over several minutes, he was in the boat.

As this was my first steelhead, I took a good look at him. By inland trout standards he was a large fish, about 5 pounds; but he was small for a steelhead.[1] A good steelhead, I knew, would go 10 to 20 pounds. The steelhead is a peculiar kind of ocean-going rainbow, seldom called a trout by fishermen. He is born in the river, goes to sea, and like the salmon, returns to the same river to spawn. This one looked at first rather like a rainbow trout, and on second look, rather not. His scales seemed smaller and he was much darker, his stripe a deep pink against candlelight silver, a uniquely beautiful fish. Small as he was, he was a steelhead. Ben too was pleased; a man who guides you likes action. It's not every day, he said.

My time was up and we started back to the ranch. Norm came out and gave a low whoop. With your tackle, Ben's instruction, and luck, it's a fly-fishing river, I said. He smiled and nodded. At my request he took me up to the main cabin, where the night before I had seen several large steelhead on the wall. Which is yours? I said. He pointed to one that went 22½ pounds. On fly, he said. Close's Wickerbill with the orange polar-bear hackle? I said. Yes, he said, but you may have set a record. How so? I don't recall anyone ever getting his steelhead on fly in his first three hours on the river, he said.

It's the fly, I said. That's my brag. But I'm puzzled. Here you are, an inland state, perhaps a thousand miles from the sea. Do the steelhead have a schedule for their journey so far up here into the mountains?

They are in the river from September till April, he said. The season opens October 1 and closes March 15. They do have a sort of schedule. In the early fall they hold below Riggins, about 30 miles downstream from here where the Little Salmon comes in. Then they travel fast and hold again below the mouth of the Middle Fork. In the spring they hold below the mouth of the South Fork.

When do they take fly, apart from the present moment?

From opening day in the fall until the water turns cold, and it's best when the ice goes out in mid-February till closing date, he said. In April the steelhead go back to sea. They return in September. So the season is the opposite of the usual trout season.

What I'd like most to understand, I said, is this *canyon fishing*. It's not like any other. I fish the Yellowstone a lot. There's a short canyon there—

1. This catch might be thought to contradict the thesis of Chapter 8—that all the big ones got away. I wrote that chapter before this episode, but it alters nothing, not only because a 5-pound steelhead is a small steelhead, but also because the steelhead is a special fish. Even the great aquatic biologist Paul R. Needham (*Trout Streams*, 1938) calls the sea-runners "steelheads" and the non-sea-runners "rainbows," as he says, "to get rid of a lot of confusion."

Yankee Jim, up near the Park. We seldom fish it because the current is strong and the water deep, so that even a sinking line won't get down to the trout. My distant impression of steelhead fishing was that you fished fly with a sinking line in the relatively shallow riffles and in pools that weren't too deep.

We have various conditions along this river, he said. Toward North Fork at the east end of the canyon, the holes are smaller and there are more rapids. The lower end has bigger holes and fewer rapids. Steelhead seldom lie in more than 12 feet of water, except in the cold months when the ice is in the river. In early fall they sometimes lie in shallow riffles less than 12 inches deep. Steelhead in this river don't come to the surface to take a fly. No one has ever taken a steelhead on dry fly in this area to my knowledge. Sometimes the sinking line will work without lead weight on the leader, but a floating line never will. I caught my big one last April 6. The water was slow and deep, 12 feet. Manns Creek Hole, where you caught your fish, is 9 feet deep with a gravel bottom. It's a matter of . . .

Fly fishing on the bottom, I said.

With these observations, we shook hands and swore allegiance to the fly. I flew off down the canyon on the way to Boise. At the controls was Al Tice, founder and former owner of the ranch, who flies up and down and in and out of the canyon every practicable day. Paul had told me, he's the best mountain pilot in Idaho. When I mentioned this to Al, between two white peaks split by a streak of blue sky, he said, Paul is the best instrument pilot in these parts.

Chapter 10
SALMON FLIES

The resplendent classic salmon fly is a peculiar creation. Unlike the trout fly, from which its designation *fly* doubtless descended, it has no firm ground in nature. It is not meant to represent an insect and so in that generic sense is not a fly. Indeed, it is not meant to represent any particular thing in nature. It is a sheer act of the angling imagination. But behind the several departures from the classic salmon fly during the past fifty years lie determined efforts to develop a rational basis for them. All begin with the great salmon itself.

The serene, stylized lines and mystic head of the game Atlantic or "true" salmon have evoked from anglers a feeling of respect and admiration. He is a stately fish, big but not cumbrous, fast but not hasty. Nor is "dart" the word for his action in the water; from a still, fin-waving position, or a slow, invisibly undulating glide, he will suddenly jet forward or to the side with a swift stroke, turning slightly on occasion to flash a bright streak under the water, going this way and that, as if drawing phantom triangles and other geometric forms. Along the surface he sometimes pushes up a traveling bulge at cruising speed. He goes into the air with a rip and a swoosh that are music in the salmon fisher's ear, turning and twisting at a height of several feet and coming back down with a neat chug, or a plank splash that rolls away the waves. The sound of leaping salmon is to the river man as the surf is to the sea dweller. It is not generally at this time, however, that the salmon fishes well, and one might better sit down and watch his games. His fishing strike is typically a boil on the surface, swirling like a choked geyser, during which the novice more often than not is nervous with the rod and takes the fly away from him.

When the salmon run is on, out come the rod, the reel, the line, the fly, and into the water goes the hopeful fisherman, switching his rod, feeding the line through the guides until yards of it are sustained curling in the air, and then letting it go with a forward spring, looping out over the river, the fly dropping to float, drift, or "fish" in the current over the lie of the great fish.

In season along the shores and up the rivers of Ireland, England, Scotland, Norway, and northeastern North America, the salmon is the talk of the countryside. Why he forsakes the salt sea to spawn in vulnerable upriver freshwater shallows no one can quite explain. The salmon, says Izaak Walton, "like some persons of honor and riches, which have both their winter and summer houses [has] the fresh rivers for summer, and the salt water for winter to spend his life in, which is not, as Sir Francis Bacon hath observed in his *History of Life and Death,* above ten years."

Modern observation—from scale reading—reveals that he has five stages of life. In the first he is known as an *alevin,* a tiny emerging fish that hides in the crevices of the river. In a few months he is a colorful *parr,* five or six inches long, with dots of red along the back, a silver underbelly, and a row of black bars along the sides. Salmon fishermen often see many parr chasing their flies. After a period of from one to five years, but usually two, he descends the river as a somewhat larger silvery *smolt,* and is lost to sight for several years. He has lush feeding grounds in the ocean and grows rapidly there. If he, or she, returns to the river in a little more than a year, with a weight up to five pounds or so and a forked tail, he is a *grilse,* pound for pound as fighting a fish as one will meet. If he stays longer—as many as five years, with corresponding increases in weight—he comes back, usually to the same river, the great square-tail silver-and-blue salmon. He finds the river after the spring rains or summer or fall freshets discharge fresh water into the sea, and comes in not to feed but to complete his life cycle, most likely in the headwaters where he was born. He may die then, as the Pacific salmon do immediately after spawning; but he may live through a starvation winter upriver and go out with the spring rains again, black and emaciated, a "slink" (sometimes, unfortunately, fished), to go round his cycle and return again in silver bloom.

He meets the angler on the way up to the spawning beds; and the question as to whether he truly feeds during the run agitates the angler in search of a theory for his fly. The salmon's stomach at this time rarely shows much in the way of food. A complex argument by able scientists shows that he does not and cannot feed in the river. He is said on excellent authority to lose his digestive enzymes in fresh water (the reason why he can be packed in ice and shipped whole without deterioration). An equally complex argument by equally able scientists says that he digests so rapidly that an autopsy can reveal little, but that one does find traces—such as fly wings, fish scales, and ribs—as proof that he has eaten. The argument

93

is a scientific one, but fishermen are generally prone to take sides, and neutrality is regarded as weak-mindedness by either side. It is widely believed that the salmon fly may resemble a struggling minnow or insect or the brilliant underwater colors of the unknown food upon which the salmon feeds in the sea. The temporizer attributes to the fly the quality of *attraction*, whether because of hunger, ferocity, curiosity, flash reflex, temperature, tides, or old memories.

The art of salmon fishing, in common with the art of fly-fishing in general, consists of equipment, knowledge of stream life, and presentation. In their particulars, however, these three elements are distinctive in the game. Equipment centers on the fly. A great master of the game, Eric Taverner (*Salmon Fishing*, 1931), has argued that the salmon fly comes from the fifteenth-century imitation trout flies in *The Treatise of Fishing with an Angle*. "Humour . . . the fish," said Richard Franck (*Northern Memoirs*) in 1694, and toward this end advises the angler to use glittering tinsel and multiple wings. This was the beginning of the fancy salmon fly and its theory. It did not wholly come into fashion, however, until the nineteenth century. We see it first in color in George Bainbridge's *Fly Fisher's Guide* (1816). Since then the fashion has shifted back and forth from somber to brilliant colors, the latter in outright abstract patterns.

Salmon-fly brilliance is the work of the Irish, whose flytiers lived near seaport markets where they found gold and silver tinsel, colored silks, bright feathers, and other delights of man's eye. A standard salmon fly today is an international affair, with hooks from England and Scandinavia, jungle-cock and peacock feathers from India, wild duck from the United States, silk from Italy, tinsel from France, golden pheasant from the Orient, and hair from Canadian moose hocks or Rocky Mountain bear. One fly may contain twenty different materials of as many colors from as many different countries. The salmon fly is the most complicated in fly-fishing and the most difficult to tie well. Yet no one understands what it means to the fish or how it got that way, although we do know that the Irish tendency won out against conservative local flytiers on the rivers.

The dispute crossed the Atlantic. "Barnwell"—Robert Barnwell Roosevelt (*Game Fish of the Northern States of America, and British Provinces*, 1862), Theodore's uncle, and a distinguished and now neglected American fisherman, conservationist, and writer—reported in his time that the flies "in vogue in Canada are much gayer than those of New Brunswick . . . and in the end we may find that handsome, gaudy feathers answer best." Thad Norris (*The American Angler's Book*, 1864) resisted this notion: "The gaudy Irish flies tied for the Shannon would frighten the salmon on this side of the Atlantic . . . flies for American rivers—except when the water is discolored by a freshet—as a general rule, should be of darker and more sober tints than those used in Scotland and Ireland." As it turned out, gaudy flies came to be used in New Brunswick for an extended period. Then, not long ago, the somber tones of the 1860's returned with a vengeance in the form of plain hair flies and even imitations of insects—the stone fly, sedge, and May fly.

A McFarland (*Salmon of the Atlantic*) has hazarded this theory of Scottish influence on salmon flies:

> In the early years of Scotland, the clan with the gayest tarletan made the gaudiest flies and the wearer of an unusually bright kilt had to sleep in it when near a salmon stream. But evil days fell upon the land and its sons began to travel and bring home fine feathers and tinseled cloth inappropriate to the climate and offensive to the religious dignity of the race. So a bawble too braw for the kirk became the makings of a salmon fly with such arrangements and additions as might appeal to the alcoholic imagination of a gillie, or the mellow humor of a laird.
>
> With flies produced in this manner, anything approaching classification would have been impossible, had the first tourists not confined themselves to conventional vintage routes and returned with feathers plucked from the same birds and cloth cut from the same bolts. As it was, there appeared certain bright and drab creations, more or less uniform in composition and named Jock Scott for the maker [?] or some kind of a dose if possessed of unusual killing powers. Such flies brought willing fish, and the dour Scotch are too canny to imagine that anything will move the unwilling ones, so they were content with their labors. . . .
>
> Unfortunately, there are and always will be in the world, a number of people who insist on trying to paint the lily, hence by English, Irish, Canadian and American "fly cubists" we have had foisted upon us, multitudes of hybrid flies named for their originators, or for some stream to whose fish it is fondly imagined they prove unusually attractive.

More has happened to salmon-fishing tactics in the past fifty years than in the previous two centuries. Berners and Walton preferred bait for salmon. It is most discouraging to the fly-fisher's estimation of the fish that he still loves bait, especially a gob of worms. Some time after Walton, the fly took precedence over bait, and for two centuries was fished for the most part with the standard motion, suggested above, of an angle cast downstream with the fly fished well under the surface. A modest but fine literature of this game developed after the beginning of the nineteenth century, its two classic general works being William Scrope's witty and readable *Days and Nights of Salmon Fishing in the Tweed* (1843) and Alfred Chaytor's informative *Letters to a Salmon Fisher's Sons* (1910). Eric Taverner did his modern omnibus summary of the old game along with hints of the new in 1931.

QUILL GORDON

The trouble with the old game was that although it afforded a wide scope for contending with the fish through knowledge of his habits, there was little one could do about the fly except to consider its size and the general tone of its color palette in their relation to weather and river conditions. Presentation of the fly to the fish was routine: across and down; across and down. It was a simple game, requiring a minimum of tactical skill, and for spring fishing when the water is high and the salmon run is on, it remains the best recommended approach. Its similarity to downstream wet-fly trout fishing is apparent. It may be recalled that trout fishing broke out of this rut in the late nineteenth century with intensive upstream surface fishing, followed by the specially constructed dry or floating fly. In downstream fishing, the fly fishes itself against the current. Upstream fishing is more skillful and exploitable, as it places the angler in complete control of his fly. Somewhat later—publicly, in the 1920's—equally revolutionary and not dissimilar refinements were introduced into salmon fishing simultaneously in England and North America.

The first big change in modern salmon fishing took place when A. H. E. Wood (*Greased Line Fishing for Salmon,* prepared by "Jock Scott," 1935), distinguished British sportsman and gardener, did what the title of his posthumous book suggests: greased and floated his line. This may not seem like much, but it was everything. For the first time in history salmon fishing really got to the surface. The old school never dreamed of an across-stream or upstream cast, for the simple reason that the sunk line would immediately be caught up with the currents and eddies, thus dragging the fly through the water in a series of unnatural and unattractive gyrations obnoxious to the salmon. The same thing, of course, happens to the greased line lying across varying currents, but something now could be done about it.

The crux of Wood's innovation consisted in an adaptation of a technique well known to anglers as "mending the line." Just as the floating line at some place along its lie is about to pull the fly unnaturally, the angler flips or rolls the line lying on the surface into a more favorable position that will allow the fly to proceed unhindered on its course. In other words, he manipulates the line in the various currents to stabilize the drift of the fly, without jerking it. With salmon fishing brought to the surface, the angler could now cast to particular salmon wherever they lay. It was revolution. And once again, distance from the bottom proved to be an influential rule for the development of angling art.

Greased-line fishing brought a change also in construction of salmon flies, resulting in the long-shanked, short-dressed fly (see picture portfolio) for low water, which had always been considered almost impossible to fish. The sunk fly is natural to high spring water, and is generally considered the proper technique for such conditions. Thus the greased line not only developed a new angling art but in effect opened up a new season for rivers that turn very quiet in the summer.

Not long after Wood began experimenting on the Dee in Scotland, Colonel Ambrose Monell, George La Branche (*Salmon and the Dry Fly,* 1924), and Edward R. Hewitt (*Secrets of the Salmon,* 1925) were experimenting with the dry fly for salmon on the Upsalquitch, a tributary of the Restigouche. Theodore Gordon (*The Complete Fly Fisherman,* 1947) had tied dry flies for a friend on the Restigouche before 1903, and they took fish; but his move, while enterprising indeed and the first on record, was seemingly without influence until Monell years later persuaded La Branche to extend his dry-trout-fly efforts to salmon. Hewitt conducted extensive studies of the salmon and tackle for it that made him the most noted American salmon angler in the United States and England, and the greatest influence in getting this country's salmon fishing out of the doldrums.

Now there occurred a remarkable event, unresolved to this day. La Branche developed a high-floating dry fly, floated it a "sacred inch" from the salmon's nose without drag, and took many Restigouche salmon, so many that he concluded that brown trout were more difficult to fish. Whereupon Wood, hearing of all this over on the Dee, invited La Branche—or rather challenged him—to come over and try to take one of *his* salmon on a dry fly. In the mid-twenties La Branche did so, and his efforts were catastrophic: many rose to his fly but none stayed with the hook. Finally after several return trips, he managed to take one salmon. The subsequent published correspondence between Wood and La Branche is the most rarefied apologia in fishing literature for "Why I didn't catch him." The dry fly, even in the smallest sizes, is now established American salmon-fishing practice; but it is said that British salmon will only play with the dry fly and rarely hook themselves.

A "secret weapon" developed and widely used in modern times on the Restigouche is "fishing the Patent," an American method adapted, it is believed, from Rocky Mountain hair-fly fishing for trout. Like other modern techniques it allows the angler to place his fly where he wishes, and is a great killer on some rivers. Lee Wulff (*Leaping Silver,* 1940), one of the best-known salmon anglers in the United States, has led a movement to further scale down the size of rods to trout-fishing proportion and weight, and to increase the use of the dry fly, particularly his own Grey and White Wulffs, two of the most remarkably successful dry salmon flies ever created. The American salmon fisherman today plays all the fly-fishing angles to get into contact with his great and puzzling quarry.

Chapter 11

THE FIRST MODERN TROUT FLIES

The Treatise of Fishing with an Angle introduced the first modern trout flies. They were not the first known in history. Before the treatise, the artificial fly was described possibly twice in literature, once for certain by Aelian in the third century A.D., and once, less certainly—depending on your scholar—by Martial about two hundred years earlier. Before Martial the fly is without record. The twelve hundred years between Aelian and the *Treatise of Fishing* are the dark ages of the fly. Something went on, but we do not know what until it turns up in the treatise, modern and almost complete. But the fly-fishers of antiquity, who were not necessarily sport fishermen, had no influence in modern times—Aelian's fly was first noticed in the second half of the nineteenth century—and so the flies of the treatise stand alone as the ancestors of the modern trout fly.

As the author of the treatise calls these flies "the XII," we presume that they were entrenched in the fishing practices of the fifteenth century and earlier. This has long been the accepted interpretation. However, the authoritative ring of "the XII" could also be the author's own declaration of choice in flies. If the curse of classicism was not on them at the time they were first set down in writing, it came upon them afterward. For two centuries they ruled the sport, so far as writing is concerned. The trout fly is still subject to a constant pull between classicism and innovation. In recorded history the score now is even: three dominantly classical centuries, the fifteenth, sixteenth, and eighteenth, and three innovating, the seventeenth, nineteenth, and twentieth. The widespread search today for a small-number set of basic trout flies suggests the beginning of a new classicism.

The record of the rule of the XII is clear. Just seven books on angling, as we saw in Chapter 2, are known to have been published from the *Treatise of Fishing* in the early fifteenth century to *The Compleat Angler* in the middle of the seventeenth century. Look at these again for their bearing on the development of the trout fly.

After the *Treatise of Fishing* came the recently discovered *The Arte of Angling* (1577) by an anonymous author, from whom Walton seems to have borrowed information on baits, keeping baits, and other matters. This long-lost and worthy writer mentions the trout and the fly only once and then surreptitiously: "I dare not well deal in the angling of the trout, for displeasing of one of our wardens, which either is counted the best trouter in England, or so thinketh, who would not (as I suppose) have the taking of that fish common. But yet thus much I may say, that he worketh with a fly in a box." Another curious avoidance of trout flies occurs in an edition of the *Treatise of Fishing* published in 1586 and reprinted in 1614 under the title *A Jewell for Gentrie*, which omits the whole fly list. Other writers, however, used it freely.

The third book, Leonard Mascall's *A Booke of Fishing with Hooke and Line,* published in 1590, pirates and edits the twelve flies from the treatise.

The fourth book, John Dennys's *Secrets of Angling,* a treatise in verse published in 1613, treats the trout but not the fly; however, the second edition of the poem, published in 1620, contains a remarkable observation written by its felicitous editor William Lawson, perhaps the only man to have been made famous by writing a single footnote.

Angle with a made fly, he says, and with a line of three hairs at least twice the length of your rod; counterfeit the May fly and change his color month by month from dark white to yellow. Lawson gives a dressing, the first new trout-fly dressing after the XII—a period of about two hundred years, counting from the probable date of the original manuscript—as follows: "The head is of black silk or haire, the wings of a feather of a mallart, teele, or pickled hen-wing. The body of Crewell according to the moneth for colour, and run about with a black haire; all fastned at the taile, with the thread that fastned the hooke."

Lawson then offers an illustration of a trout fly—the first in angling history—but we can't count on it. It corresponds not to the dressing but to a natural that the engraver must have caught on his windowpane.

The fifth book on angling is Gervase Markham's *The Pleasures of Princes,* published in 1614. The trout flies in this prose version of *Secrets of Angling* are from the *Treatise of Fishing*, pirated, with revisions and additions, from Mascall. The historian John Waller Hills (*A History of Fly Fishing for Trout,* 1921) is inclined to believe that the editing of Markham's flies is the work of Lawson, and that by his work the flies of the treatise were brought to perfection, "complete and unambiguous, neither of which they originally were." Hills's high opinion of this version of the flies accounts for some of the differences between his conception of the original flies and ours presented here.

The sixth book, Thomas Barker's *The Art of Angling*, published in 1651, is the first to say how to tie a fly. His fly dressings are generalized.

The seventh is *The Compleat Angler* (1653). Walton seems not to have been a fly-fisher; he took his artificial flies from the *Treatise of Fishing* via Mascall. But Part Two of the fifth edition of *The Compleat Angler*, subtitled "Being Instructions How to Angle for a Trout or Grayling in a Clear Stream," written by his friend Charles Cotton and published in 1676, is a masterful specialized treatise on fly-fishing. Cotton published an original list of sixty-five flies with their dressings.

Three other works need to be mentioned here: *The Experienced Angler* by Robert Venables (1662), who, like Barker, gives generalized dressings; James Chetham's *The Angler's Vade Mecum* (1681); and Richard Franck's *Northern Memoirs* (written in 1658, published in 1694).

Thus from the *Treatise of Fishing* through Walton, with the minor exceptions noted, the only flies in print are the XII. The revolution in fly-fishing, breaking this classicism-by-plagiary, was performed in the 1650's, 1660's, and 1670's by Barker, Cotton, and Venables.

So long as the XII ruled, the art of the fly scarcely moved. When their rule was broken, fly-fishing returned to firsthand imitation of nature, and a large variety of flies were invented. Barker and Venables introduced the idea of choosing flies for their relationship to weather and water. Fancy flies (flies imitative only of the generality of flies) came on, beginning with Cotton, and with him, too, fly-fishers entered the universe of minutely imitative fly dressings, where they have been ever since. Cotton fished fine and tied fine. For example, his fourth fly for March: "There is also for this month a fly, called the Thorn Tree Fly, the dubbing an absolute black mixed with eight or ten hairs of Isabella-colored mohair; the body as little as can be made, and the wings of a bright mallard's feather, an admirable fly, and in great repute amongst us for a killer."

This killer is a simple fly, as simple as a *Treatise of Fishing* fly, except for the color of the mohair. Sir John Hawkins, who edited an edition of *The Compleat Angler* in 1760, explains the reference as follows: "Isabella," he says, is "a kind of whitish yellow, or, as some say, a buff colour a little soiled." Soiled was the point. A generation before Cotton, in the year 1602, the Infanta Isabella, daughter of Philip the Second, King of Spain, accompanied her husband the Archduke Albertus on a campaign. When he laid siege to Ostend, then held by heretics, she made a rash vow that she would not change her clothes until the city was taken. This happened to require three years. So Isabella's linen came to be the right color for the cavalier Cotton's trout fly.

The revolution steered by Cotton, Barker, Venables and, perhaps in some degree, Franck, ended in the seventeenth century. With one exception—Charles (1744 edition) and Richard (1747 edition) Bowlker's *The Art of Angling*—the eighteenth, like the fifteenth and sixteenth, went classical again so far as flies are concerned, though it was a lively century in what it did to create the modern rod, reel, line, and leader. Bowlker wrote off several of the treatise flies in "A Catalogue of Flies Seldom Found Useful to Fish With," and created a new list of "the most useful flies" which was promptly classicized for the second half of the eighteenth century. The nineteenth and twentieth centuries returned to the creation of new flies. Isabella buff had nothing on the body of the Green Drake by Alexander Mackintosh (*The Modern Angler or, Driffield Angler*, 1810): "a little fine wool from the ram's testicles, which is a beautiful dusty yellow." That this tradition has not let up is shown by a dubbing for the Hendrickson fly by our contemporary Art Flick (in his book *Streamside Guide*, 1947), which calls for belly fur of the vixen fox stained a little pink with urine burns.

The real work of the nineteenth century was in the creation of entomologies, the decisive shift to upstream fishing, and the invention of the dry fly, which together formed the greatest revolution in fly-fishing history since the sport has been known.

With the dry fly came a new brand of classicism, an effort led by Frederic Halford (*Floating Flies and How to Dress Them*, 1886, and other works) to create a definitive "scientific" set of imitation flies. But no action without a reaction. G. E. M. Skues, a great angling writer of a generation ago, successfully attacked dry-fly purism and the new classicism with the weapons of the old wet fly, the new nymph, and the urge to create. In the United States at about the turn of the century, Theodore Gordon introduced the dry fly, designed with an impressionism like Monet's and a streamside empiricism that altered forever the American weakness for imitating not our own natural flies but the established English artificials. He took his stand on mimesis as the ground of the art, but he was not a stickler for precise imitation: "If we have faith in the trout's ability to distinguish colors and shades of those colors, we have firm ground under our feet, a rational basis of action, and satisfactory explanations of many puzzles. Such a belief need not limit us to strict imitation of the natural in all cases." The range of the Quill Gordon fly is evidence of this liberality.

In the arbitrariness of the sport, however, some anglers specify extremely refined rules. For Sid Neff of Pittsburgh, a promising young angling writer with awesome flytying artistry and learning (in Montana they call him "Einstein"), the essence of the sport lies in the exact correlation of fly and insect. He gives a clear description of this approach to fly-fishing in a letter to the author:

After our conversation I began to think how I might better explain what I consider the fine art of angling. Without a doubt, the art of fishing with an angle came from the English. Through the centuries they evolved various rules, which, in order to play the game in its purest way, must be followed. As anglers gained a better understanding of the game, they began to modify these rules. As the world changes, rivers, trout, insects, and even anglers change—so must the rules. What I consider to be the highest form of the art (and men like Marinaro, Harris, and Sawyer are in full agreement with me) is attempting to catch individual trout that are rising to specific insects (at specific times and in specific stages). When one encounters a riser, one must immediately identify the rise-form. From this one is to identify the active insects. Should there be several insects active, the rise-form should be a strong indication of the specific insect (and stage) that the riser is taking. From this information, the angler can choose the proper representation from his box. Before his fly is presented, he must be aware of the exact rise-position of the trout. The fly is then presented to the riser—if the fish takes the fly with the same rise-form (as he was taking insects), then the angler wins the game. Should the riser take the fly with a different rise-form (thus indicating the angler has chosen the wrong representation—possibly because of improperly identifying the rise-form or the insect), he loses the game. Catching a trout is not an end in itself, but rather a means to the end. One modification I would suggest to the rule is the differentiation between fly and insect. An insect is an animate creature, a fly is lifeless. With reference to the above, a fly is a creation of metal, fur, and feathers that represents the insect. Without the insect a fly is not of any use. For example, when the various Caenidae [the smallest May flies, about 4 mm in size] are active, the many Caenis representations are awfully effective. Should one attempt to use a Caenis fly, say in April or May (or any time the Caenis is not active) the results are disastrous.

Most fly fishermen today would agree that angling is not primarily a question of how many fish one catches but of how they are caught. Sheer effectiveness is dominated by style, and style—how you choose to fish—is defined by one's own rules. Hence the proliferation of styles and of well-tempered argument over them.

The tension between classicism and innovation is still with us, and doubtless always will be. Today in the United States, Easterners, with their perennial Quill Gordons and Cahills, usually are more classical than Westerners, with their experiments in new types as well as patterns of flies. But the issue is not sharp. Two innovators, Lee Wulff in the East and Dan Bailey in the West, both of them professionals who have invented many new flies, especially for fast, rough water, may often be found fishing the old flies. And the traditionalist Sparse Grey Hackle ("angling is tradition"), who has given us idylls on sympathetic if fishless streams, will try any new fly so long as it is a May fly.

Opinion on flies, however, has not always been so peaceable. In the wars between classicists and anticlassicists in times past, the *Treatise of Fishing* was sometimes held up as the bad example. In the course of assailing all forms of classicism, Hewett Wheatley (*The Rod and Line,* 1849), a brilliant advocate of the fancy fly, "Water-Witches," and other new artificial baits, said: "That the 'Jury of a dozen flies,' written about by our ancestors, may have condemned a few fins to death, I cannot dispute; but I believe they were mercifully pleased to acquit forty-nine out of every fifty that were arraigned before them. The moderns are not so merciful."

And Skues says: "The famous twelve flies for trout and grayling are described as if they were the laws of the Medes and Persians and altered not."

That the *Treatise of Fishing* flies were classicized to the absolute limit for perhaps two centuries is clear from the evidence, but it must be remembered that classicism is not the fault of the classic. It was an important moment for fly-fishers when the author of the treatise wrote down the twelve dressings in the first manual of the art. The great defense of the treatise flies is Hills's history, which traces eleven of the twelve down to the present. Our work in constructing the flies for the illustrations in this book would have been more difficult but for Hills, though we are forced to disagree with him in some important respects.

So much for the historical setting. We turn now to the business at hand, which is the actual tying of the XII trout flies. We present our argument (and travail) first with regard to the general elements as they relate to all the flies, and then with regard to each fly in particular.

The general elements follow:

Style

The treatise tells us the ingredients but does not tell us how the flies were tied, nor does it give a hint as to their general appearance. There is no known description of the act of tying a fly until Barker, Cotton, and Venables, and we have searched them and the other early writers for clues.

Markham, a little over a century away from the printing of the treatise, said this about their style: "Now for the shapes, and proportions of these flies, it is impossible to describe them without paynting, therefore you shall take of these severall flies alive, and laying them before you, try how neere your Art can come unto nature by an equall shape, and mixture of colours."

The assumption that the treatise flies were modeled on nature is our clue to size, but this only shifts the difficulty to one of identifying the naturals represented by these artificials. In only two of the flies is there certainty, namely, the Stone Fly and the Wasp Fly; these are the same today, and there is no reason not to take fish with them now on the Beaver-kill or the Madison. The Dun Fly No. 1 could be either the February Red or the March Brown. The coloration of the Shell Fly makes it acceptable as a caddis; the Shell Fly and grannom are identified by Alfred Ronalds in *The Fly-Fisher's Entomology*, 1836. For the rest we know of nothing better to do about the natural models than to present the often contradictory intuitions of Hills and Skues, two fly-fishers of one sensibility who spent their lives observing both English stream insects and their imitations. Our policy is to dress the fly to the size of a possible natural proposed by either or both of these masters.

It is not surprising that the treatise does not give us a word picture of the appearance of the flies. Modern fly dressings do not usually specify style in this respect, and most professional flytiers today are not particularly conscious that their "exact imitation" imitates no fly in hand but may be a convincing impression of the fly on the water. We have concluded from its fur-and-feather materials that the treatise flies too are impressionistic, but that they were slightly rougher than modern flies; for the equipment was cruder, the professional was unknown, and the flies were tied by hand. To some extent the style is fixed by reverse wings. The most noticeable difference from the modern style is dictated by the shape of the hooks illustrated in the treatise. The shanks are so short and the bite of the hook so deep that the fly bodies must have extended well onto the bend.

The flies illustrated here vary in the "set" of the wings. This is partly intentional, partly chance resulting from the feathers used and random variations in the tying of each fly. We wished to avoid making a case for a uniform style.

Tying Thread

The treatise gives no directions. But in one instance, the Dun Cut, the wings are bound on with barked hemp, indicating that a dark effect was desired. A possible inference is that unless, as in this case, something was done about it, tying off the fly ordinarily left a light or neutral effect. Venables says: "First, I begin to set on my Hook . . . with such coloured Silk as I conceive most proper for the Flie." Hence we suppose the rule for the treatise was merely to pick a harmonious silk.

Tails

Here the most obvious departure from most modern flies is in the absence of tails. The word *tail* is mentioned in two treatise flies (Dun Fly No. 2 and Stone Fly) but each time as a reference point. In the Stone fly the reference is unmistakably to the insect; in the Dun Fly No. 2 the reference may be to part of the bird.

The argument *for* tails is this: (1) The treatise and later books counsel the fly maker to copy nature. Tails are conspicuous on many insects. (2) Venables specifically gives instructions on the point: "Let me add this only, that some Flies have forked tails, and some have horns, both which you must imitate with a slender hair fastened to the head or tail of your Flie . . . and in all things, as length, colour, as like the natural Flie as you can possibly." (3) Cotton dressed one of the treatise flies (the Stone Fly) with tails. (4) The earliest illustration of a fly (*Secrets of Angling,* 1620) has a tail, although the text doesn't specifically ask for one.

The argument *against* tails is this: (1) No directions to this effect are specifically given, and if one assumes tails are implied, what material should be used? (2) Neither Mascall nor Markham adds tails in his several changes of the treatise dressings. (3) In Cotton's list of sixty-five patterns, tails are specified in only three: the Green Drake (the whisks of the tails or long hairs of the sable or fitchet), the Grey Drake (the whisks of the tails of the beard of a black cat), and the Stone Fly (place two or three hairs of a black cat's beard on the top of the hook). The Dun Cut calls for horns. Since many of Cotton's flies must have simulated May flies, they should also have been tailed, but this does not seem to have been the fashion. Of one fly that is definitely a May fly he says: "the Little Yellow May-Fly, in shape *exactly the same with the Green Drake* [our italics], but a very little one, and of as bright a yellow as can be seen; which is made of a bright yellow camlet, and the wings of a white-grey feather dyed yellow." No tails.

Our conclusion is that by *tail* the treatise means the hind or tail end of the fly. This is justified by the usage of the day, according to the *Oxford English Dictionary*.[1] But we must admit that the word could mean simply a tail-appendage.

Body

The basic body material for all flies is wool. Six of the patterns call for black; the others call for dun, ruddy, yellow, tawny, dusky, and green, respectively. To get ruddy, yellow, green, and perhaps tawny colors, natural wool must have been dyed. It could have been used as yarn or spun on as dubbing. The only problem is the black. Black could have been dyed or used natural. It seems strange that so many dressings call for black, as this is not a particularly common color for naturals. Natural black sheep's wool would be an off-black, even a dun, especially when held against sun-

1. The great classic of lexicography, otherwise known as *A New English Dictionary on Historical Principles* or the *O.E.D.*, deals with all periods of the English language. (Oxford: Clarendon Press, 1884–1933)

light, and so we surmise that perhaps when dark hues were wanted, natural wool from the black sheep was used in the old flies.

In modifying the basic hue of the wool body, two flies call for ribbing of black silk, one for ribbing of yellow thread. Two call for peacock herl "lapped around" the body. The Dun Cut has a black body with a yellow stripe down either side. The Stone Fly has a bicolored body with yellow under the tail and wings of an otherwise black body. The problem lies in techniques for achieving mixed body colors.

Venables and Cotton give detailed directions on the techniques for tying some types of multicolor bodies, and these directions are clues. Venables says: "If your Flie be of divers colours, and those lying longways from head to tail, then I take my Dubbing, and lay them on the hook long-waies one colour by another (as they are mixt in the natural Flie from head to tail) then bind all on, and make it fast with silk of the most predominant colour."

Cotton's method was different: he spun his different furs first on the thread (as it is usually done today); for example, the Stone Fly: "the dubbing of bear's dun with a little brown and yellow camlet very well mixed; but so placed, that your fly may be more yellow on the belly and towards the tail underneath than in any other part."

There is no knowing how the author of the treatise dubbed, but it is plausible to suppose that it was done as either Venables or Cotton did it. Cotton's method gets more blending and is more suited to the Stone Fly than the Dun Cut, for the latter suggests a precise yellow stripe along the body.

As to the Stone Fly, we are indifferent between the two techniques, except for the intuition that Venables's technique is the older. We therefore tied this fly more or less along his lines. For the Dun Cut, the mechanics of the operation make Venables's the only reasonable one to follow.

Fly Wings

The plumage from at least seven birds is specified for dressing treatise flies: partridge, jay, the red cock (rooster), capon, drake, buzzard, and peacock. All except the peacock are given as fly-wing materials. Two birds, the drake and the buzzard, need explanation.

In fifteenth-century England and since then, the word *drake* has the special meaning of the male of the common waterfowl (and domesticated duck), the mallard. The word was also applied to males of waterfowl in general, but it is most likely that the word *drake* in the treatise is used in the restrictive sense of the male mallard. In two flies, Maure and Tandy, there is no contention. The treatise specifies for them "the wild drake," which unquestionably is the male mallard.

In another instance it specifies "black drake" (Drake fly), but it is not explicit as to whether the meaning is feather color or species of bird. We conclude feather, and give our reasons later in the discussion of the twelve flies.

"Buzzard" means the common hawk (and closely related species) in Great Britain, whereas in the United States the term is often used for another group of birds, the vultures. The buzzard members of the hawk family were considered inferior because they were useless in falconry (suggesting why it is uncomplimentary to be called one). The red-tailed hawk is the closest North American species to the common European buzzard. The plumage of juvenile buzzards differs from the adults in being lighter on the breast and parts of the feathers. This increases the range of feathers that could be used in dressing the treatise flies. (The specimen used in our illustration—a juvenile—was provided by the well-known British angling writer Major Richard Waddington.) Two types of markings are found on the flight feathers, white mottled with dark, and dark mottled with darker. The various effects are illustrated in the flies tied.

The problem of the specific feather to be used in treatise flies is more often than not difficult to decide. Only three specific types of feathers are clearly mentioned: (1) herl of the peacock's tail, (2) mail, or light and dark breast feathers, from the drake, (3) hackle feathers from the red cock or capon. These feathers are easily recognized. The distinction between rooster and capon hackles, however, is puzzling. Capon hackles would of course be softer; but we do not know how meaningful such subtle distinctions were to the author.

In eight of the twelve flies, the author mentions no specific feather (at least by present-day usage). These all take the form of "wings of the partridge" (i.e., wings of the fly to be made from the partridge), wings of the buzzard, or wings of the drake. The treatise makes qualifications in two cases: "wings of the blackest drake" and wings "of the drake dyed yellow." The problem: What specific feather of the bird is intended for the fly wings in these eight patterns?

It is exasperating, and interesting, that the treatise should be vague on this point and so specific on the others. Perhaps in the language of the day the phrase was meaningful as it stands. Aside from breast feathers, wing or flight feathers are the common mallard feather called for in fly dressings since the seventeenth century. But even Cotton is vague on this specification. He says, for example, "the wings, of the pale grey feather of a mallard." It was apparently understood to be a flight or wing feather; only one of Cotton's dressings specifies mail: "the wings, of the male of a mallard as white as may be." (In the English of this period, "mail" and "male" were both used to designate breast feathers.) Hills concludes as regards the treatise's mallard feather, "I think [that the fly had] wings from the quill feather of a drake: not the dark mottled feather, usually called dark mallard; for I think (though it is only a matter of opinion) that when the mottled feather, light or dark, is intended, the *Treatise* uses the word 'mail,' which would be an appropriate word for a body feather" (p. 151). Hills consistently follows this interpretation, except for Dun Fly No. 1, where he assumes that the direction "wings of the partridge" means hackle or body feather.

The immediate successors of the treatise offer little assistance in this area, possibly because they too had trouble in interpreting treatise dressings and thus improvised; or they were drawing on the experience or practice of their times, which would not necessarily correspond with those of the treatise. Reading flight feathers into the vague treatise instruction, as we do, is purely deductive, but there is no strong argument against it and no satisfactory alternative.

Dual wings follow from one interpretation of three treatise flies (Dun No. 2, Ruddy, and Yellow Fly). Venables makes it clear that multiple-winged flies existed in his time: "Flies made for the Salmon are much better being made with four Wings, than if of two onely and with six better than them of four."

Hills, in his analysis of early fly construction, points out that in the first description, wings made of quill feathers were not matched slips of feather cut from right and left quills as they are today. Rather, a section from one feather was folded over or rolled into a tube and then attached to the hook.

In the matter of attaching wings one is completely at the mercy of writers after the treatise. Barker, Cotton, and Venables are consistent in that they attach the wings in reverse fashion; that is, they put on their wing materials with the ends of the feathers pointing away from the end of the hook. Then when the body was completed, they pulled the wings up and bent them back—how far back is not specified—and wedged them into place with a few turns of the working silk. Hills at best is obscure in his interpretation of the way Barker bent back his wing.

Barker is the first writer in history to provide any instruction on attaching wings, and we would have appreciated more lucidity from him. Read for yourself what he says: "Cut so much of the browne of the Mallards feather as in your owne reason make the wings, then lay the outermost part of the feather near the hook, and the point of the feather next toward the shank of the hook, so whip it three or four times about the hook with the same silk you armed the hook with. . . . [Instructions for adding body and hackle, palmer-tied, given here.] Then you must take the hook betwixt your fingers and thumb in the left hand, with a needle or pin part the wings in two, so take the silk you have wrought with all this while, and whip once about the shank that falleth crosse betwixt the wings; then with your thumb you must turn the point of the feather towards the bend of the hook, then whip three or four times about the shank of the hook, so view the proportion."

The rule of imitation suggests offhand that some wings should be up and some down, as they are in nature. But we do not assume that the rule is liberal, and here we are stymied by our decision on other grounds, mentioned above, to tie reverse wings, and therefore up wings. Conceivably reverse wings could be shaped down, but it would be a difficult and a backward way to get down wings. An argument against down wings is given by Venables: "If you set the points of the wings backwards, towards the bending of the hook, the stream (if the feathers be gentle as they ought) will fold the points of the wings in the bending of the hook, as I have often found by experience."

We expect this to remain a controversial subject, but the act of tying the flies forces a conclusion. Venables's disapproval of down wings, and the logic of reverse-wing tying, lead us to conclude that the treatise fly wings took on a more or less upright form.

To Hackle or Not to Hackle

The treatise seems to regard hackle feathers as wings. The phrasing of both dressings is alike. It says "wings of the drake and of the red capon's hackle." It does *not* say wings of the drake and hackle of the red capon. In two patterns (Ruddy and Yellow flies) where hackle feathers are mentioned, the literal interpretation would be wings composed of two different wing materials. The alternative is that hackle feathers were wound on in the conventional modern way but were still classified as a sort of wing. Hills and Skues both apparently make this assumption.

There is no clue in Mascall or Markham that the hackle should be wound on, but Barker and Venables both describe the tying of palmer-type flies. In Cotton's list there are two types of flies, palmer and winged. Hills quotes without comment Franck's ambiguous directions to hackle: "And among the variety of your Fly-adventurers, remember the Hackle, or the Fly substitute, form'd without Wings, and drest up with the Feather of a Capon, Pheasant, Partridg, Moccaw, Phlimingo, Paraketa, or the like, and the Body nothing differing in shape from the Fly, save only in ruffness, and indigency of Wings."

Has he hackled only at the throat of the fly or all along the hooks, palmer tie? It appears that, a century and a half after the treatise was printed, there is still no certain evidence of flies hackled only at the throat, as they are today. The first definite evidence of conventional hackling that we have found is Bowlker in the mid-eighteenth century.

When Bowlker wants a palmer tie, he is explicit; for example, his Black Palmer: "The body is made with the black ostridge's feather, ribbed with silver twist, with a black cock's hackle *over the body*" [our italics]. When he wants hackle around the neck of the fly, he says "hackle . . . for the legs" or "hackle wrapt twice or thrice under the but of the wing."

We conclude that the treatise flies should be unhackled, Hills notwithstanding.

Fly Heads

One treatise direction (Black Leaper) ends "with a blue head" and another (Drake Fly) "with a black head." These could refer equally to the head of the bird or to the head of the fly.

We know this much, that fly heads of different colors were known to later writers. Lawson gives his fly a head in the famous footnote. Cotton gives us flies with brown, black, and red heads. And Venables is clear on the subject: "The Head is made after all the rest of the body, of silk or hair, as being of a more shining glossy colour, than the other materials, as usually the head of the flie is more bright than the body, and is usually of a different colour from the body."

Mascall and Markham give us both interpretations of the treatise's ambiguity as between head of fly and head of bird. For the Black Leaper, Mascall modifies the text from "wings of the red capon with a blue head" to "the winges are made of the winges of a browne capon, with his blew feathers in the head," an intent even less clear than the treatise's. And Markham changes the dressing further to "his wings with the browne feathers of the Mallard, and some of his blew feathers on his head." Thus Markham inexplicably changes the bird, and furthermore, implies a dual wing (the metallic, iridescent-green head feathers could be construed as blue). Neither writer gives us this fly with a blue head.

In the Drake Fly, Mascall inconsequentially adds a comma to the text, but Markham makes a drastic change: "wings of the under mayle of the Mallard, and his head made blacke." So here we have a black-headed fly.

Note how one gets out of trouble if the interpretation of "head" is as head of the fly: two knotty ornithological problems are neatly solved. (1) The wings of the Black Leaper are from a red capon rather than an uncertain blue mongrel chicken. (2) The wings of the Drake Fly are brown mallard breast instead of some aberrant color phase or another species. The interpretation—fly head—is simplest and clarifies both dressings. It makes sense, and we adopt it.

As to the treatise flies being wet flies there is no question. But some critics have believed that the dry fly is indicated in some of those who adopted the treatise flies. We don't think we can improve much on Hills's interpretations and discussion of this subject. With one exception, all the passages in the old literature leave considerable room for subjective interpretation. Therefore, when Mascall says the Ruddy Fly is good to use "aloft on the water," or Barker that "hogs wool floats best" or "fly at the top of the water," etc., we don't think one can go any further than admit a direction to fish in an upper stratum of water, including the surface. This certainly would not have been difficult by raising the rod and even using a dapping technique. The point is that this is a far cry from what we imply by dry-fly fishing, starting with the specialized construction and all the rest. It is only by the wildest stretch of the imagination that one could envision the existence of the dry fly in the seventeenth and eighteenth centuries and not have something more specific said about it.

The troublesome "exception" often mentioned is the cork-bodied flies of Barker. There is no way to get away from the implications here, even though the result is more like a bass bug than a dry fly. However, that is immaterial insofar as the treatise flies are concerned and is only a Mascall innovation, as there is no hint of it later. Hills's interpretation is as good as any.

Difficult Renditions

In the present stage of knowledge, secure conclusions cannot be made on several critical points. In instances where it is impossible to render a logically strong judgment between choices, we present our first choice as the most likely, and alternatives as possible but less likely. The alternatives are offered in the illustrations and the table of our dressings.

Now look at the flies and our argument for the dressing of each. We use the original fifteenth-century language rather than the modernized version given in Chapter 12.

No. 1 Dun Fly (March)

The treatise: "The donne flye the body of the donne woll & the wyngis of the pertryche."

Does "dun" imply May fly? The *Oxford English Dictionary* indicates that *dun* was a descriptive adjective in the fifteenth century. The *Middle English Dictionary*[2] has the adjective *don,* "dun," but no example referring to flies. Reference to *dun* meaning subimago May flies seems to have come later in history through association with the fly's general hue. Our assump-

2. Edited by Sherman Kuhn, Hans Kurath (retired), and staff (Ann Arbor: University of Michigan Press, 1952–   ). This is a more specialized dictionary than the *O.E.D.* and is designed to give a fuller treatment of the language of the Middle English period (i.e., from about 1100 to about 1500, excluding the early printed books). Thus far, the letters *A–K* have been published, and the files of the *M.E.D.* contain the materials which are now in process of becoming the published letters *L–Z.* The *M.E.D.* includes the vocabulary of the manuscript *Treatise of Fishing with an Angle* (1450), but not that of the 1496 print.

tion is that *dun* refers to color only and does not imply a life stage of a May fly.

"Partridge" we assume to refer to the common (Hungarian) partridge. Is a wing or body feather intended? Markham specifies "male," and Hills must thus have got his body feather from Markham, and not the treatise; Hills further suggests that the feather was tied on as hackle. Since we assumed that a wing feather is implied if mail (breast) is not specified by the treatise, we make the partridge wing feather first choice.

Hills believes that this fly is an imitation of the February red, a stone fly; Skues says March brown, a May fly. Either of these insects could readily be the prototype. Hills seems to have been influenced by the connotation of the modern fly Partridge and Orange, a hackle fly, even though the use of partridge as hackle in the treatise fly is not apparent.

No. 2 Another Dun Fly (March)

The treatise: "A nother doone flye. the body of blacke woll: the wynges of the blackyst drake: and the Jay vnder the wynge & vnder the tayle."

"Wings of the blackest drake" we construe to mean a dark section of flight feathers.

Two interpretations can be made of the phrase "and the Jay under the wing and under the tail." One is that the reference means jay feathers placed under wing and tail end of the *fly*. If this is followed (as Hills recommends), what feathers from the jay are used (blue feathers?) and how are they placed? There is no answer.

The alternative is that the text refers to the bird and not to the fly. That is, the fly wings are to be made from feathers from under the wing and tail of the jay, as well as from the drake. Thus, a dual- or multiple-winged fly would result. This makes more sense in terms of construction. Mascall changes the bird but understands the meaning to be "feathers under the wings of his taile."

We choose to stay with the jay and take a feather from under his wing, thus making a dual-wing fly.

Both Hills and Skues believe Dun Fly No. 2 is the olive or blue dun.

No. 3 The Stone Fly (April)

The treatise: "The stone flye. the body of blacke wull: & yelowe vnder the wynge, and vnder the tayle & the wynges of the drake."

This fly and its dressing have an unbroken history to modern times. It is one fly that is unmistakable in identification and one where the directions show the treatise clearly imitating nature.

Making the black-wool body yellow under wing and tail pinpoints a conspicuous feature in the color pattern of some of the larger stone-fly adults. This interpretation seems inconsistent with our interpretation of the text of Dun Fly No. 2; if it is in fact inconsistent, then the error lies with Dun Fly No. 2 rather than here; for this fly is known without question. However, order of directions differs: in the case of the Stone Fly the phrase "and yellow under wing and tail" follows "body" and hence should be related to the body in some way. In the case of Dun Fly No. 2 the phrase "and the Jay under wing and tail" follows the wing instruction and so seems to call for jay feathers in the fly wing.

"Wings of the drake" we again construe to mean sections of flight quills. The wings of the stone fly (in flight) are large and conspicuous. They could have been dressed large. Cotton gives this specific instruction and we follow it.

No. 4 Ruddy Fly (May)

The treatise: "In the begynnynge of May a good flye. the body of roddyd wull and lappid abowte wyth blacke sylke: the wynges of the drake & of the redde capons hakyll."

The archaic word *roddyd*, probably the past participle of the verb *rud* (*O.E.D.*), meant red or ruddy; and the word is clarified by Mascall, who gives the fly the title Ruddy Fly.

"Wings of the drake and of the red capon's hackle" can be interpreted as a dual wing, and "wings" could be conventional wings of hackle wound on. If they are hackle wings, they could be conventional hackle or palmer. Hills does not say so outright, but implies a conventional hackle for this fly as well as for the others where hackle is mentioned: "The basis of the fly, red hackle, is the same in both: the wings are not different."

This is a critical point. If the fly is tied with a conventional hackle, it must be done without specific instruction from the treatise to do so. If it is a hackle fly, it seems more likely to be a palmer, since the palmer tie appears to be the only hackle fly known to the seventeenth century.

If, on the other hand, it is a dual-wing fly, the order of placing the materials is important. It makes sense to veil the mallard quill sections with red-hackle points.

Hills considers the Ruddy Fly to have a modern counterpart in the Red Spinner (imago of the blue dun); Skues in the Great Red Spinner (imago of the March brown).

No. 5 The Yellow Fly (May)

The treatise: "The yelow flye. the body of yelow wull: the wynges of the redde cocke hakyll & of the drake lyttyd yelow."

113

QUILL GORDON

The instruction "wings of red cock's hackle and of drake dyed yellow" again presumably refers to a dual wing. Some of Cotton's flies call for this dyed quill. The order of hackle and quill is reversed from that of the Ruddy Fly, but we assemble the materials as before: dyed quill veiled by hackle points. Hackle points on the inside are useless, as they would be obscured by the more opaque mallard quill.

No. 6 The Black Leaper (May)

The treatise: "The blacke louper. the body of blacke wull & lappyd abowte wyth the herle of þe pecok tayle: & the wynges of þe redde capon wt a blewe heed."

Does "with a blue head" refer to the bird (red capon) or the fly? As noted previously, if it refers to the fly an ambiguous direction becomes quite clear.

Taking the alternative interpretation, that it is the red capon which has the blue head, what feather and what color feather is implied? Both Hills and Skues take this alternative (without explanation), and both adopt hackle feathers. They do not specify the color of the hackle, although Skues implies red (Red Palmer). The argument could be advanced that a blue feather was intended. But the case for any hackle feather is weak in the absence of the word *hackle* in the directions. It is specified in two other dressings, so why not here too, if it is actually intended?

All in all, a blue-feather interpretation is subjective and seems to be tinged with wishful thinking from the flytier's point of view. A blue-headed fly is not the most satisfying creation for a purist to contemplate. But a blue-headed fly is not much more startling than a yellow stripe down the side of a body, yellow under wing or tail, or wings tied on with brown hemp.

No. 7 Dun Cut (June)

The treatise: "The donne cutte: the body of blacke wull & a yelow lyste after eyther syde: the wynges of the bosarde bounde on with barkyd hempe."

The yellow stripe down the side and wings wrapped with barked hemp are, doubtless, clues to the identity of this fly. The bodies of many insects give the impression of being divided by a lighter line in the distribution of the back and belly color patterns.

"Wings of the buzzard" we take to mean sections of flight feathers. These are specified in Markham (and likewise by Mascall) as "the wings of the wings of a *Buzzard*."

"Barked hemp" is a rope cord steeped in a dye made of the bark of certain trees (for the preservative action).

Hills thinks the Dun Cut is the yellow dun; Skues, "beyond question" the sedge fly or Welshman's Button of Halford.

No. 8 Maure Fly (June)

The treatise: "The maure flye. the body of dolke wull the wynges of the blackest mayle of the wylde drake."

Dolke does not appear in the *Oxford English Dictionary*. Dusky is the interpretation evident or implied in Mascall and Markham.

Maure, for them, becomes "moorerish" and "morish." Hills believes Mascall misread *maure.* Actually, *maure* and *moor* are legitimate synonyms in fifteenth- and sixteenth-century English. The *O.E.D.* gives *maure* and *moure* as obsolete forms of *moor* and the connotation of the word as dusky, with a 1489 example of usage: "He became as blacke as a moure." *Maure* also meant "ant," but elsewhere in the treatise the word *pysmire* is used for ant.

Hills seems to make a good case here for the subimago of the May fly (green drake, *Ephemera danica*) as the natural meant by the treatise. Skues thinks it is the alderfly.

No. 9 Tandy Fly (June)

The treatise: "The tandy flye at saynt Wyllyams daye. the body of tandy wull & the wynges contrary eyther ayenst other of the whitest mayle of þe wylde drake."

Tandy becomes "tawny" in Mascall and Markham.

This is the only fly with directions for the form, or forming, of the wing. The literal translation would be "wings opposite, one against the other." This Hills interprets as meaning feathers set "back to back," which seems reasonable. The implication of these instructions seems to be that the identity of the two light mallard breast feathers should be preserved after they are set on the hook.

As with the Maure Fly, Hills makes a case for the imago of the May fly (gray drake, *Ephemera danica*). Skues thinks it is the oak fly.

No. 10 Wasp Fly (July)

The treatise: "The waspe flye, the body of blacke wull & lappid abowte wt yelow threde: the winges of the bosarde."

This fly's name and dressing are obviously related and provide another example of the treatise copying nature. (Skues says "probably a crane fly.") The *O.E.D.* gives only a primary meaning of *wasp* as referring to the natural insect.

Should the body be formed in an hourglass shape? It would not take much ingenuity or imagination to tie it that way. Perhaps the wings would also have been tied flat. We have presented an alternate Wasp Fly so tied. This fly and the following Shell Fly will give the reader examples of the down-wing interpretation, which generally we have rejected.

"Wing of the buzzard" is presumed to refer to flight feathers. By Markham's time the directions called for "wings of the downe of a Buzzard."

No. 11 Shell Fly (July)

The treatise: "The shell flye at saynt Thomas daye. the body of grene wull & lappyd abowte wyth the herle of the pecoks tayle: wynges of the bosarde."

The fly has a history that may be associated with the present grannom. The color and material fit this insect rather well. As Hills points out, the treatise date of the fly (July) is late for the actual emergence dates, but many of the caddis would be grannomlike in general appearance. Skues says the Shell Fly is "probably one of the green-bellied sedges."

The name Shell Fly is curious. If it is the grannom, or other caddis, could this refer to the case or "shell" or the larva?

Wings of buzzard flight feathers would be tied-down wings if the fly were a strict imitation, but we have not assumed such strictness, and, as we said above, we find that the weight of the evidence is for uprights.

No. 12 Drake Fly (August)

The treatise: "The drake flye. the body of blacke wull & lappyd abowte wyth blacke sylke: wynges of the mayle of the blacke drake wyth a blacke heed."

Drake (like *dun*) has a specialized meaning in fly-fishing. It refers to adult May flies. As in the case of *dun*, it seems likely that *drake* in the entomological sense was not intended in the treatise. The earliest *O.E.D.* example of this usage is in 1658 (Franck's *Northern Memoirs*): "It was only with dracks that I killed these trouts." The *O.E.D.* also gives *Drake-Fly*, meaning "an artificial fly dressed with breast feathers of a drake," and cites the treatise as an example.

Cotton gives another plausible reason for the association of ornithological and entomological meanings: "and his [green drake] tail turns up towards his back like a mallard, from whence, questionless, he has his name of the green drake." *Drake*, as synonymous with the May fly, or May flies in general, was evidently well established by the mid-seventeenth century.

One has to dispose of precisely what is meant by "mail of the black drake with black head." There seem to be at least four possibilities: (1) As proposed by Hills: "some specially coloured dark mallard feather, only to be found on a black headed drake." (2) Also by Hills: "black head refers not to the bird but the feather, and means one with a black or dark base." (3) The reference was to the drake of another species of duck that had a black head. (4) "With a black head" refers to the fly, not the bird (the interpretation spelled out in Markham: "and his head make blacke").

Of these, number 2, favored by Hills, seems a far-fetched interpretation. Hills apparently intuitively assumes that "black drake" means "black mail of the drake," and this would not be unreasonable if one could dispose of "with a black head." Alternative 4 can be considered on the same basis as "red capon with a blue head" (Black Leaper), and we have followed it with a black-headed fly. Alternatives 1 and 3 are in effect the same except that Hills held to a variation of the mallard rather than a different species of duck.

The problem with changing the species of bird is that *drake* has the special meaning of male of the mallard, and it does not seem reasonable that the treatise would expect breast feathers from a different duck to be used. *Drake* does have the more generalized meaning of males of any species of duck. In British fauna the choice of alternative species is not great. It narrows to two alternatives, and of these, the tufted duck is an easy first choice. But because the fly is named Drake Fly, one needs to be cautious about going against the primary connotation of the word as used elsewhere in the treatise.

One last question. The trout-fly dressings are taken from the first printed version of the *Treatise of Fishing*, published in 1496. They occur near the end of the treatise. The earlier manuscript version of the treatise, about 1450, has no trout flies. This is not surprising, for the manuscript version is only a large fragment of the whole; its last several pages have not survived. The question is, were the flies in the original treatise? There are three possibilities: (1) Wynkyn de Worde copied the list from the original manuscript exactly, except for his usual changes in spelling, punctuation, syntax, etc. (2) He took a simpler list from his original and added to it from other sources. (3) He got the entire list somewhere else. We are inclined to accept the first because the descriptions of the flies sound like the writer of the manuscript, and the printed text contains abbreviations which de Worde might copy but which he would be less likely to write himself. There are also indications in the manuscript that the writer intended to describe the dubbing of hooks. After listing all the things that an angler must know (including how to dub the hooks), the author promises that they will be depicted: "All þese ȝe schall fynd expressed openly to your ye." From this one might conclude that it is possible that the original manuscript contained not only descriptions of the flies but also pictures of them. In the Middle Ages *dub* meant "disguise."

Chapter 12

DAME JULIANA

The Treatise of Fishing with an Angle, though strictly speaking anonymous, is usually attributed to Dame Juliana Berners who, according to legend, was a nun and a sportswoman in the fifteenth century. She was, as the legend goes, noble in birth and spirit, sociable, solitary, dashing, beautiful, learned, and intellectual. In some accounts she fled to field sports to avoid love; in another she might have retired to a convent "from disappointment." The seeming conflict between nun and sportswoman, together with the scarcity of evidence for assertions made about her, have been the occasion for spirited argument among generations of antiquaries.

If Juliana is a myth, she is a myth not of anglers but of these antiquaries. She was neither discovered nor invented by anglers, nor have they added anything to her story. Anglers are almost alone responsible, however, for adopting her as the author of the *Treatise of Fishing*. She is still the only candidate, and is entrenched now in both libraries and legend. The history of the Juliana legend, and the association of her legend with fishing—two separate matters—are the subject of this chapter.

There is no doubt, if by-lines mean anything, that Dame Juliana was a hunting writer or compiler. The solid fact about her is that her name, in the spelling "Barnes," is attached to the first hunting treatise printed in English in 1486; and it is repeated, in the spelling "Bernes," in another printing in 1496. On that evidence she is the first woman writer to publish in print in the language. In the first printing the hunting treatise was part of a larger compilation, dealing with hunting, hawking, and heraldry, known as the *Book of St. Albans*. In the second it was again part of this book, to which had been added *The Treatise of Fishing with an Angle*. Hence the connection, whatever its merits, between Juliana and the first writing on sport fishing. Two and a half centuries passed without notice of this connection by anglers, while antiquaries developed the legend. That legend, completed in its essentials, appears to have been brought into fishing literature in 1760 by John Hawkins in his introduction to the eighth edition of *The Compleat Angler*.

This was at the time of the first Walton revival. Hawkins was a London lawyer and a friend and biographer of Samuel Johnson. Johnson, it is said, encouraged him to edit Walton, and for a long time his was the standard reissue of the famous idyl, reprinted many times down into the nineteenth century. Dame Juliana came into the book only incidentally. Reviewing early writing on fishing, Hawkins made the following observations on the second *Book of St. Albans* (1496). "This book," he said, "was written by Dame *Julyans Bernes*, prioress of the nunnery of *Sopwell*, near St. *Albans;* a lady of noble family, and celebrated for her learning and accomplishments, by *Leland, Bale, Pits,* and others." Since that time Juliana has been an angling personality. Sir Henry Ellis, who made the first bibliography of angling books in 1811, repeated more or less the same information, and the ascription was followed thereafter by other angling bibliographers, though often with some sign of skepticism.[1]

The sources given by Hawkins are eminent early English antiquaries. The legend had only recently been rounded out by other antiquaries in their chambers, as far from field and stream as one can get. They left behind a historical riddle and a suspicion among some people in favor of a colorful Juliana.

The *Book of St. Albans,* in which Dame Juliana first appeared, is the most celebrated book on field sports in English, the first English sporting book to be printed, and one of the earliest English printed books, issued nine years after Caxton's first in England. Its subjects—hunting, hawking, and heraldry—were among the fundamentals of a polite education and necessary for the competent discussion of literature as well as correct behavior. The book appears to have been meant to assist newly risen persons of means in learning these arts, especially their terminologies, as aristocratic graces. It begins simply, "In so moch that gentill men and honest persones haue grete delite in hawkyng and desire to haue the maner to take hawkys. . . ." Only the hunting treatise, which is placed between the others, has an indication of an author or compiler. It concludes: "Explicit [i.e., finished] Dam Julyans Barnes in her boke of huntyng." No more information about her is given in the book.

---

1. Pickering contradicted Hawkins in his notable little separate edition of the *Treatise of Fishing* in 1827, but Hawkins's assertions prevailed in the angling world.

The code of hunting in Juliana's treatise was thought by some to have come down from Tristram, the legendary knight who was long believed to have invented the terminology of hunting. Listen to your dame, she says, in one place, and in another, pay heed to Tristram. There is no conflict between these injunctions. Learning hunting terms was part of the upbringing of a page, so that "dame" in the hunting treatise would be a natural expression for the mistress-tutor he would attend in training for knighthood. By calling his attention to Tristram she would remind him of the chivalric tradition of hunting.

The fifteenth-century attitude toward Tristram as hunter and provider of a glossary of gentlemanly terms was stated clearly by Sir Thomas Malory in his story *Isode the Fair*, written probably in the 1460's:

> And so Trystrams lerned to be an harper passyng all other, that there was none suche called in no contrey. And so in harpynge and on instrumentys of musyke in his youthe he applyed hym for to lerne. And aftir, as he growed in myght and strength, he laboured in huntynge and in hawkynge—never jantylman more that ever we herde rede of. And as the booke seyth,[2] he began good mesures of blowynge of beestes of venery and beestes of chaace and all maner of vermaynes, and all the tearmys we have yet of hawkynge and huntynge. And therefore the booke of [venery, of hawkynge and huntynge is called the booke of][3] sir Trystrams.
>
> Wherefore, as me semyth, all jantyllmen that beryth olde armys ought of ryght to honoure sir Tristrams for the goodly tearmys that jantylmen have and use and shall do unto the Day of Dome, that thereby in a maner all men of worshyp may discover a jantylman frome yoman and a yoman frome a vylayne. For he that jantyll is woll drawe hym to jantyll tacchis[4] and to folow the noble customys of jantylmen.

Juliana's hunting treatise, in fact, was not for the most part an original work. A. L. Binns has shown that it is difficult to single out one stage of its development and call it "authorship";[5] the term "compiler" is more appropriate than "author." The manuscript used by the printer has not survived, but Binns has compared the printed version with two extant

---

2. The modern editor, Eugène Vinaver (*The Works of Sir Thomas Malory,* 1947), says: "Malory's description of a gentleman's education is to a large extent original; and the phrase 'as the booke seyth' is used merely to conceal a departure from the source."
3. Vinaver notes that the words in brackets were added by Caxton in his edition of Malory in 1485.
4. Qualities.
5. A. L. Binns, *A Manuscript Source of the Book of St. Albans,* John Rylands Library, 1950. See also E. F. Jacob in *Bulletin of the John Rylands Library,* Vol. 28, 1944.

independent manuscripts which have similar texts,[6] and concluded that all three are copies, with variations, of a lost parent original. He traces the tradition of Juliana's hunting treatise in the *Book of St. Albans* as follows: Some of it was taken from an Anglo-Norman treatise, Twici's *L'Art de Venerie* (c. 1328). This treatise with some other materials became Twici in English (c. 1425). From there much went into the unknown but postulated treatise that would be the parent of the *Book of St. Albans*. Into this parent went also matter from *Livre de Chasse* (c. 1387) via its English translation, *Master of Game* (c. 1406). *Master of Game* had in it also some new material. So did the parent of the *Book of St. Albans* hunting treatise. From this parent then came the three similar extant treatises. The question of "authorship" of Juliana's treatise thus extends over two centuries of development. Whether she compiled the version in the *Book of St. Albans*, or an earlier one, is not known.

The manuscript possibly was in a monastic library, though more likely on a merchant's sparse bookshelf; copies of it were surely in circulation in manuscript at the end of the century. Early printers turned to such old surviving manuscripts, having before them the prospect of converting into the new medium of communication all the writing in existence that was within reach and profitable to publish, together with new writing for which there was demand. The demand for treatises had been proved: they were a prominent form of manuscript writing and publishing in the vernacular, and were widely circulated in the fifteenth century.

The printer of the first *Book of St. Albans* disdained to identify himself, merely setting down the information that it was "translatyt and complytyt togedyr at Seynt Albons" in 1486. He was the second printer in England, the first to print color; and he printed eight books. His identity has been determined, in part, by indirect means. One of his books was reprinted in 1497 by Caxton's apprentice and successor, Wynkyn de Worde, who referred to its first printer as the "one sometime schoolmaster of St. Albans," and by that appellation he has since been known. It is assumed that his shop was in the Hertfordshire town of St. Albans, twenty miles northwest of London, that he had access to the library of the famous Abbey of St. Albans, if he was not himself a monk, and that he may have found his manuscripts there, monasteries being then the principal repositories of learning. Nearby was the nunnery of Sopwell and the river Ver, which were to figure in the legend to come. The book of hunting, hawking, and heraldry having, according to a custom of the time, no title or title page, came to be called the *Book of St. Albans*.

The second printing, in 1496, was made by Wynkyn de Worde in small

6. MS. Lambeth 49 (unprinted) in Lambeth Palace Library, and MS. Rawlinson Poet. 143 (unprinted) in the Bodleian Library.

folio in his shop at the sign of the Red Pale at Westminster, London. Wynkyn de Worde is generally regarded as the first English commercial printer. Caxton, though a merchant and bookseller, was also a scholar and an editor. A modern student of Wynkyn de Worde, Henry Plomer (*Wynkyn de Worde and His Contemporaries*, 1925), says that de Worde would not have been capable of writing the prologues and epilogues to his books and that these were probably written by his assistant, Robert Copland, who later became a notable printer on his own. If that was indeed the case, Copland has the distinction of being the first employed professional editor of printed works. Wynkyn de Worde in 1496 had just begun an extraordinarily successful business which would publish some eight hundred books before his death in 1534, most of them printed "At the Sign of the Sun" in Fleet Street, where he operated after 1500. The *Book of St. Albans*, which he reprinted several times in whole and in separate parts, led the entire list in popularity.

The most important departure de Worde made from the 1486 St. Albans edition was to add to his edition the illustrated treatise, never before printed, to which he gave the title *Here Begins the Treatise of Fishing with an Angle*. Below this title he placed the woodcut of the angler. There was no sign of its author.

In announcing the fishing treatise at the end of the preceding treatise on coat armor, Wynkyn de Worde explained that it belonged in the volume because like hawking and hunting, fishing is a gentleman's sport. In a similar vein, in another note at the end of the fishing treatise, the printer added the information that he had put the fishing treatise into the larger volume of treatises, instead of publishing it separately, to keep it out of the hands of idle persons, that is, persons who were not gentlemen. Perhaps Copland actually drafted these notes (and edited the fishing treatise). They have been accepted by scholars for the past two centuries as suggesting that the printer regarded the *Treatise of Fishing* as a separate and independent work by an author unknown to him, and so constitute formidable evidence against Juliana's authorship. Sometime later, about 1532–1534, Wynkyn de Worde made a separate quarto, or pocket-size, edition of the fishing treatise, probably for streamside use, again giving no author.[7]

The first printer of the fishing treatise, however, is late on the scene. The treatise was written closer to the beginning of the century in which it was printed. The sole surviving manuscript copy of this earlier version of the treatise (now in the Yale Library) is incomplete, without illustration, and varies in detail from the 1496 version; the consensus of specialists who

7. Eloise Pafort, *Notes on the Wynkyn de Worde Editions of the* Boke of St. Albans *and Its Separates*, Vol. 5 in "Studies in Bibliography" (University of Virginia Bibliographical Society, 1952–3), pp. 43–52. The only surviving copy of the 1532–4 quarto edition of the *Treatise of Fishing* is in the Morgan Library in New York.

have studied the characteristics of the writing places it as a copy transcribed around 1450. It has long been believed that both the printed and manuscript versions were derived from a lost parent manuscript written early in the fifteenth century.[8] The manuscript copy has no sign of its author; the end, where the author's name might have been placed, is missing. Thus both the manuscript and the first printing of the fishing treatise appear anonymous.

Juliana, however, as noted earlier, reappeared in Wynkyn de Worde's *Book of St. Albans* as the only author mentioned. He confirmed her authorship of the hunting treatise as follows: "Explicit dame Julyans Bernes doctryne in her boke on huntynge." The spellings Barnes, Bernes, and later, Berners, have been believed by some authorities to be variations of the same name; this belief has been questioned by others. Spelling aside, hers being the only author's name in the *Book of St. Albans*, it is not surprising that the whole book should have eventually been ascribed to her, if only for convenience.

The *Book of St. Albans* was reprinted many times by different printers in the sixteenth century. The first reprint of the first edition which ascribed the whole work to Juliana was in 1595; the editor, Gervase Markham, called it *The Gentleman's Academie; Or, The Books of St. Albans: . . . All compiled by Juliana Barnes, in . . . 1486.*

Here the simple facts end.

The first pieces of the legend of Juliana appeared in 1559, sixty-three years after the fishing treatise was first printed. In the interim came Henry VIII, the Reformation, the expropriation and abolition of monasteries, the beginning of what is called the Renaissance, and the rise of antiquaries and chroniclers seeking to preserve and celebrate the record of medieval England as it dissolved into the modern era.

Among these antiquaries was John Bale (1495–1563). One of his books, published in 1559(?), was *Lives of the Most Eminent Writers of Great Britain (Scriptorum Illustria Majoris Britanniae . . .)*, a series of short biographies. About Juliana he was flowery:

---

8. The reason for dating the parent manuscript early in the fifteenth century is as follows: The treatise reference to Edward, Duke of York, speaks of him as "late called Master of Game." Edward—grandson of King Edward III—succeeded to his title in 1402, became Master of Game to Henry IV in 1406. Henry IV died in 1413. Edward died in 1415. His biographer-editor, Baillie-Grohman, surmises that he probably wrote *Master of Game* while at leisure in prison in 1405. The fishing treatise thus could not have acknowledged *Master of Game* earlier than 1406, and so could not have existed in the form we know it before that year. The word *late* is ambiguous. If, as it seems, it means "lately," the date of the fishing treatise could be any time after 1406. If it means that Edward is deceased, the date is after 1415. Since the surviving copy of the manuscript is placed at about 1450, the author must have written the original copy between the extreme dates of 1406 and 1450. The word *late* in reference to the Duke of York suggests a date close by, say between 1406 and 1420.

JULIANA BARNES. XXXIII

She was an illustrious female, eminently endowed with superior qualities both mental and personal. Amongst the many solaces of human life she held the sports of the field in the highest estimation. This heroic woman saw that they were the exercises of noble men after wars, after the administration of justice, or the concerns of the state. She had learned, perhaps, that Ulysses instituted such diversions after the conquest of Troy, and that they received commendation from Plato, as the sources of renewed enjoyment to those who suffered, either from domestic calamities, or the injuries of war. These arts therefore this ingenious woman was desirous to convey in her writings as the first elements of nobility; with the persuasion, that those youths, in whose hearts resided either virtue or honour, would cultivate them to guard against vain sloth. Since, as Seneca says, "love is generated in youth by luxury; and nourished by idleness basking in the lap of fortune." And Ovid says, "Take away idleness, and the arts of Cupid perish." To these treatises she added the Art of Heraldry. Hence she wrote in her native tongue, I. The Art of Hawking. II. The Art of Hunting. III. On the Laws of Arms; and is said to have edited a small work on Fishing. She flourished in the year of our Lord 1460, in the reign of Henry the VIth.[9]

This vignette started a story which has run through four centuries. Here were Juliana's fine personal qualities, the subjects and elevated themes of her writing, a specific date when she was living, and, weak as it is, a connection between her and the fishing treatise. To what extent is Bale reliable?

He offers no means of verifying what he says. Yet within the conventions of panegyric, he exerts some accuracy of expression. His praise is transparently interpretative; it could be based on inferences from the *Book of St. Albans*. He makes a nice distinction between weak and strong statements. She "perhaps" learned about Ulysses and Plato, but she definitely wrote three treatises. She "is said" to have edited a small work on fishing. It is possible that Bale wrote this after a perusal of the 1486 edition of the *Book of St. Albans*—he spells her name "Barnes," as it is in that edition—and with indirect knowledge of the 1496 edition and its fishing treatise. If, as some later scholars have believed, his mention of the fishing treatise means that he saw only the 1496 edition, why did he change the spelling of her name from "Bernes" to "Barnes"? Aside from which book he read, he may be

9. Translation as given by Joseph Haslewood. From the notes to his facsimile edition of the second *Book of St. Albans*, London, 1810, p. 5. The translation is slightly biased. For example, it says Juliana was "eminently endowed with superior qualities both mental and personal." The Latin, *corporis & animi dotibus abundans, ac formae elegantia spectabilis,* would be more exactly translated as "abounding in gifts of body and spirit, and remarkable for her physical beauty." Haslewood's translation is more compatible with the theory of the nun. One could bias it the other way by emphasizing the grace of her figure.

reporting literally that he heard it said that she wrote the fishing treatise. The connection is as weak as he makes it. But the date when she "flourished," 1460, he asserts as a fact without qualification. Except for this, one might dismiss Bale as simply the troubadour of an old English writer. Certainly he leaves an impression that he knew something—not much, but something persuasive enough to inspire him to these distinctions in expression.

Bale has always been a controversial personality. Some modern authorities hold his antiquarian works in high esteem. C. S. Lewis (*English Literature in the Sixteenth Century*, 1954), says of them, "Here Bale is sincerely concerned with fact, and is free both from literary adornment and scurrility, which elsewhere, for Bale, are much the same thing." The scurrility Lewis speaks of was in religious conflict: Bale, a Carmelite monk turned against the Church, was a bitter campaigner for the Reformation. He is also credited with visiting monasteries and saving important records from them when they were banned by Henry VIII, but several early scholars say that much of what Bale reported on the contents of monasteries, he took from a contemporary, John Leland (1506–52), who is the ghost in the Juliana story.

Leland, who called himself "Antiquarius," was Henry VIII's librarian and chaplain; he has been called court antiquary to Henry VIII, though he may not have had such a title. He was the first English antiquary and is usually acknowledged as the "father" of the art. Modern antiquaries regard him, and most early antiquaries—as credulous, but thank him for precious records of the past. Though his manuscript notes were not printed until the early eighteenth century, the importance of his work was immediately recognized, and demonstrated by the use made of his notes by several other antiquaries, among them Bale. Leland's collection of the lives and works of about six hundred English writers and scholars before 1500 lay behind Bale's work in that field.

Leland, it appears, saw the great disaster to learning in the disorderly closing of the monasteries, and planned a great work on the glories of England's past. He persuaded the king to give him a commission—in his own words, "to peruse and diligently to serche al the libraries of monasteries and collegies of this yowre noble Reaulme, to the intente that the monumentes of auncient Writers as welle of other Nations, as of this 'yowr owne Province mighte be brought owte of deadly darkenes to lyvely lighte.' " (*The Itinerary*, ed. by Thomas Hearne, 1710–12) From about 1534 to 1542—a period during which hundreds of religious houses were closed, or, as in the case of great abbeys like Westminster and St. Albans, surrendered—Leland traveled through England and Wales, searching through the fast disappearing records of the past. He examined and made notes on books, manuscripts, catalogues, and other records, and reported not only on religious houses, churches, and libraries, but also on towns, houses, castles, bridges, and streams. The kind of detail he noticed (to give a fisherman's example) was this: "Dour in Ewys Land a great House of Whyt Monkes suppressed, and thereby runneth a Broke cawlled Worme." He had a fisherman's eye too for the "trouts" and other fish to be found in the many waters. Reporting on his visit to the Abbey of St. Albans, he recorded a controversy between town and Abbey over the Abbey's great fishpond, as a consequence of which the pond was drained.

Leland's work is arranged mainly in three parts: the *Itinerary*, which is the field work, the *Collectanea*, which is the library work, and *De Viris Illustribus*, *Sive de Scriptoribus Britannicis*, his biographies of writers. No one has presented any direct evidence that Leland found anything at St. Albans concerning Dame Juliana or that he wrote anything about her from any source. Yet his presence in the legend was to become pervasive. Leland went insane in 1550, or perhaps a little earlier, after which his notes fell into other hands. He died in 1552—it is said in the house of a London printer-historian, Reginald Wolfe, a strange coincidence, as we shall see.

Not long after Bale wrote about Dame Juliana, aspects of her character were described in similar terms by Raphael Holinshed (d. 1580), Shakespeare's principal source for the historical plays. In his chronicle of Edward IV, Holinshed wrote: "Julian Bemes, a gentlewoman endued with excellent giftes bothe of body and minde, wrote of certaine treatises of hauking and hunting, delighting greatly hirselfe in those exercises and pastimes: She wrote also a book of the law[s] of arms, and knowledge apperteynning to harolds." Bemes is easily recognized as a likely misprint for Bernes. Fifteen lines above this item, Holinshed makes a statement, in another connection, with the double acknowledgment, "as Bale noteth out of Lelande." The question is, did Holinshed note Juliana out of Bale, Leland, or some other source? The spelling "Bemes," corrected to "Bernes," might suggest that it was not out of Bale, who called her "Barnes." Holinshed worked as translator for Reginald Wolfe, who had come into possession of some of Leland's notes. After Wolfe died in 1573, Holinshed, working in part from Leland's notes, carried on Wolfe's work, which in 1577 became the famous chronicles.

The next words on Juliana came from the Catholic priest and antiquary John Pits (1560–1616). Pits, on leaving Oxford in 1578, went into voluntary exile on the Continent, chiefly in Germany and France, where he spent most of his life teaching and writing. Curiosity about lives of writers, which existed in antiquity and has not since abated, occupied Pits as it had Leland and Bale. Pits's lives of English writers (*De Illustribus Angliae Scriptoribus*, published in Paris in 1619) made him in a way Bale's opposite number in a Protestant-Catholic contest to establish biographies of writers of worth. Pits claimed that Bale was not original and merely misrepresented Leland. Critics in turn say Pits himself very likely never saw Leland's work. He drew on Bale but left out of his list some of Bale's Protestant writers, adding some Catholic writers whom Bale had ignored. Both, however, were agreed in their appreciation of Juliana. The following is a translation of Pits on Juliana from the Latin:

CONCERNING JULIANA BARNES

Juliana Barnes, born of a noble rank, was a manlike woman endowed with brilliant gifts of nature. She was a Minerva in her studies and a Diana in hunting, lest by pursuing leisure she might be involved in the charms of Venus. For they say that at home she was almost always studying the chase and fowling, and often followed those exercises in the forests and fields. Entertaining her mind with these honorable delights and training her body, she so arranged the whole course of her life that she either prudently might avoid illicit desires or vigorously overcome them. She also is said not to have overlooked fishing. Moreover, she engaged in military matters and read and wrote much concerning the art of heraldry; surpassing her sex in talent, constancy, and fortitude, *you may even say that she surpassed the male sex.* Accordingly she wrote certain works in the English language that afterward were rendered into Latin.

Concerning the Art of Fowling, one book. That it is for one who is noble and respectable.

Concerning the Art of Hunting, one book. As in the case of the Art of Fowling.

Concerning the Art of Fishing, one book.

Concerning the Laws of Armor, etc., one book. It is treated in the work following [i.e., after the fishing treatise].

I find nothing concerning other arts or subjects. She flourished in the year 1460 after the Incarnation, when Henry VI was in danger with regard to the throne of England.[10]

In being long on rhetoric and short on fact, Pits is very like Bale: but did Pits get his information from Bale or Leland or from some other source? He does not say.

The Leland mystery continued on toward its climax through William Burton (1575–1645), Robert Burton's elder brother, a topographer and antiquary best known for his *Description of Leicestershire* (1622). Burton had means and retired to the country to devote his life to his researches. In his book he takes his crack at Bale, saying that Bale "collected almost his whole worke [on writers] out of Leland" and that Bale suppressed this fact. Among Burton's credentials for making an observation on this subject is the circumstance that he owned several volumes of Leland's original

10. John Pits, *Relationum Historicarum*, 1619, p. 649.

manuscripts and had access to others. He was, it appears, an incessant Leland scholar, preserving some of the old antiquary's decaying pages by making transcripts of them. Burton acknowledges his debt to Leland in his book on Leicestershire in these words: "This John Leland . . . had a Commission granted him by King *Henry* the eight, in the 25. yeare of his raigne; to view, peruse, and take to his owne use any Record or Manuscript, in any Abbey or religious house within the Realme: Out of which Records he collected many things together into diuers Bookes, foure volumes of which I haue in my custody, and most truely acknowledge them to haue afforded mee many worthy notes of antiquity."

The Leland documents, it appears, came to Burton by a circuitous route. When Leland was declared a lunatic, his elder brother, who oddly had the same name and is called John Leland Senior, was given possession of Leland's properties. The story is that the boy-king Edward VI, whose brief reign coincided with the time of Leland's unhappy end, heard of them, presumably from his scholarly tutor, Sir John Cheke. He commanded Sir John to seize the documents. (It is not clear how Reginald Wolfe managed to keep some of them.) Sir John afterward gave four of Leland's Latin volumes to Humphrey Purefoy, a cousin of William Burton, and at one time a member of Queen Elizabeth's Privy Council. From him they passed to his son, Thomas Purefoy of Barwell in Leicestershire, who in 1612 bequeathed them to Burton. These were three volumes of the *Collectanea* and one on writers, *De Viris Illustribus.* After working on them and other Leland manuscripts for a number of years, Burton in 1632 presented his Leland manuscripts to the Bodleian Library at Oxford, where they were eventually edited and published, and where the originals still remain.

These men went to the grave with their secrets, as even antiquaries do, and most of the seventeenth century passed without event in this sphere. Another generation of antiquaries arose and began to examine the signs of the past. In the year 1700 the county historian Sir Henry Chauncy (1632–1719) had a few words to say about Dame Juliana in his account of St. Albans in his book *The Historical Antiquities of Hertfordshire.* He reviewed the history of printing in England as follows:

> William Caxton, Mercer of London, brought this noble Art of Printing into England, which was first practiced in the Abby of St. Peter at Westminster; then John Insomuch, a Monk and Schoolmaster in this Town [St. Albans], erected a Printing Press in this Monastery, where several Books were printed; one entitled the *Fruit of Time,* another *The Gentlemans Recreation,* or the *Book of St. Albans,* so term'd because printed here in a thin Folio, *anno* 1481. and compiled by Julian Barnes the Abbess of Sopwell. (p. 449)

In another place (p. 160) unrelated to this, Chauncy gives the pedigree of the ancient family of Berners, without Juliana. Chauncy's information about the *Book of St. Albans* is shaky, his title for the book and date of publication both being incorrect. And the name he gives to the printer, John Insomuch, has never been verified; scholars have observed that he may have obtained it by mistake from the opening words of the *Book of St. Albans*: "In so much that gentill men . . ." Yet Chauncy's remarks have attracted attention from scholars. The most interesting thing he does is to identify Juliana as "Abbess of Sopwell." He seems to have had his own independent source for this information—Hertfordshire was his home county. But Chauncy was not the first to make Juliana a nun and head of Sopwell.

This truly novel addition to the story of Juliana was first printed in 1697. A scholar, Edward Bernard, published at Oxford a catalogue[11] listing early printed books and manuscripts in the library of Dr. John Moore, Bishop of Ely (1646–1714). Owing to his possession of this great library, which is said to have contained about 29,000 books and 1,800 manuscripts, Moore has been known as the "father of black-letter collectors." One of Moore's books, listed in Bernard's catalogue,[12] was a copy of the *Book of St. Albans* (1486). The catalogue entry has the following printed annotation: "It is said to have been made by the Lady *Juliana Berners*, Lady Prioress of Sopwell Nunnery, near St. Albans; in which Abby of St. Albans it was first printed in the year aboveasaid [i.e., 1486]."

Three important events occurred in this passage: for the first time, so far as one knows, Juliana's name appeared in print in the variation "Berners"; for the first time she was identified in print as a nun, specifically prioress of Sopwell; and for the first time it is said in print that the *Book of St. Albans* was first printed in the Abbey.

The origin of this note can be determined by a surmise which would seem difficult to fault. Bishop Moore's library was bought in 1714 by George I and given to Cambridge. The copy of the *Book of St. Albans* which was listed in the 1697 catalogue is still in the University Library at Cambridge.[13] On a blank leaf at the beginning of the book, but not part of the collation, the following observations are written in longhand:

This Booke was made by the Lady Julian Berners, daughter of Sr James Berners, of Berners Roding, in Essex, Knight, & Sister to Richard Lord Berners. She was Lady Prioresse of Sopwell, a Nunnery neere St. Albons, in wch Abby of St. Albons this was first printed 1486, 2 H. 7. She was living 1460, 39 H. 6. according to John Bale, Centur.8 Fol. 611.

11. *Catalogi Librorum Manuscriptorum Angliae et Hiberniae*, Bodleian Library, Oxford, 1697.
12. No. 9419.233.4, on page 367.
13. No. 4214 in the published *Catalogue of the Fifteenth-Century Printed Books in the University Library, Cambridge*.

This note must be the source of the annotation in the 1697 catalogue of Moore's library, and whatever its merits, it provides the earliest source of the information that Juliana was Lady Juliana Berners and prioress of Sopwell, and that the book was first printed in the St. Albans Abbey. It also identifies the Berners family and places her in it; and repeats the information from Bale that she was living in 1460.

On other pages in this copy of the *Book of St. Albans* are further notes in the same hand: one set quotes the opening lines of Bale's description of Juliana and attributes them more or less equally to both Bale and Leland; another note says that this copy of the *Book of St. Albans* belonged to William Burton, who received it from "my cousin" Thomas Purefoy in 1612. It was from Thomas Purefoy, as we have seen, that Burton inherited the Leland manuscripts; presumably the copy of the *Book of St. Albans* came along with them. These notes were written by William Burton in his own hand and so carry his high authority for their content. There can be no doubt that the Juliana legend rests on Burton's assertions written into his copy of the *Book of St. Albans*.

Here we are at dead center of the Juliana mystery. All the essential elements of the legend have been laid down. They hint that Leland found records concerning Dame Juliana at the St. Albans Abbey, which he is known to have visited, and wrote about her in his notes, after which these notes were in part used by Bale and later seen by Burton, who drew further upon them. Whether or not the Burton notes are believed, we are clearly dealing here with legend, since they remain unverified in Leland's records or elsewhere. Yet it is a peculiar origin for a legend, because Burton can hardly be supposed to have written the notes with such conviction without having seen some evidence that convinced him. Perhaps someday this evidence will turn up.[14]

The contents of the Burton notes reached the antiquarian public almost simultaneously by two routes. One was by way of Thomas Hearne (1678–1735), Oxford antiquary and editor of the first published editions of Leland's works. The other was by way of Conyers Middleton (1683–1750), Cambridge antiquary and historian.

First, Thomas Hearne.

Hearne is known chiefly for publishing for the first time Leland's *Itinerary* (1710–12) and *Collectanea* (1715). He worked for years with Leland's manuscripts, many of them the transcripts made by Burton. In 1731 Hearne edited another work, in the preface to which he discussed, largely in Latin (which scholars still used in the early eighteenth century), the question of Juliana Berners and the *Book of St. Albans*.[15] He wished to praise the

---

14. We have had Leland's printed works searched without avail. However, many of Leland's manuscripts were lost, and we have not searched his unprinted manuscripts.
15. *Walteri Hemingford, Historia de Rebus Gestis Edwardi I. Edwardi II. & Edwardi III.*, ed. by Thomas Hearne, Oxford, 1731.

good life of the monks of the Middle Ages, which, he says, included playing games. But into later editions of their written works, he charges, their enemies sometimes introduced alien words to bring the religious into disrepute. So with the *Book of St. Albans* by Juliana Barnes, "or rather Berners," prioress of Sopwell. To account for the earthly language of parts of the hunting treatise, he supposes that some Wyclifist editor inserted into its inventions of collective nouns such phrases as: a pontificality of prelates, a dignity of canons, a discretion of priests, a superfluity of nuns, and an abominable sight of monks, the last of which in one version he reports was written, "An hominable (sic) shyt (sic) of mocks." Purged of this mischief, the treatise, he has no doubt, is the text of Juliana Barnes, "than which prioress," he asserts, "there was no other either more beautiful or even more learned."

The source of his knowledge of Juliana's title and connections, Hearne tells us, is William Burton in the notes in Bishop Moore's copy of the *Book of St. Albans*. He has also some new information from memoranda by a contemporary, John Bagford, "that illustrious man, by far the greatest expert on the origin of the art of printing." Bagford (1650–1716), a shoemaker and well-known professional collector of books, had written, according to Hearne, this interesting note about the *Book of St. Albans*: "The first that I ever saw had been the book of John Leland, after it came into the hands of Burton of Leicestershire, and is now in the collection of the bishop of Ely (Dr. Moore)." Thus if one wishes to believe Bagford's unsupported but plausible word, Burton's copy of the *Book of St. Albans,* in which he wrote the founding words of the legend of the nun, had appropriately come down to Burton from Leland. If this were a proven fact, it would prove nothing, and yet it seems to add another connecting link to the past. The important matter is what Burton wrote in the book when it was his.

A few years later Hearne recorded the Burton notes in his own copy of the *Book of St. Albans,* and these were to reach another antiquary in the next century and form the cornerstone of a study of Juliana in a great work on the second *Book of St. Albans*. Before we come to that, the eighteenth century has more to offer.

The second route by which the legend of Juliana was spread, and the one that appears to have brought it into fishing literature, was through Conyers Middleton, Cambridge University librarian, who had charge of Bishop Moore's library there. Middleton studied the "Burton" copy of the *Book of St. Albans*. In 1735 he published *A Dissertation Concerning the Origin of Printing in England,* later reprinted as *The Origin of Printing*. In it, Middleton identifies the copy of the *Book of St. Albans* and says:

> After the first Treatise of Hawking and Hunting &c., is added, *Explicit Dam Julyans Barnes in her boke of huntyng*. Tho' her Name be subjoin'd to the first Part only, yet the whole is constantly ascribed to her,

and passes for her Work. She was of a noble Family, Sister to *Richard* Lord *Berners* of *Essex*, and Prioress of *Sopwell* Nunnery near *St. Albans*: She lived about the year 1460, and is celebrated by *Leland* and other Writers for her uncommon Learning and Accomplishments, under the Name of *Juliana Berners*. (P. 14.)

Middleton did not provide his sources—even so late as this, antiquaries seemed to think it sufficient to make unsupported assertions—but it appears from the similarity of the information and even language that his statements derive from the Burton notes. Of the early authorities he specifies only Leland, and fails to give the tie. As this was the first publication of the information about Juliana for a moderately wide audience, it is a landmark in the legend. Indeed, it appears that the legend went directly from Middleton into angling literature. It was just twenty-five years later that John Hawkins, as we have seen, described Dame Juliana in almost identical words in the introduction to his edition of *The Compleat Angler*. Hawkins, however, made one important departure from Middleton. Whereas Middleton (out of the Burton) dealt only with the first edition of the *Book of St. Albans*, Hawkins attributed the whole of the second edition to Dame Juliana, thereby attaching the legend of the nun and noblewoman to the fishing treatise. Hawkins gives no source, but his assertions about Dame Juliana clearly derive from Middleton (or Middleton's source); and presumably he made the connection with the fishing treatise via Bale and Pits.

Thus, in sum, although Bale is factually weak, and Pits is weaker, and Holinshed is cryptic, and Chauncy is full of error, and the Burton notes provide no verification, and Leland (to whom better knowledge of Juliana is ascribed) remains silent in the background, the legend crystallized publicly in Hearne, Middleton, and Hawkins.

From Middleton, it appears, the legend spread to numerous works of biography and reference, and provoked opposition. William Oldys (1696–1761), a free-lance London antiquary of distinction—to whom anglers owe a debt for his life of Izaak Walton's fly-fishing companion Charles Cotton, in Hawkins's edition of Walton—became the first influential critic of the legend. In a note appended to his life of Caxton in *Biographia Britannica* in 1748, Oldys made an analysis of the prevailing beliefs about Dame Juliana and the *Book of St. Albans*. Here in the mid-eighteenth century a new and more demanding sense of proof had entered the antiquarian mind —as represented by Oldys—together with disbelief in the old authorities. Oldys scoffs:

This book [*Book of St. Albans*] . . . is ascrib'd to an illustrious and heroic Lady of great gifts in body and mind; a second Minerva in her studies, and another Diana in her diversions; in short, an ingenious *Virago,* as Bale and Pits call her, who lived about 1460, and yet she was no less than an Abess, as Sir Henry Chauncy, or Prioress, as Dr. Middleton calls her, of the strict and mortified Nunnery at Sopwell in Hertfordshire; who says also, that she was sister to Richard Lord Berners of Essex. But that the said Juliana Barnes was such a religious Lady, and so nobly descended, no author, as yet, has attempted to prove.

Oldys offers, as he himself notes, the first detailed description and critique of the individual treatises in the *Book of St. Albans.* He allows Juliana only the hunting treatise; but oddly, he thought she versified it from a tract on hunting by Sir Tristram; his source, John Manwood's *Laws of the Forest* (1665 edition), enabled a later scholar (Haslewood) to trace the error to a sixteenth-century reprint of the *Book of St. Albans.* Although Oldys knew the original editions of the book, and the writings on the subject from Bale to the catalogue of Bishop Moore's library to Chauncy to Middleton, he apparently was not aware of the Burton notes. He regards Chauncy as important enough to attack him directly. Oldys takes no stock in the St. Albans printer as either monk or schoolmaster. He doubts Chauncy saw the original editions, since the title and date are wrongly given. Moreover, he says, Chauncy contradicts himself, calling Juliana the abbess of Sopwell in one place, "when he has a distinct chapter upon the religious foundation there and only calls it a Priory; but mentions nothing of Juliana Barnes, in that place." Nor can Oldys find a sister to Richard Lord Berners in a pedigree anywhere.

For Oldys, Dame Juliana is "Mrs. Barnes," a term that did not necessarily mean married. Unlike Hearne and his predecessors, he cannot tolerate the notion that Juliana could be both nun and sportswoman. He says:

And indeed, such a contrast of characters in one person, is apt to raise very contesting ideas. One cannot reconcile the notions those subjects inspire, of their authors being so expert and familiarly practiced in those robust and masculine exercises, with the character of such a sedate, grave, pious, matronlike Lady, as the Prioress of a Nunnery is imagined to be; a conjunction of such extreams, seeming quite unnatural. Indeed, we have, and so we may have had, your romping, roaring hoydens, that will be for horsing and hunting after the wildest game, in the most giddy company; but to join so much of these rough and impetuous diversions, as is required to obtain the proficiency aforesaid, with the most serene and solemn profession of a mortified and spiritual life in herself, and the charge or care of training it in others, must make an unaccountable mixture. In that light, there appears such a motley masquerade, such an indistinction of petticoat and breeches, such a problem and concorporation of sexes, according to the image that arises out of several representations of this religious

Sportswoman or Virago, that one can scarcely consider it, without thinking Sir Tristram, the old Monkish Forester, and Juliana, the Matron of the Nuns, had united to confirm John Cleveland's *Canonical Hermophradite*.

Oldys is the first scholar categorically to contradict the statements of Bale and Pits linking Juliana to the fishing treatise. He says: "It is neither ascribed to her, nor anybody else; but only printed in this larger volume of those subjects relating to the Gentry and Nobility; that every idle and ordinary person might not be able to purchase it, as they would if it had been published in a little pamphlet by itself."

This did not, as we have seen, deter Hawkins twelve years later from declaring her the author of the fishing treatise. Nor did Oldys stop the legend of Juliana, even among antiquaries. On the contrary, his arguments against the reasonableness of supposing that a nun could be a sportswoman were to provoke a new train of thought in support of the legend.

In 1810 a genial London antiquary, Joseph Haslewood (1769–1833), reprinted Wynkyn de Worde's edition of the *Book of St. Albans* in facsimile, and wrote the master collection of notes on the book and Juliana. Although Haslewood advances a point of view with which one might not agree, and makes a few errors in detail, his work is in a class by itself. No student of the *Treatise of Fishing* or the second *Book of St. Albans* could well do without consulting it. Although only 150 copies were printed, the book became the basis of all scholarship on Juliana until the latter part of the nineteenth century, when it was put into eclipse by an unfair attack which will be discussed later. Haslewood paid the price for the extent of his belief in Juliana.

Haslewood built on the foundation of scholarship laid by Oldys, and made further researches that brought into public view the Burton notes, the contents of which Middleton had relayed without giving the authority. Haslewood put them into print, explained them, and wove his thesis about Juliana around them. He did not, however, print the notes directly from the Burton copy of the *Book of St. Albans* (the one in Moore's library), but indirectly from the accurate record of them left by Thomas Hearne in 1733.

Though his diary makes no mention of it, Hearne, it appears, had obtained for himself a copy of the first edition of the *Book of St. Albans*; this copy is now in the Bodleian Library. He inscribed his name on a blank leaf with the date, September 28, 1732. Below his name he made some notes about the Burton copy of the *Book of St. Albans*, based on a letter he had received in 1732 from an antiquary friend, Thomas Baker, who lived at Cambridge.

Like Hearne before him, Haslewood found the Burton notes persuasive, and saw no difficulties in Juliana's supposed dual role of nun and sportswoman; indeed it was his counterargument to Oldys on this point that got him posthumously into trouble. Haslewood is cautious and precise. He begins his review of the legend in the passive voice:

> Julyans, or Juliana, Barnes, otherwise Berners, who has been generally designated as the authoress of the present volume, is supposed to have been born, towards the latter end of the fourteenth century, at Roding-Berners, in the hundred of Dunmow and county of Essex. The received report is, that she was daughter of Sir James Berners, of Roding-Berners, Knight, whose son Sir Richard was created Baron Berners, temp. Hen. IV. and that she once held the situation of Prioress of Sopwell Nunnery, in Hertfordshire.

He then cites the texts of Bale, Holinshed, and the Burton notes (as reported by Hearne) that make her a prioress and member of the Berners family, as "the only biographical incidents which can now be traced in the life of this lady." And, he says, "Wherever the canvas has been enlarged, or the colours given with higher tints, by later writers, the attempt has uniformly proceeded from the desire of producing novelty. Even these scanty materials have been doubted in several particulars, so far as to render necessary some further observations on her family, title, station, and authorship."

The Berners family, he says, is old and honorable; its pedigree comes from Chauncy and others. Barnes, Bernes, and Berners, he finds, are variations of the same name, with Barnes most frequent. Sir James married Anna, daughter of John Berew. With a nice euphemism for the politics of that era, Haslewood says of Sir James:

> He fell a victim to the turbulence of party, and was beheaded in 1388, as one of the evil counsellors of his imbecile master, Richard II. He left issue three sons; Richard, Thomas, and William; and, as now supposed, a daughter named Julyans. Of his estates in Essex, which became confiscated under the attainder, there was a partial restoration to the widow, the year after execution . . . the family still appear to have retained their rank among the wealthy, and shared in the courtly favours of the Monarch. The widow took for her second husband an illegitimate branch of royalty, in Sir Roger Clarendon, knight, natural son of Edward Prince of Wales.

Haslewood neglected to add that in another turbulence of party, Sir Roger was hanged in 1402 by Henry IV.

Observing that doubt about Juliana as a Berners had arisen owing to the absence of a female offspring in the Berners pedigree, Haslewood launches a conjecture: the silence of the pedigree "might well arise from the final circumstance of her entering a convent, and taking the requisite vows of celibacy. From that period it was usual for the relatives to consider such monastic devotees as no longer branches of the family stock; and if they became strangers to their own kindred, much more so were they likely to become to the world at large. Hence, perhaps, her name would scarcely be preserved beyond the archives of her own society."

Here Haslewood calls upon Leland to extend his chain of conjecture. Leland, he recounts, visited religious houses and made notes of manuscripts; perhaps such notes—upon the Sopwell Nunnery, where the superior survived Leland—came into the hands of Burton, who possessed four volumes of Leland, which Burton acknowledges "to have afforded mee many worthy notes of antiquity." The fact that Burton troubled to make this note on Juliana's authorship in his copy of the *Book of St. Albans* impressed Haslewood. He thought Burton would not "retain such an entry in his own copy, unless assured of its correctness." "Her being 'Lady Prioress of Sopwell,'" Haslewood observed, "is corroborated by Chauncy in part, in his account of St. Albans, which adds such presumptive evidence in support of the note, as to leave the whole statement indubitable. To this may be added the confirmation derived from the unquestioned repetition of all our best antiquaries."

With this position established, Haslewood makes further conjectures entirely of his own. He sets forth the Berners family tree and enters into it Juliana's name "as a new bough." He describes his handiwork as "a pedigree that swells the extinct peerage; and in which the name of another descendant, John Lord Berners, *the translator of Froissart*, has long appeared, like the solitary arm of a decayed tree still bearing fruit, all that remains to awaken interest or enquiry of the parent stem. Together then let them be placed, equally honourable to the respective periods they adorned; and stand, like remaining columns which once graced the portal of a desolated mansion, still, amidst ruins, mocking the violence and destructive ravages of time." The pleasure of mocking time is a clue to the passion—and perhaps the folly—of the antiquary.

Haslewood goes on, with qualifications. Juliana's title "Dame," from the colophon to the hunting treatise, is sometimes confused with "Lady." But in her time it meant "neither rank, age, nor character," and could be applied equally to a concubine, a virgin sister of a king, a gentlewoman, or a wife. However, in the Benedictine order of nuns, a distinction was made between a nun's origin in wealth or in poverty; and in that class system, the wealthy were called "Dame," and a humble lay sister upon being elected to higher office would also be called "Dame." "The title of 'Dame Julyans Barnes,'" he says, "was therefore of no real importance; it was neither hereditary, nor derived from nobility or power; it was a local term, serving as a proper and respectful address to 'a gentlewoman,' and might be plainly modernized to 'Mrs. Julyans Barnes.' " The title "Dame," he says, neither confirms nor conflicts with the story, but is consistent with it.

Haslewood is prepared now for what gagged Oldys: the inconsistency of character in the roles of nun and sportswoman. He quotes Pits's description of Juliana—as repeated ironically by Oldys—as a "second Minerva in her studies, and another Diana in her diversions." The conceptual difficulty of reconciling nun and sportswoman, Haslewood thinks, arose from the use of the first person in the hunting treatise. Presumably he had in mind such lines as, "Lystyn to yowre dame, and she shall yow lere." Haslewood agrees with Oldys that no nun of Sopwell would likely have been out in the field hunting and hawking in the manner taught by the "dame." He cites the history of this nunnery:

> The monastery of Sopwell was founded about the year 1140. Two women, religiously inclined, having made themselves an habitation by wradling boughs of trees with wattles, and stakes, close to Einwood, and within the precincts of the Abbey of St. Albans, where they passed their time in continual acts of devotion, severe abstinence, and strict chastity, Jeoffry, then Abbot, was induced to erect them into a cell, subordinate to the mother abbey, appropriating convenient buildings to their use, and directing the women to adopt the vest of nuns, according to the Order of St. Benedict. "Moreover the Abbot, tender for the credit and safety of his Nuns, ordained that they should inclosed in their house under locks and bolts, and the seal of the Abbot for the time being; and that none should be taken into their college but a select and limited number of virgins": [16] which were not to exceed the number of thirteen. How long they continued to live under lock and seal is not recorded. The laws certainly fell into some disregard, as in 1338, Michael, then Abbot, revived certain of the rules, eleven in number, enjoining a more rigid observance of them in future. By these rules it was, amongst other things, ordained, "That a little bell do ring in the morning, as notice to rise and appear; and that none leave the dormitory before the bell rings. That the garden door be not opened (for walking) before the hour of prime, or first hour of devotion; and in summer, that the garden and the parlour doors be not opened until the hour of none [nine] in the morning: and to be always shut when the curfew rings. That no sister hold conversation in the parlour without her cowl on, and her face covered with a veil. No nun to lodge out of the house, and no guest within it."[17]

Notwithstanding the variation, suspension, or trifling relaxation of such restrictions, usually arising from the progress of time, in all

16. Quoted from Chauncy, p. 466.
17. [Footnote from Haslewood.] *History of the Ancient and Royal Foundation, Called the Abbey of St. Alban, &c. by the Rev. Peter Newcome,* 1795, p. 468.

institutions; yet was it the duty of the Superior of Sopwell Priory, to enforce some remnant of its laws;—*her* manners formed a model to the monastic votaries; and her presence was uniformly necessary to regulate the daily acts of devotion.[18] Under such restrictions it is impossible to believe that the staid prioress could, while in the exercise of such an important station, devote her time, without impeachment, to the diversions of the field. That resignation and strict piety might indulge in partial and innocent amusements, may be credited; but to hold familiarity with hawks; to study thir singular propensities; to collect recipes for the destruction of their vermin; exceed the attention of a menial ostreger in their care; or, by following the pleasures of the chace, surpass a huntsman in knowledge of the art and technicalities of venery; and withal, to suppose a holy prioress wandering over champaign and through woodland, as the prey either on wing, or of fleet foot, might deviously guide, is forming a character of such inconsistent shreds, that, when blended together, it appears rather fitted for some partial creation of fiction, than the faithful delineation of real life.

Oldys was equally eloquent in denouncing the idea of a nun in the field.[19] But Haslewood did not need the argument. He had another line of thought which would explain the prowess of a nun.

Haslewood, like Oldys, declined to attribute all the treatises in the *Book of St. Albans* to Juliana. In addition to the hunting treatise in Wynkyn de Worde's edition, he gives her, on a "probable" basis, a small part of the hawking treatise, a short list of beasts of chase, and another short one of persons, beasts, fowls, etc.

18. [Footnote from Haslewood.] It seems certain that the Abbot for the time being (or his deputy, the prior), in whom alone, according to the History of the Abbey, (p. 220) "was the power to make the prioress, without any consent or leave of the sisters," always selected those not too far advanced in life to perform the duties of the office in person, and when they became disqualified by age, they were removed. The following are all the names of the ladies holding the office, that I have met with; but the list must be incomplete.

    Domina Johanna prioresse de Soppewelle.

1330. Domina Philippa died, and was succeeded by Alice de Pekesdene.

1416. Domina Matilda de Flamstede is mentioned as formerly prioress. She probably resigned the situation from age, as she died in 1430, and had "lived in the rules of religion 60 years and 18 weeks; and in the whole, 81 years and 8 weeks" —Ib. p. 311.

1426. Domina Leticia Wyttenham.

1480. Joan Chapell, from the infirmity of age set aside, and Elizabeth Webb appointed in her stead.

1553. Joan Pigott, prioress at the time of abolishing of the convents, and living at this period.

    No date has anywhere been assigned for the period that Dame Julyans is supposed to have held the office; she might be an intermediate prioress between Leticia Wyttenham and Joan Chapell.

19. Both were mistaken, according to A. L. Binns, who says that nuns did hunt and bishops tried to stop it.

"Even these compilations," he says, "upon examination, will be found to display a varied and extensive knowledge of the passing world. The terms of familiarity applicable to the ordinary classes of society, prove them to have been collected by one mixing unreservedly with mankind; and not the local or casual gatherings, of a simple recluse in a nunnery. But why should it be believed that our authoress passed her whole life immured in a cloister? If conjecture may supply the absence of facts, how easily can a more consistent outline be furnished?"

Here for the first time in the long history of increments provided by the eminent antiquaries of Britain, Haslewood brings Juliana to life:

> Let us suppose her educated in a convent [and a footnote from an old manuscript says that before the Reformation young women were educated at nunneries in needlework, confectionary, surgery, physic, writing, drawing, and the like]; the teens passed with relations in the vicinity of the court; at times partaking of the amusements of the field, then a favourite pursuit with ladies of family; forming a commonplace book, according to the literary plan of that period, on various subjects; from disappointment retiring to a cloister, where an advancement to the office of superiour commonly attended courtly connections; amidst the hours of listless solitude, either seeking amusement by the translation of a treatise upon hunting, from the French language; or versifying the general rules of the sport from her own collections; whereby it became set forth with the affixture of "Dame Julians Barnes";—and the sketch is at least plausible. It unites all the supposed characteristics of our authoress, without violating probability, or distorting consistency.
>
> To conclude, the facts resolve themselves into very few particulars. Her name to the Book of Hunting stands most prominent. Next, the date given by Bale, whose delineation of her appears to have been drawn from the second edition of the work, as he attributed to her pen the *Treatise on Angling* then first printed: her being prioress of Sopwell, which rests on the united authorities of Burton and Chauncy, though the date remains to be discovered by some more fortunate investigator: and lastly the probability of her being related to the Berners family.—Such is the extent of information of the life of our authoress, who, if the above separation of the pieces which were really written by her prove just, will have the literary claim materially narrowed; yet this is a circumstance rather to her advantage than otherwise . . . by freeing her character from the weight of censure, by which it has long been shadowed, and giving it a fairer claim to be considered as feminine.

The peculiarity of Haslewood's reasoning is that he makes precise statements about the historical record, varied in strength and weakness according to circumstances; and in arriving at conclusions, he appears to believe, on the principle of corroboration, that a number of weak observations add up to a strong, "indubitable" one. His long conjecture about Juliana's possible life at court makes more legend, and yet it is also a logical reply to the reasoning of Oldys that a nun could not reasonably be supposed to have a knowledge of sports. Haslewood shows that if you believe Bale and Chauncy and believe in the Burton notes, there is no inconsistency between sportswoman and nun, the first role being at court, the second in the cloister.

But Haslewood is categorical in denying Juliana authorship of the fishing treatise. He says:

> While the unbusied and volatile spirits of the age unite in exhilarating the passions by the chase; the philosopher, student, and sedentary man, need a less boisterous recreation; and therefore become anglers. Hence the works extant upon that art display the erudition of its pursuers. Knowledge and philanthropy, acting under the genial influence of the solitude attached to the diversion, combine to enforce the best moral principles, while the novice is in eager pursuit of technical instruction. No works that treat upon subjects of art surpass, in this particular, the interesting essays upon angling: and to precede near seventy different English writers, who have more or less thus judiciously enlarged upon the science, stands the anonymous author of the present treatise: a treatise supposed to be the earliest didactic attempt upon the subject, printed in any language.
>
> Neither for Juliana Barnes, the monkish schoolmaster, nor anyone who assisted in compiling the original Book of St. Albans, can there be consistently advanced a claim of authorship in this "little pamphlet." The treatise of hawking is formed, without adornment, by recipes promiscuously gathered; that of hunting is a string of technical phrases attached to venery; and neither of them is interspersed with judicious and sentimental precepts, like the introduction and end of the present tract. It commences with a parable from Solomon, not in the dull and grave monotony that might appear the dubious and fanatical progeny of a gloomy cloister, but with an interesting and candid familiarity discussing what is "good disport," and "honest game"; and enforcing the mild principles of virtue and rational piety, for the obtainment of a cheerful, or, as it is quaintly termed, "a merry spirit." Whatever ravage or spoilage birds, dogs, and horses, might create, is not antecedently considered: neither check, limitation, nor regret, is given to the destructive pursuits of hawking and hunting: but here, at the conclusion, the peaceable angler, whose instrument of pleasure and mischief is converted into a walking staff, is solemnly charged not to seek amusement by fishing in the poor man's several water, without license; nor to break any gins, or wears; nor take any fish there found; neither break any man's hedge; nor open gates without shutting again; and, finally, not to pursue this disport ravenously, by taking too much at one time. Such simple and inartificial observa-

tions form a strong and illustrative fact, of a pen superior to any concerned in the other more laboured compilements.

The period of writing this [fishing] treatise may be fixed, with some confidence, to have been early in the fifteenth century.

After Haslewood almost everything widely known about Juliana had its source directly or indirectly in his book. Then toward the end of the nineteenth century Haslewood was accused by William Blades (1824–90), printer-antiquary and Caxton specialist, of having written a "sham biography" of Dame Juliana. This occurred in a chapter on authorship in Blades's 1881 facsimile edition of the first *Book of St. Albans*, which is still the standard modern edition of that work, as Haslewood's is of the second *Book of St. Albans*. Blades wrote almost nothing on the authorship that could not have been drawn from Haslewood, made no acknowledgment of his borrowings, and misrepresented Haslewood's opinions. One would never know from Blades, for example, that both Haslewood and Oldys had declared the *Treatise of Fishing* anonymous; or that both of them had observed that "Dame Juliana Barnes" could mean "Mrs. Barnes."

At the center of his attack, Blades says that Haslewood "supplied a full-blown biography of the authoress, giving particulars of her birth and education, the occupations of her youthful days, and a most imposing pedigree." Haslewood, he says:

> . . . attributes to her the authorship of all four works in the Book of St. Albans. The difficulty of accounting for a lady so placed writing upon such subjects, is cleverly, if not satisfactorily settled by assuming that she passed her teens at court, partaking of the amusements of the field, and writing for her own use a common-place book on various subjects. Then retiring through disappointment (doubtless a love affair) to a cloister, her rank raised her to the position of prioress. There in her seclusion, writing amidst the solitude of listless hours and vain regrets, she versified the general rules of sport from her own pleasant recollection, and from the diaries of her youthful happiness, which fortunately she had preserved. If we remember the mania which seized all classes for diary-keeping at the beginning of the century, when Haslewood wrote this, it will deepen our sense of humour to note that he attributes private diary-keeping to a young lady who lived *ante* 1450.

Haslewood, as we have seen, in fact allowed Dame Juliana not all four works but only the hunting treatise, and parts of others. The "difficulty of accounting for a lady so placed writing upon such subjects" had been raised first by Oldys and again by Haslewood, not incidentally but as a central part of their reflections. For Oldys—as later for Blades—the difficulty was insuperable. Haslewood offered a reconciliation of the conflict.

"But why," said Haslewood, "should it be believed that our authoress passed her whole life immured in a cloister?" To eliminate the nun and her pedigree, one has to dispose not merely of Haslewood's conjectures but of the basic elements of the "biography" as set forth in the Burton notes and Chauncy. Haslewood obtained the pedigree of the Berners family from Chauncy and developed the Sir James Berners branch, entering Juliana in the specified place in dotted lines. The place was specified neither by Chauncy nor by Haslewood, but by the Burton notes. Blades incorrectly states that Chauncy united Dame Juliana with the Berners family. Blades does not deal with the Burton notes, upon which Haslewood chiefly rested. Finally, Blades describes Haslewood's Juliana as keeping a diary, when in fact Haslewood supposed her "forming a common-place book." Blades appears not to have been aware of the difference between a diary and a common-place book (a collection of passages and reference notes), or that forming common-place books was in fact a popular pastime before 1450.

It is difficult to account for the low level of Blades's attack. For although Haslewood asked for trouble when he brought Juliana to life with imaginative detail, he did not distort the materials in support of his thesis. Possibly the "scientific" bent which in crude form was the fashion in Blades's time gave him such contempt for Haslewood's temporizing with the centuries of antiquarian gossip about Dame Juliana that he was carried away by the emotion. His conclusion—like that of Oldys—was reasonable. He also expressed it well: "She [Dame Juliana] probably lived at the beginning of the fifteenth century, and she possibly compiled from existing MSS some rhymes on Hunting."

Blades's ironic aside concerning Dame Juliana's supposed retirement through disappointment—"doubtless a love affair"—suggests a new possibility for the legend that should make Blades turn over in his grave. If Juliana had a love affair, who was her lover? A plot for Juliana could be imagined as follows: The daughter of Sir James Berners and Anne Berew would have had to be born no later than 1388, since Sir James was executed in that year for conspiracy against Richard II, son of the Black Prince and grandson of Edward III. A few years later her mother married Sir Roger Clarendon, bastard son of the Black Prince and so half-brother of the king who executed her father. In 1399 Henry IV deposed his cousin Richard II and seized the throne. Three years later Henry IV executed Juliana's stepfather, Sir Roger, as a possible pretender to the throne. Although her natural father had lost his head on behalf of Henry IV and her stepfather had been hanged by Henry IV, let us presume that the remaining family was in favor at court.

In and out of this court and its prison was Edward, the second Duke of York, author-translator of *Master of Game*, the first book on hunting in the

English language. In it he praised hunting as a good sport for warriors. Edward, cousin of Henry IV and archconspirator against both kings, managed to keep his head and almost wore the crown; he had a blood claim to the throne, and at one time his cousin Richard II considered abdicating in his favor. As it was, he held some of the highest offices in England, including that of Master of Game. Suppose that Juliana as a girl hunted and fished with him. For various reasons—lack of dowry or the exigencies of the court—she did not marry. After Edward died in battle at Agincourt in the year 1415, at the age of forty-two, a hero, Juliana, sorrowing, entered the nunnery. There she reflected and wrote on sport. In the fishing treatise she wrote, with a touch of humor, that the right noble Duke of York, later called Master of Game, had described the joys of hunting; she, however, would describe its griefs. Turning from the pursuit of glory, she finds peace in the art of angling. This fantasy unites the first fishing writer and the first hunting writer in English as tragic lovers, with a certain symbolic merit.

The legend of Dame Juliana as it was actually created by that line of eminent antiquaries, Bale, Holinshed, Pits, Burton, and Chauncy, and adopted by Hearne, Middleton, and Haslewood, is not much believed by their professional descendants. The hunting treatise, taken as a compilation, is not denied her; so we presume she lived. Bale, Holinshed, and Pits, living in the century after hers, celebrated her, but we do not know for certain that they knew any more than a person walking into a library and taking down the *Book of St. Albans* today. The Burton notes in which she becomes a nun and a Berners fade into the mystery of their origin, with implications about Leland, and the faint possibility of a discovery being made someday. Chauncy, taken at his word, corroborates her presence at Sopwell; but he might also have seen the catalogue of Bishop Moore's library and changed "Prioress" to "Abbess." In a sense it seems we owe the riddle of Juliana to Henry VIII; the gap in knowledge created in the disorders of the Reformation is the basis of the antiquaries' suspicion that the record of the nun existed and was lost.

But whatever one chooses to believe about the Dame Juliana legend and the hunting treatise, the authorship of the fishing treatise is a different matter. For their connection we have only the unsupported remarks of Bale and Pits. Against it are Wynkyn de Worde's notice that he included the fishing treatise in the *Book of St. Albans* only for social reasons, and the fact that he named no author. Against it too is the opposition of antiquaries from Oldys to the present. Even more formidably in the way is the text of the *Book of St. Albans* itself. Assuming Dame Juliana wrote the hunting treatise, how could the same person be supposed to have written the fishing treatise? The styles of the two, as Haslewood and others have noticed, are very different.

QUILL GORDON

The opening passages of the two treatises illustrate their differences. The angler begins with an English quotation from the Book of Proverbs, which is presently supported by a Latin medical aphorism. So far from being mere ornament, these quotations serve to announce the main themes of the introductory section: a long life and a flourishing one, the importance of a cheerful spirit, sobriety, and moderation. These are fully developed in the introduction, the angler never losing sight either of Solomon or of the teachings of medicine. In a very different manner, in the hunting treatise, Dame Juliana begins:

> Wheresoeuere ye fare, by fryth or by fell,
> My dere chylde, take hede how Tristram dooth you tell;
> How many maner beestys of venery ther were,
> Lystyn to yowre dame, and she shall yow lere.

Tristram, never mentioned after the second line of Juliana's book, appears, as we have seen, to serve as the announcement of a lesson in chivalry. Alternatively, he serves a purely decorative function. In any case, the knight is quickly lost sight of, and the real instructor in hunting is "your dame" (referred to three times), who addresses herself to my child, my dear child, child, my children, my lief children, my son, sons, my sons, dear sons, my dear sons (twenty-eight times outside the dialogue of the master huntsman and his man). Although this conceit, or formalism, of the "dame" and "children" is maintained throughout most of the hunting treatise, it contributes nothing to the discussion of hunting. At times her phrases, "my dear sons" and the like, seem to be mere padding, and such padding is the most striking feature of Juliana's style, unlike the economical style of the fishing treatise. The hunting treatise is sprinkled with tags, like "by fryth or by fell" in the first line. The technical distinction between "enclosed woodland" and open country is important, yet the only function of the words here seems to be to complete the line and perhaps give a rhyme for "tell."

All medieval poets resorted to such tags (even Chaucer occasionally), but it is difficult to find a poet whose verse is so full of them as this one. Everywhere are lines ending with as I you tell, as I you bid, as I you say, as I you ken, so tell I my tale, the sooth for to say, the sooth I thee say, I thee pray, as ye may, as ye see, as thou mayst see, so shall ye say, all have I bliss, that is no leas [i.e., lie], in frith or in field, and the like. In the hunting treatise there are many other tags like these, which anyone familiar with English poetry of the fourteenth and fifteenth centuries will recognize at once. In long stretches of the hunting verse almost every couplet is eked out by some invention of this sort, and the rhymes for dozens of other couplets are provided by the addition of an otherwise functionless also,

144

echone (each one), anon, so free, or the like. Somewhere between a quarter and a third of the work consists of such verbal padding.

In the matter of organization the two works are altogether different. The author of the *Treatise of Fishing* had a great deal of information to impart concerning the methods and instruments of angling, the times, seasons, places, baits, flies, and all the rest. Some is miscellaneous and fragmentary, consisting of brief hints to the angler as to the best procedures to follow under certain circumstances. Although it does not always follow a strictly logical form of presentation, its materials are set forth in an orderly manner, each subject being presented, concluded, and left for the next. Closely related matters are grouped for discussion. Without exaggerating this feature of the treatise, it is clear that the angler's mind was basically systematic in its operations.

In contrast, the hunting treatise, viewed as practical instruction in hunting, is a hodgepodge having no discernible guiding principle. It begins with a miscellaneous group of stanzas explaining nine different sets of hunting terms; tells how to cut up a roe; gives correct names for boars of different ages and tells how to reward the hounds after the killing of the boar; describes and discusses the hare; gives some general instructions in hunting; explains two more sets of terms; describes the roebuck, hart, and hind; gives the seasons for hunting various beasts; tells how to hunt the hare; gives the dialogue of the master huntsman and his man; tells how to cut up the boar and the hart. This summary is considerably simplified; if it seems chaotic, the hunting treatise itself is much more so. There is no organization by beasts; the hart is dealt with in three widely separated places, the roebuck in two, the hare in two, and the boar in two. There is no organization by techniques or subjects; the cutting up of animals is discussed in three separate places, proper terms for horns and antlers of different sorts appear in two places, and terms for animals of different ages are given in four places.

The most obvious flaw in the arrangement of the hunting treatise has already been noted by several writers. It is a seven-page dialogue of the master huntsman and his man, which interrupts the monologue of the dame to her children. Following it, we find the discussions of the cutting up of the boar and of the hart (four pages), which clearly belong somewhere among the matter preceding the dialogue. The printer may have mislaid this and set up the dialogue in the belief that the amorphous dame-and-children part was finished; then perhaps he discovered the missing item and tacked it on at the end. The dialogue seems, however, to have been put into its present form by Juliana; it is similar in style and organization (or lack of it) to the rest of the treatise.

The two treatises differ also in content and in spirit. The fishing treatise begins with a sophisticated and rather philosophical defense of the special

145

claims of angling as a sport—its physiological and spiritual values. The hunting treatise shows little interest in the values of hunting to the hunter's body or soul. After the introduction, the fishing treatise is concerned with the tools and the techniques of the angler (presented with at least an attempt at completeness), hardly at all with matters of terminology. The chief difficulty in interpreting the fishing treatise stems from the way in which the author takes the terms for granted, as though everyone would know what a "dor worme" is and what is the "bayte that bredyth on an oke leyf." The hunting treatise seldom bothers to describe the animals or their habits (two passages, three animals briefly dealt with) or give instruction in the art of hunting (two passages, only the hunting of the hare treated at any length).

Dame Juliana's interests lay, not in the animals or the hunting as such, but in the words and phrases connected with them. The hunter must never speak of "a fair hart"; he must learn to say "a great hart" and "a fair doe." In referring to groups of animals he must take care to say "a herd" of harts or hinds or bucks or does, but "a bevy" of roes, "a sounder" of boars, "a route" of wolves. He must know when to say that the hart "profers," when he "reprofers," and when he is "defoulant." The hare may "sore" or "resore," "prick" or "reprick," and the well-bred huntsman must know when to use each term. He must also learn how to use words like "allay," "relay," and "vauntelay"; and he should know which animals are "beasts of venery," which "beasts of chase," and which merely "rascaille." In a word, the hunting treatise is snobbish; it presumes a hierarchic scheme of society in which the higher orders are marked by a codification of expression; whereas the fishing treatise is natural, plain, philosophic, and a manual of angling operations.

A number of the hunting terms have a distinctly foreign cast. The fishing treatise uses homespun terms, for the most part words which had long been familiar to ordinary Englishmen. Many are of strictly native origin (staff and crop, smite and strike), while others are thoroughly naturalized borrowings from Latin, French, or Scandinavian (trout, tench, bleak). But the hunter setting his hounds on the track must say three times, "So ho, so ho"; and after that, "Sa, sa cy avaunt, so ho." If the hounds run too fast and get too far ahead of him, he shall say, "How amy" and then "Sweff, mon amy, sweff." If a particular hound, let us say Bemounde, picks up the scent, the hunter cries: "Oyes a Bemounde le vallant" and "Que guide trouers la cowarde ou la court cowe." And so it goes. The French terms are usually spelled according to the conventions of Anglo-French, the French of England rather than that of France. Parisian French, which could be learned abroad, would not have served the social purpose.

The foreign terminology is due as much to the sources used by Dame Juliana as to her own linguistic preferences. As we have seen, she compiled her hunting treatise from French sources, chiefly Twici, which was written in England in Norman-French, and the *Master of Game*, which was largely translated from the French of France. Perhaps she used translations rather than the sources themselves, since these works had been turned into Middle English shortly before her time, and in the translations the French hunting cries and much French terminology are retained intact.

The terminology in the hunting treatise may be explained through its social aspect. The education of a noble youth, serving his apprenticeship as a page, would require knowledge of the correct phrases, whether or not he actually hunted; and the children of merchants would at least want to know them. Juliana's hunting treatise, which lacks practical organization, may have been designed not for practical instruction in hunting but only for instruction in its sporting language. From that point of view the hunting treatise might be said to have linguistic organization. This theory would make some sense too out of the constant reiteration of expressions that otherwise appear only as padding. The hunting treatise thus may be conceived as a treatise on the conversation of a gentleman. This too would explain its French character, a noble English family of the time would have an Anglo-Norman tradition. The difference between the styles of the hunting treatise and the fishing treatise in the *Book of St. Albans* may be explained on the grounds that the fishing treatise was not part of a traditional, corporate, dignified way of life hardening into formalized literary convention, as the hunting treatise was. The *Treatise of Fishing* may show the new class of merchants and others turning away from the courtly past, as reflected in purely chivalric literature, to a more individual and empiric approach to recreation.[20]

The plain English of the *Treatise of Fishing* suggests that there never was—as has sometimes been thought—a foreign original, although, as we have seen in Chapter 2, its aesthetic structure appears to have been drawn from earlier continental hunting models. Juliana's hunting treatise, with its detached linguistic bias, is decadent by comparison with the older hunting treatises.[21] With respect to authorship, the difficulty here is in imagining the Juliana of the hunting treatise changing her spots to write the fishing treatise—a not impossible but not likely happening.

If it was not Juliana, what kind of person might have written the fishing treatise? There is no good reason to exclude the possibility of either a priest or a nun. Yet there is nothing to suggest monastic or priestly authorship; the tone is not even that of an especially devout layman. The writer evidently had a rather good education; at least he had an orderly mind, and

20. A line of thought suggested by A. L. Binns.
21. See Chapter 2 for the identical firm structure to be found in Xenophon's treatise on hunting (c. 400 B.C.?), the *Art of Falconry* (c. 1240–50), *La Chace dou Cerf* (c. 1245?), *Livre de Chasse* (c. 1387), and *Master of Game* (c. 1406).

he could quote a Latin couplet and interpret it correctly. His education would be exceptional for a country squire of the fifteenth century, and it is a question whether any squire of that day could have resisted the social pressure in favor of the fashionable sports of hunting and hawking.

Although the tone and spirit of the treatise do not suggest a priest, it is possible that the author was a clerk in minor orders. A lawyer or a schoolmaster could have written it. Two small points suggest a physician. The treatise quotes from a highly regarded medical authority, the *Regimen Sanitatis Salernitanum* (*c.* 11th century; extant manuscripts date from about 1260 to 1300), treating it with almost as much respect as the Bible. It also echoes the common *probatum est* formula of the medical books (i.e., the remedy has been proved or tested), when it remarks that "thyse baytes ben well prouyd baytes for the samon." There is nothing in the treatise that could not have been written by a physician—a country doctor, who would have lived in town. In any case, the vision of angling which the treatise reflects is that of a townsman returning to nature.

We have plausibly proved, we think, that as author of *The Treatise of Fishing with an Angle*, Dame Juliana is a myth. But in elevating our recognition of her from legend to true myth, we have perhaps provided anglers with what they really want.

Chapter 13

THE FIRST KNOWN ESSAY ON SPORT FISHING:
THE TREATISE OF FISHING WITH AN ANGLE

The Treatise of Fishing with an Angle *was written in England sometime between 1406 and 1420. It survives in two early versions, each of which, it appears, was transcribed independently from the now lost original. The older of the two was copied by a scribe in about 1450 and survives in a single manuscript copy, now at Yale. The other version is the first printed text, which appeared in the second* Book of St. Albans *in 1496. The text below was put into modern English by Professor Sherman Kuhn of the University of Michigan, editor of the* Middle English Dictionary. *We made this version by combining the 1450 manuscript version with portions of the later one. Our reason for doing this is as follows:*

We think the surviving manuscript version of 1450 has a superior claim to authenticity in detail, since it is closer in time to the lost parent manuscript. But this 1450 version is incomplete. If the 1496 printed text added nothing to the lost parent, it shows that about half of the 1450 manuscript has been lost. The loss occurred mainly in two sections, one of six pages at about the middle of the manuscript, the other after its end. The end section, as it appears in the 1496 version, contains two important passages, namely, the descriptions of the twelve trout-fly dressings and the concluding charge to anglers to follow a code of good behavior.

Hence we took the 1450 version as the foundation of our text and merely spliced into it the missing sections, which we took from the 1496 version. The manuscript also lacks illustrations, and so we inserted the illustrations from the 1496 version in their appropriate positions. We have noted the points at which the texts are joined, and have indicated occasional inserts

149

from the 1496 text in brackets. The result, we believe, is a unique complete modern version based on the best of the old sources.

THE TREATISE OF FISHING WITH AN ANGLE

Solomon in his Proverbs says that a glad spirit makes a flowering age—that is to say, a fair age and a long one.[1] And since it is so, I ask this question, "What are the means and cause to bring a man into a merry spirit?" Truly, in my simple judgment, it seems to me, they are good and honest sports and games in which a man's heart takes pleasure without any repentance. Then this follows—that good and honorable recreations are the cause of man's fair old age and long life. Therefore, I will now choose among four good sports and honorable pastimes, that is to say, among hunting, hawking, fowling, and fishing, particularly angling with a rod or a pole, a line, and a hook. And thereof I will treat as far as my simplicity will permit, both for the above-mentioned saying of Solomon and also for the statement of medical science made in this manner:

1. Proverbs 17:22 (Vulgate): Animus gaudens aetatem floridam facit.

Si tibi deficiant medici, medici tibi fiant
Haec tria—mens laeta, labor et moderata diaeta.[2]

That is to say: If a man lacks physicians or doctors, he shall make three things his doctors or physicians, and he will never have need of more. The first of them is merry thought. The second is work in moderation. The third is a good diet of pure foods and suitable drinks. First, then, if a man wishes to be merry and have a glad spirit, he must avoid all contentious company and all places of disputes and quarrels, where he might have a cause of melancholy.[3] And if he will have a labor which is not excessive, he must then arrange for himself, for his heart's pleasure—without care, anxiety, or trouble—a merry occupation which may rejoice his heart and his spirit in a respectable manner. And if he wishes to be moderate in diet, he must avoid all places of debauchery, which is the cause of overindulgence and sickness, and he must withdraw himself to a place of sweet and hungry[4] air, and eat nourishing and digestible foods.

I will now describe the said four sports or games to find out, as well as I can, which is the best of them; albeit, the right noble Duke of York, lately called the Master of Game,[5] has described the joys of hunting, just as I think to describe (of it and all the others) the griefs. For hunting, to my mind, is too much work. The hunter must run all day and follow his hounds, laboring and sweating very painfully. He blows on his horn till his lips blister; and when he thinks it is a hare, very often it is a hedgehog. Thus he hunts, and when he comes home in the evening, rain-beaten, sorely pricked by thorns and with his clothes torn, wet-shod, befouled, some of his hounds lost, some crippled[6]—such griefs happen to the hunter and many others which, for fear of the displeasure of those that love it, I dare not report in full. Truly, it seems to me that this is not the best recreation or sport of the four mentioned.

Hawking

This sport and pastime of hawking is laborious and right troublesome also, as it seems to me, and that is the honest truth. The falconer often loses his

2. This seems to be a variant of a maxim in the eleventh-century *Regimen Sanitatis Salernitanum:* Si tibi deficiant medici, medici tibi fiant Haec tria, mens laeta, requies, moderata diaeta. For one of the best-known versions of the proverb, see Robert Burton, *The Anatomy of Melancholy* (1621), Part 2, Sec. 2, Mem. 6, Subs. 4.
3. An excess of black bile in the body, a pathological condition which could produce all manner of dangerous ailments—as well as a gloomy frame of mind.
4. Hunger-producing, conducive to a hearty appetite.
5. Edward of Norwich, second Duke of York, 1373–1415, Master of Game to Henry IV and translator of the book called *The Master of Game.*
6. *Surbatted,* bruised in the feet, footsore from too much running on rough ground.

hawks, the hunter his hounds; then all his sport is gone and finished. Very often he shouts and whistles till he is painfully thirsty. His hawk goes above[7] and does not choose to pay him any attention when he would have her fly at the game. At last she will consent. Then, with improper feeding, she will get the frounce, the ray, the cray,[8] and many another sickness that brings her to the souce.[9] These sports seem to me to be beneficial, but they are not the best of the four mentioned.

Fowling[10]

The sport and game of fowling seems to me poorest of all, for in the summer season the fowler has no luck. And in the hardest and coldest weather he is sorely vexed, for he would go to his traps, but he cannot because of the cold. Many a trap and many a snare he makes, and many he loses. In the morning he walks in the dew; he also goes wet-shod and very cold to dinner the next day and sometimes to bed, before he has eaten well on anything that he gets by fowling. Much more of the same I could tell, but my displeasure[11] or anger makes me leave off. It seems to me that hunting, hawking, and fowling are so toilsome and unpleasant that none of them can succeed in bringing a man into a merry frame of mind, which is the cause of a long life according to the said proverb of Solomon.

Fishing

Undoubtedly then, it follows that it must needs be the sport or game of fishing with an angle-rod—for every other kind of fishing is also right

7. Or, she takes to a bough of a tree; the Middle English can be read either way.
8. *Frounce*, a disease of hawks, characterized by sores in the mouth and throat. *Ray* (or *rye* or *ree*), a disease which produces a swelling of the hawk's head and legs; cf. also the modern dialectal *ray* "diarrhoea in cattle and sheep." *Cray*, a sort of constipation, in which the excrements are hard, chalklike, and difficult to pass. The choice of two diseases which rhyme and can have opposite meanings may suggest that the writer had a flippant attitude toward hawking. All three diseases will be found together, however, and in the same order as above, in two fifteenth-century books on hawking; see the *Book of St. Albans* (1486), sig. a4, and British Museum manuscript Harley 2340 in Thomas Wright and J. O. Halliwell, *Reliquiae Antiquiae* (London, 1845), I, 294–5. These books are later than the treatise.
9. Or *source*, rising or mounting up of a bird, in this case, probably the mounting up of a hawk getting into position to swoop on the prey. According to some writers, the word (cf. French *sous*, "under, beneath") refers to the hawk's downward flight upon its prey; see John Hodgkin, *Proper Terms* (Supplement to the Transactions of the Philological Society, 1907–10), p. 100. Either way, the writer of the treatise seems to have misused the word here, for the diseases mentioned would not assist the hawk to fly in any direction—quite the contrary. Possibly the writer was not an expert in hawking terminology.
10. Trapping or snaring birds.
11. *Magyf*, a variant of *mawgre*, displeasure, ill-will. Perhaps the displeasure and anger are due to the author's own experience with bird catching; or perhaps the author has left out something and means to say "for fear of provoking displeasure and anger."

toilsome and unpleasant, often causing men to be very wet and cold, which many times has been seen to be the main cause of sickness and sometimes of death. But the angler can have no cold nor discomfort nor anger, unless he be the cause himself, for he cannot lose more than a line or a hook, of which he can have plenty of his own making, or of other men's making, as this simple treatise will teach him; so then his loss is no grievance. And he can have no other grievances, unless some fish breaks away from him when he[12] is on his hook, in the landing of that same fish, or in any case, he does not catch him. This is no great hardship, for if he fails with one, he cannot fail with another, if he does as this treatise which follows will instruct him—unless there are no fish in the water where he is angling. And yet, at the very least, he will have his wholesome and merry walk at his own ease, and also many a sweet breath of various plants and flowers that will make him right hungry and put his body in good condition. He will hear the melodies of the harmony of birds. He will also see the young swans or cygnets following their brood swans, the ducks, the coots, the herons, and many other birds with their broods, which seems to me better than all the noise of hounds and blasts of horns and other amusements that falconers and hunters can provide, or the sports that fowlers can make. And if the angler catches the fish with difficulty, then there is no man merrier than he is in his spirits. Also, whoever wishes to practice the game or sport of angling, he must pay heed to the sense of the old proverb, that is, these verses:

> Surge, miser, mane sed noli surgere vane,
> Sanctificat, sanat, ditat quoque surgere mane.[13]

This is to say, he must rise early, which thing is right profitable to a man in these ways. One is for health of the soul, for it shall cause a man to be holy, if anything can make him pleasing to God.[14] The second cause is that it will produce bodily health and will cause him to live long. The third, it will cause him to be rich, temporally and spiritually, in goods and in goodness. Thus I have proved, according to my purpose, that the sport of angling is the true means that causes a man to be merry-spirited, which (according to the said proverb of Solomon and the teaching of medicine) makes a flowering age and a long life. And therefore, to all those that are virtuous, gentle,[15] and freeborn, I write this simple treatise, by following which you can have the whole art of angling to amuse yourselves as you

12. The fish. Fish are masculine in this treatise.
13. An old schoolbook aphorism; cf. Anthony Fitzherbert, *The Book of Husbandry* (1534), edited by W. W. Skeat for the English Dialect Society, Vol. 37, p. 101. For other variants of it, see *Twelfth Night,* II, iii, 3, and *Poor Richard's Almanac.*
14. If he is ever to be on good terms with God.
15. Having noble qualities, or being of gentle birth.

please, in order that your age may be the more flourishing and last the longer.

Then if you want to be crafty in angling, you must first learn to make your tackle, that is to say, your rod, your lines of different colors, and your hooks. After that, you must know how you should angle and in what places of the water; how deep and what time of the day for what manner of fish in what weather; how many impediments there are to angling; and especially with what baits for each different fish in every month of the year; how you must make your baits-bread,[16] where you will find the baits, and how you will find them, and how you will keep them; and the most difficult thing, how you are to make your hooks of steel and of iron,[17] some for you to dub[18] and some for the float, as you will afterward hear. All these things you will find openly depicted to your eye.

How You Must Make Your Rod

And how you should make your rod skillfully, I will tell you. You must cut, between Michaelmas and Candlemas,[19] a fair, smooth staff six feet long, or longer if you wish, of hazel, willow, or aspen; and heat it in an oven when you bake, and set it as exactly straight as you can make it; then let it cool and dry for four weeks or more. Then take and bind it tight with a good cord to a bench or to an exactly squared timber. Then take a plumber's[20] wire that is straight and strong and sharp at one end. Heat the sharp end in a charcoal fire till it is hot, and pierce the staff with it through the pith of the staff—first at the one end and afterward at the other until it is all the way through. Then take a bird spit[21] and burn the hole as you think fit, until it is big enough for your purpose and like a taper of wax;[22] and then wax it. Then let it lie still for two days afterward, until it is thoroughly cold; then unbind it and let it dry in a smokehouse or up under the house-roof till it is thoroughly dry. In the same season, take a rod of white hazel and beath it[23] even and straight, and let it dry in the same way as the staff; and when they are dry, make the rod fit the hole in the said staff, so

16. That is, bait-food, food used as bait. It might include baits made of various ingredients and baked like bread. But *brede* in this passage could also be *breed* (propagate) or a variant of *braid* (how you must make the trick, or stratagem, of your bait). The interpretation given above seems slightly more plausible than the others.
17. *Osmund,* iron of high quality imported from the Baltic area.
18. To clothe, dress up. This seems to be the earliest instance of dubbing, or dressing up, a hook; it evidently means to put an artificial fly on the hook. This promise of flies was fulfilled in the 1496 printed version. The text above suggests that the flies were in the lost pages of the manuscript.
19. That is, between September 29 and February 2.
20. A plumber, a worker in lead.
21. A spit or skewer for roasting birds.
22. That is, make the hole decreasing in size, tapering.
23. That is, soak it in hot water to make it pliable, so that it can be straightened.

that it will go halfway into the staff in a continuous line. And to make the other half of the crop,[24] take a fair shoot of blackthorn, crabtree, medlar, or juniper, cut in the same season and well beathed and straightened; and bind them together neatly so that all the crop may exactly enter into the above-mentioned hole. Then shave the staff down and make it taper-wise waxing.[25] Then ferrule the staff well at both ends with hoops of iron or latten,[26] with a spike in the lower end fastened with a removing device for pulling the crop in and out. Then set your crop a handbreadth inside the upper end of your staff in such a way that it will be as big there as at any other place above. Then, with a cord of six hairs, strengthen your crop at the upper end as far down as the place where it is tied together; and double the cord and tie it firmly in the top with a noose to fasten your fishing line on. And thus you will make yourself a rod so perfect and suitable that you can walk with it, and no one will know what you are going to do; and it will be light and nimble to fish with at your pleasure and desire. [And for your greater convenience, behold here a picture of it as an example]

To Color Your Lines

After you have made your rod, you must learn to color your lines of hair in this manner. First you must take, from the tail of a white horse, the longest hair that is to be had, and the rounder it is the better. And when you have separated it into six bunches, then color every part by itself in a different color, such as, yellow, green, brown, tawny, russet, and dusky color. First, to make your yellow hair: Take a half-gallon of small ale and crush in it three handfuls of walnut leaves and a quarter of alum, and put them all together in a brass pan and boil them well together.[27] And when it is cold, put in your hair that you wish to have yellow, until it is as dark as you want to have it, and then take it out.

To Make Green Color

You must take small ale, the quantity of a quart, and put it in a little pan, and add to it half a pound of alum. Put your hair in it, and let it boil

---

24. The top part of anything; the upper section of the fishing rod, to be made of the two kinds of wood.
25. Increasing in size like a taper.
26. An alloy resembling brass.
27. Small ale is probably weak or inferior ale (like the expression "small beer"). The word *quarter* probably stands for a quarter of a pound.

half an hour. Then take your hair and let it dry. Then take a half-gallon of water and put it in a pan, and add two handfuls of weld[28] or waxen,[29] and press it down with a heavy weight, and let it boil softly half an hour. And when it turns yellow in the scum, put in your hair and with it half a pound of copperas well beaten to powder. And let it boil half-a-mile-way.[30] Then set it down and let it cool five or six hours, take out your hair and let it dry, and there you will have the best green that ever was for the water. And the more copperas you put in, the greener it will be.[31]

Another way, you can make a brighter green, thus. Dye your hair with blue dye[32] until it is a light blue-gray color. And then seethe it in yellow vegetable dye as I have described, except that you must not add to it either copperas or verdigris.

To make your hair yellow, prepare it with alum as I have explained before, and after that with yellow vegetable dye without copperas or verdigris.

Another yellow you shall make thus. Take a half-gallon of small ale, and crush three handfuls of walnut leaves, and put them together. And put in your hair till it is as deep a yellow as you want to have it.

To make russet hair, take a pint and a half of strong lye and half a pound of soot and a little juice of walnut leaves and a quart[33] of alum; and put them all together in a pan and boil them well. And when it is cold, put in your hair till it is as dark as you want it.

To make a brown color, take a pound of soot and a quart of ale, and seethe it with as many walnut leaves as you can. And when they turn black, set it off the fire. And put your hair in it, and let it lie still until it is as brown as you wish to have it.

To make another brown, take strong ale and soot and blend them together, and put therein your hair for two days and two nights, and it will be a right good color.

To make a tawny color, take lime and water, and put them together; and also put your hair therein four or five hours. Then take it out and put it in tanner's ooze[34] for a day, and it will be as fine a tawny color as is required for our purpose.

The sixth part of your hair, you must keep still white for lines for the

---

28. Or *olds;* a yellow dye made from the plant *Reseda luteolo.*
29. Or *wyxen;* apparently another name for weld.
30. The time it would take to walk half a mile.
31. *The first break in the manuscript occurs at about this point. There is no apparent lacuna in the manuscript, but there is a gap in the text equal to about six manuscript pages. The 1496 print fills this gap and is sole authority for the text of the following section of the treatise. We note the point ahead where the manuscript resumes.*
32. Literally: Let woad your hair in a woad-vat.
33. Error for *quarter,* i.e., a quarter of a pound.
34. The liquid from a tanner's vat, a mixture of tanbark juices, etc.

dubbed[35] hook, to fish for the trout and grayling, and to prepare[36] small lines for the roach and the dace.

When your hair is thus colored, you must know for which waters and for which seasons they will serve. The green color in all clear water from April till September. The yellow color in every clear water from September till November, for it is like the weeds and other kinds of grass which grow in the waters and rivers, when they are broken. The russet color serves for all the winter until the end of April, as well in rivers as in pools or lakes. The brown color serves for that water that is black, sluggish, in rivers or in other waters. The tawny color for those waters that are heathy or marshy.

Now you must make your lines in this way. First, see that you have an instrument like this picture drawn hereafter. Then take your hair and cut off from the small end a large handful or more, for it is neither strong nor yet dependable. Then turn the top to the tail,[37] each in equal amount, and divide it into three strands. Then plait each part at the one end by itself, and at the other end plait all three together. And put this last end in the farther side of your instrument, the end that has but one cleft. And fix the other end tight with the wedge the width of four fingers from the end of your hair. Then twist each strand the same way and pull it hard; and fasten them in the three clefts equally tight. Then take out that other end and twist it sufficiently in whichever direction it is inclined. Then stretch it a little and plait it so that it will not come undone. And that is good. And to know how to make your instrument, behold, here it is in a picture. And it is to be made of wood, except the bolt underneath, which must be of iron.

When you have as many of the lengths as you suppose will suffice for the length of a line, then you must tie them together with a water knot[38] or else a duchess knot. And when your knot is tied, cut off the unused short ends a straw's breadth from the knot. Thus you will make your lines fair and fine, and also very secure for any kind of fish. And because you should

35. Covered with an artificial fly.
36. *Rye*, i.e., *ray*, "to array, dress up, prepare."
37. That is, the top to the bottom; reverse half the hair so as to make each strand of uniform strength from end to end.
38. Probably the knot later known as the fisherman's knot.

know both the water knot and also the duchess knot, behold them here in picture. Contrive them in the likeness of the drawing.

[Illustration missing[39]]

You must understand that the subtlest and hardest art in making your tackle is to make your hooks, for the making of which you must have suitable files, thin and sharp and beaten small; a semiclamp of iron; a bender;[40] a pair of long and small tongs; a hard knife, somewhat thick; an anvil; and a little hammer. And for small fish, you must make your hooks in this manner, of the smallest square needles of steel that you can find. You must put the square needle in a red charcoal fire till it is of the same color as the fire is. Then take it out and let it cool, and you will find it well tempered for filing. Then raise the barb with your knife and make the point sharp. Then temper it again, for otherwise it will break in the bending. Then bend it like the bend pictured hereafter as an example. And you must make greater hooks in the same way out of larger needles, such as embroiderers' or tailors' or shoemakers' needles, or spear points; and of shoemakers' awls, especially, the best hooks are made for great fish. And the hooks should bend at the point when they are tested; otherwise they are not good. When the hook is bent, beat the hinder end out broad, and file it smooth to prevent fraying of your line. Then put it in the fire again, and give it an easy red heat. Then suddenly quench it in water, and it will be hard and strong. And that you may have knowledge of your instruments, behold them here in picture portrayed.

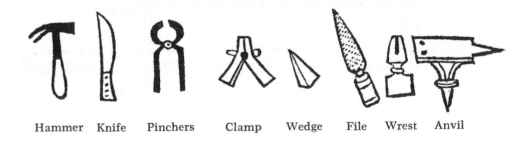

Hammer   Knife   Pinchers   Clamp   Wedge   File   Wrest   Anvil

When you have made your hooks in this way, then you must set them on your lines, according to size and strength in this manner. You must take fine red silk thread, and if it is for a large hook, then double it, but not twisted. And otherwise, for small hooks, let it be single. And with it, bind

39. Probably missing because the printer was unable to reproduce the knots.
40. An instrument for bending, called a *wrest* below.

the line thick for a straw's breadth from the point where the one end of your hook is to be placed. Then set your hook there, and wrap it with the same thread for two-thirds of the length that is to be wrapped. And when you come to the third part, then turn the end of your line back upon the wrapping, double, and wrap it thus double for the third part. Then put your thread in at the hole[41] twice or thrice, and let it go each time round about the shank of your hook. Then wet the hole and pull it until it is tight. And see that your line always lies inside your hooks and not outside. Then cut off the end of the line and the thread as close as you can, without cutting the knot.

Now that you know with what size hooks you must angle for every fish,[42] I will tell you[43]

With How Many Hairs You Shall Angle for Every Fish

First, for the minnow,[44] with a line of one hair. For the growing roach,[45] the bleak,[46] the gudgeon,[47] and the ruff[48] with a line of two hairs. For the dace[49] and the great roach, with a line of three hairs. For the perch,[50] the flounder,[51] the bream,[52] with a line of four hairs. For the chevin-chub,[53] the tench,[54] the eel,[55] with a line of six hairs. For the trout,[56] the grayling,[57] the barbel,[58] and the great chevin,[59] with a line of nine hairs. For the great trout, grayling, and perch, with a line of twelve hairs. For a salmon,[60] with fifteen. For the pike,[61] you must take a good fine line of packthread, made in the manner of a chalkline made brown with your

41. The loop made by doubling the line and wrapping it.
42. Something omitted (?).
43. *The manuscript resumes at this point.*
44. The European species *Phoxinus phoxinus;* perhaps also, the stickleback (*Gasterosteus aculeatus*).
45. The European *Rutilus rutilus*. The great roach farther on in the list is probably the full-grown roach.
46. The freshwater bleak (*Alburnus lucidus*).
47. *Gobio gobio,* or *G. fluviatilis.*
48. The freshwater ruff (*Acerina cernua*).
49. The European *Leuciscus leuciscus.*
50. The European *Perca fluviatilis.*
51. One of the European flounders; probably *Flesus flesus.*
52. The European freshwater *Abramis brama.*
53. Same as chevin or chub (*Leuciscus cephalus*). Perhaps *chub* is an explanatory synonym, i.e., "For the chevin (chub)," etc.
54. *Tinca tinca,* or *T. vulgaris.*
55. The European *Anguilla anguilla.*
56. Brown trout (*Salmo trutta*), the only trout in England at the time.
57. The European *Thymallus thymallus.*
58. *Barbus fluviatilis.*
59. Probably the full-grown chub.
60. The Atlantic salmon (*Salmo salar*).
61. *Esox lucius.*

coloring as described above, strengthened with wire to prevent biting asunder. Your lines must be plumbed[62] with lead, and the plumb[63] nearest the hook must be a full foot and more away from it, and every plumb of a size in keeping with the thickness of the line. There are three ways of weighting. First, for a running ground-line[64] and for the float set upon the lying ground-line,[65] ten plumbs all running together. On the lying ground-line, ten or twenty[66] small plumbs. For the float, weight it so heavily that the least pluck of any fish can pull it down into the water. And make the plumbs round and smooth so that they will not get caught on stones or weeds, which would hinder you greatly in your sport of angling. And for the better understanding, behold them here in picture.

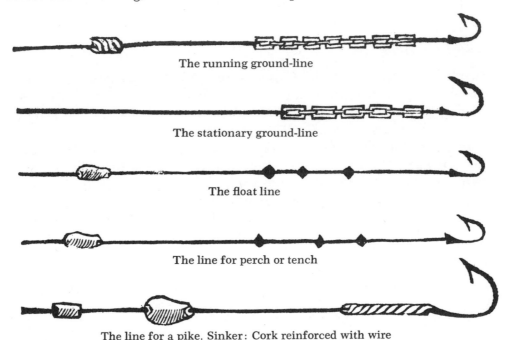

The running ground-line

The stationary ground-line

The float line

The line for perch or tench

The line for a pike. Sinker: Cork reinforced with wire

How You Shall Make Your Floats

You are to make your floats in this manner. Take a good cork that is clean, without many holes; bore it through with a small hot iron; and put a quill in at the larger hole. Then shape them in the manner of a dove egg, smaller and larger as you like, and make them smooth on a grindstone.[67]

62. Weighted with lead weights.
63. A weight, usually of lead; generally used like a sinker.
64. A ground-line free at one end, so that it could move upon the bottom.
65. A fixed, stationary line for bottom fishing.
66. Perhaps an error for "nine or ten."
67. Gynston, literally "machine stone," which sounds like some kind of grindstone. Or this could be an error for *grynston*, a spelling variant of *grindstone*.

And your float, for one hair, should be no bigger than a pea; for two hairs, like a bean; for twelve hairs, like a walnut; and so forth, for every line according to its size. Every sort of line must have a float for angling, except only the ground-line—and even the running ground-line must have a float. The lying ground-line without float.[68]

How Many Kinds of Angling There Are

Now that I have taught you to make your tackle, I will tell you how you must understand that there are six ways of angling. One is at the bottom for the trout. Another, at the bottom of an arch of a bridge or at a standing[69] (where it ebbs and flows) for bleak, roach, and dace. The third is without a float for all kinds of fish. The fourth, with a minnow for the trout, without any plumb or float; the same way for roach and dace with a line of one or two hairs baited with a fly.[70] The fifth is with a dubbed hook for the trout and the grayling.[71] And for the principal point of angling, always keep yourself away from the water and from the sight of the fish— far back on the land or else behind a bush or a tree—so that the fish may not see you. For if he does, he will not bite. And take care that you do not shadow the water any more than you can help, for that is a thing which will frighten the fish, and if he is frightened, he will not bite for a good while afterward. For every kind of fish that feeds at the bottom, you must angle for him in the middle of the water,[72] and somewhat more beneath

68. Was there supposed to be an illustration in the manuscript here, or was the verb dropped?
69. Standing water by the seashore. Or perhaps a standing-place, such as a pier, a dock, or a sea wall.
70. Probably a natural fly.
71. The corresponding passage in the 1496 version is as follows: The fourth, with a minnow for the trout, without plumb or float. The fifth is running in the same way for roach and dace with one or two hairs and a fly. The sixth is with an artificial fly for the trout and grayling.
72. The corresponding passage in the 1496 version: For all kinds of fish that feed at the bottom, you must angle for them at the bottom, so that your hooks will run or lie on the bottom. And for all other fish that feed above, you must angle for them in the middle of the water, either somewhat beneath or somewhat above.

than above; for always the greater the fish, the nearer he will lie to the bottom of the water, while the smaller fish commonly swims above. The sixth good point is: when the fish bites, that you be not too hasty to smite[73] him, nor too late. You must wait till you suppose that the bait and the hook are well into the mouth of the fish, and then strike him. And this is for the ground-line. And for the float: when it seems to you to be pulled softly under the water or else carried softly upon the water, then smite him. And see that you never oversmite[74] the strength of your line, lest you break it. And if you happen to hook a great fish with a small line, you must lead him in the water and labor there, until he is overcome and wearied. Then take him as well as you can, and beware that you do not hold beyond the strength of your line. And if you can avoid it at all, do not let him go out on the end of the line straight from you, but keep him always under the rod, and always hold him strait.[75] Thus you can sustain his leaps and his dives with the help of your hand.

In What Place Is the Best Angling

Here I will declare in what places of the water you must angle to have the best luck. You should angle in a pool or in standing water, in every place where it is at all deep. There is no great choice in a pool,[76] for it is but a prison for fish, and they live for the most part in captivity and hungry like a prisoner. Therefore, it takes the less art to catch them. But, in any case, you should angle in every spot where it is deep, and clear at the bottom, as in gravel or clay without mud or weeds, and especially if there is a whirly-pit[77] of water, or a covert—such as a hollow bank or great roots of trees or long weeds floating on top of the water—where the fish can hide themselves at various times. Also in deep, swift streams and in waterfalls and weirs, floodgates and mill pits,[78] and wherever the water rests by the bank and the current runs close by and it is deep and clear at the bottom. And in other places where you can see any fish rising and feeding at the top.

What Time of the Day Is Best for Angling

You must know that the best time to angle is from the beginning of May to September. The biting time is early in the morning from four o'clock until eight; in the afternoon, from four until eight, but this is not so good

73. To hook the fish by a quick pull on the line, to strike him.
74. Overtax, strike too hard.
75. The instruction seems to mean, "keep the line taut, allow no slack."
76. A pond in which fish are penned up to be used as they are needed.
77. A whirlpool or a very strong eddy.
78. Probably millraces.

as in the morning. And if there is a cold, whistling wind and it be a dark, lowering day, then the fish will usually bite all day. For a dark day is much better than any other clear weather. From the beginning of September until the end of April, angle at any time of the day. Also, many pool fish will bite best at noontime. And if you see the trout or the grayling leap at any time of the day, angle for him with a dub[79] appropriate to that same month. And where the water ebbs and flows, the fish will bite in some place at the flood tide, although after that they will rest behind pilings or arches of bridges and in other such places.

In What Weather Is the Best Angling

You should angle, as I said before, in dark lowering weather when the wind blows softly, and in the summer season when it is burning hot.[80] From September to April and in a fair sunny day, it is good to angle. And if the wind in that season comes from any part of the north,[81] the water then is good. And when there is a great wind, when it snows, rains, or hails, or there is thunder or lightning, and also in consuming[82] heat, that is not the time to angle.

The Twelve Impediments

Which cause men to catch no fish, apart from other common causes which may happen by chance, are these. The first, if your tackle is not good and well made. The second is if you do not angle in biting time. The third, if the fish are frightened by the sight of any man. The fourth, if the water is very thick, white, or red as lees,[83] from any flood recently fallen. The fifth, if the fish will not stir either for cold or fair weather. The sixth is if the water is very hot. The seventh, if it rains. The eighth, if it hails or snows. The ninth, if there is any tempest of any storm. The tenth, if there is a great wind from any direction. The twelfth,[84] if the wind is from the north[85] or northeast or southeast; for generally, both in winter and in summer, if the wind blows from any part of these points, the fish will not usually bite nor stir. The west and south winds are right good, yet of the two the south is better.

79. An artificial fly, a hook disguised with an artificial fly.
80. Something may have been omitted here. The 1496 versions says that burning-hot weather is not good for angling.
81. The manuscript has *oriente*, i.e., "east," with *northe* written over it. On the whole, "northeast" seems more improbable here than "north."
82. *Niming*, scizing; i.e., consuming, devouring, or stupefying.
83. Dregs, sediment of wine.
84. Number eleven was omitted. This probably should be poor choice of bait, which was placed second in the 1496 version and does not appear here.
85. An error for *east*(?).

Baits to Angle With

And now that I have told you how to make your tackle and how you are to fish it, it is reasonable that you should know with what baits you must angle for every kind of freshwater fish in each month of the year—which is the most important thing in this sport of angling. Unless these baits are known, all your skills hitherto written about will avail little or nothing to your purpose, for you cannot bring a hook into a fish's mouth unless there is food on it that pleases him.

Bait for the Salmon

And because the salmon is the goodliest fish that a man can angle for in fresh water, therefore I intend to begin with him. The salmon is a noble fish, but he is cumbersome to catch, for generally he is only in very deep waters and great rivers, and for the most part he keeps to the middle of the stream so that a man cannot come at him easily. And he is in season from the month of March until Michaelmas, in which season you should angle for him with these baits, when they are to be had. First, with a bleak, just as you do for the trout with a minnow; and with a red worm[86] in the beginning and the end of the said season; and also with a worm that grows in a dunghill; and especially with an excellent bait that grows in the water-suckle.[87] But the salmon does not stay at the bottom, but at the float. Also you may happen to catch him (but this is seldom seen) with an artificial fly at his leaping, just as you do a trout or a grayling.

For the Trout

The trout is a dainty fish and free-biting. He is in the season as the season is.[88] He will not be found anywhere except in clean gravel-bottom water and in a stream. And you can angle for him at all times with a lying or running ground-line, except in leaping time, and then with an artificial

---

86. A kind of earthworm.

87. A water plant; probably a local name for the English water dock (*Rumex hydrolapathum*).

88. His biting habits depend upon the time of year (?). However, "season" here may refer to availability or edibility, in which case the interpretation should be that the trout is in season at any time of the year. In the case of salmon there is stronger reason to speak of seasons, since as a migratory fish it would not be available at all times, nor would it be particularly palatable in autumn, when it spawns. In the passage on salmon, March is given as the beginning of the season, and this corresponds roughly to the early runs into the rivers; and the season is properly ended in September, at the onset of spawning. The 1496 version gives "March to Michaelmas" as the season also for trout. For either fish, this season would correspond to the period when the flesh was in best condition for eating.

fly; and early with an early ground-line, and later in the day with a float-line. You must angle for him in March with a minnow hung on your hook by the lower lip, without float or sinker, drawing it up and down in the stream till you feel him hooked. In the same season, angle for him with a ground-line with a red worm as the surest bait. In April, take the same baits; also, in the same season, take a lamprey, also the cankerworm that grows in a dock root, and the red snail. In May, take a stone fly,[89] and the grubworm under the cow turd,[90] and the dor-worm,[91] and a bait that grows on a pine-tree leaf. In June, take the red worm and nip off the head, and put a codworm[92] on the hook in front of it. In July, take the little red worm and the codworm together. In August, take the fly,[93] the little red worm, the herlesoke,[94] and bind the hook. In September, take the red worm and the minnow. In October, take the same, for they are special baits for the trout at all times . . .[95]

. . . of the year. From April to September the trout leaps; then angle for him with an artificial fly appropriate to the month. These flies you will find at the end of this treatise, and the months with them.

The grayling, also known as the umber,[96] is a delicious fish to man's mouth. You can catch him just as you do the trout, and these are his baits. In March and in April, the earthworm. In May, the green worm,[97] a little ringed worm, the dock canker, and the hawthorn worm. In June, the bait that grows between the tree and the bark of an oak. In July, a bait that grows on a fern leaf; and the big red worm, and nip off the head and put a codworm on your hook in front of it. In August, the earthworm, and a dock worm. And all the year afterward, an earthworm.

The barbel is a sweet fish, but it is a queasy food and a perilous one for man's body. For commonly, he introduces the fevers; and if he is eaten

---

89. Probably a species of *Perla*.

90. This habitat is not so well known to modern anglers as a source of bait. The reference here could have been to a species of earthworm, but the next bait specified is the "dor-worm," clearly the larvae of some insect. According to a modern British study— "The Larval Inhabitants of Cow Pats," by B. R. Lawrence, *Journal of Animal Ecology*, 23 (2): 234, 1954—the larvae of two true or two-winged flies (Diptera) are common inhabitants, and likely the grubworms referred to in the treatise.

91. Several insects have borne this name. The *dor-worm* is the larva of some fly, beetle, or bee.

92. The larva of a European caddis fly.

93. Probably the *flesh fly,* "blowfly."

94. Some insect or worm (?). But a *herl* is the fiber from the shaft of a feather, used for making artificial flies.

95. *The rest of the 1450 manuscript is lost. From here on, the 1496 print is the sole authority.*

96. A recently borrowed French term. Most of the fish names are native formations, like *grayling,* or older borrowings from Latin, French, or Scandinavian.

97. Many of these baits cannot be identified with any certainty, although we believe that anyone living in the fifteenth century in the place where the treatise was written would recognize them instantly.

raw, he may be the cause of a man's death, as has often been seen. These are his baits. In March and in April, take fair, fresh cheese, lay it on a board, and cut it in small square pieces the length of your hook. Then take a candle and burn it on the end at the point of your hook until it is yellow. And then bind it on your hook with arrowmaker's silk, and make it rough like a welbede.[98] This bait is good for all the summer season. In May and June, take the hawthorn worm and the big red worm; nip off the head and put a codworm on your hook in front; and that is a good bait. In July, take the earthworm chiefly and the hawthorn worm together. Also the water-dock leaf worm and the hornet worm[99] together. In August and for all the year, take mutton fat and soft cheese, of each the same amount, and a little honey; and grind or beat them together a long time, and work it until it is tough. Add to it a little flour, and make it into small pellets. And that is a good bait to angle with at the bottom. And see to it that it sinks in the water, or else it is not good for this purpose.

The carp is a dainty [!] fish, but there are only a few in England, and therefore I will write the less about him. He is a bad fish to catch, for he is so strongly reinforced in the mouth that no weak tackle can hold him. And as regards his baits, I have but little knowledge of them, and I would hate to write more than I know and have tested. But I know well that the earthworm and the minnow are good baits for him at all times, as I have heard reliable persons say and also found written in trustworthy books.[100]

The chub is a stately fish, and his head is a dainty morsel. There is no fish so greatly fortified with scales on the body. And because he is a strong biter, he has the more baits, which are these. In March, the earthworm at the bottom, for usually he will bite there then, and at all times of the year if he is at all hungry. In April, the ditch canker that grows in the tree; a worm that grows between the bark and the wood of an oak; the earthworm; and the young frogs when the feet are cut off. Also, the stone fly, the grubworm under the cow turd, the red snail. In May, the bait that grows on the osier leaf and the dock canker, together upon your hook. Also a bait that grows on a fern leaf, the codworm, and a bait that grows on a hawthorn. And a bait that grows on an oak leaf and a silkworm and a codworm together. In June, take the cricket and the dor;[101] and also an earthworm with the head cut off and a codworm in front, and put them on the hook. Also a bait on the osier leaf, young frogs with three feet cut off

98. Possibly a woodlouse or a millepede, both crustaceans. J. O. Halliwell's *A Dictionary of Archaic and Provincial Words* (London: John Russell Smith, 1852) has "*Welbode*. The insect [*sic*] millepes," and "*Wolbode*. A millepes."
99. The larva of a hornet (?); more likely a "horned worm" of some kind, cf. the horned beetle, horned snail, etc.
100. This is the only bit of angling lore allegedly drawn from books. In view of the medieval fondness for citing authorities wherever possible, it seems likely that most of the treatise was written from personal experience and oral tradition.
101. The *dor-worm*, a larva of some sort.

at the body and the fourth at the knee. The bait on the hawthorn and the codworm together; and a grub that breeds in a dunghill; and a big grasshopper. In July, the grasshopper and the bumblebee of the meadow. Also young bees and young hornets. Also a great, brindled fly that grows in paths of meadows, and the fly that is among anthills.[102] In August, take wortworms[103] and maggots until Michaelmas. In September, the earthworm; and also take these baits when you can get them; that is to say: cherries, young mice without hair, and the honeycomb.

The bream is a noble fish and a dainty one. And you must angle for him with an earthworm from March until August, and then with a butterfly and a green fly,[104] and with a bait that grows among green reeds, and a bait that grows in the bark of a dead tree. And for young bream, take maggots. And from that time forth for all the year afterward, take the earthworm and, in the river, brown bread. There are more baits, but they are not easy, and therefore I pass over them.

A tench is a good fish, and heals all sorts of other fish that are hurt, if they can come to him.[105] During most of the year he is in the mud; he stirs most in June and July, and in other seasons but little. He is a poor biter. His baits are these. For all the year, brown bread toasted with honey in the shape of a buttered loaf, and the big red worm. And for the chief bait, take the black blood in the heart of a sheep and flour and honey. Work them all together somewhat softer than paste, and anoint the earthworm therewith —both for this fish and for others. And they will bite much better thereat at all times.

The perch is a dainty fish and surpassingly wholesome, and a free-biting fish. These are his baits. In March, the earthworm. In April, the grubworm under the cow turd. In May, the sloe-thorn worm and the codworm. In June, the bait that grows in an old fallen oak, and the green canker. In July, the bait that grows on the osier leaf, and the grub that grows on the dunghill, and the hawthorn worm, and the codworm. In August, the earthworm and maggots. All the year thereafter, the earthworm is best.

The roach is an easy fish to catch. And if he is fat and penned up, then he is good food, and these are his baits. In March, the readiest bait is the earthworm. In April, the grub under the cow turd. In May, the bait that grows on the oak leaf and the grub in the dunghill. In June, the bait that grows on the osier and the codworm. In July, houseflies and the bait that grows on an oak; and the nutworm[106] and mathewes[107] and maggots till Michaelmas; and after that, the fat of bacon.

---

102. A winged ant, either queen or drone.
103. Probably a caterpillar that feeds on cabbages.
104. Probably a green-colored natural fly.
105. We regret not knowing more about this remarkable observation.
106. Perhaps the larva of the nut weevil (*Balaninus nucum*), which lays eggs in green hazelnuts or filberts.
107. Worms or maggots of some kind; cf. *mathe*, "maggot," etc.

The dace is a noble fish to catch, and if it[108] be well fattened, then it is good food. In March, his bait is an earthworm. In April, the grub under the cow turd. In May, the dock canker and the bait on the sloe thorn and on the oak leaf. In June, the codworm and the bait on the osier and the white grubworm in the dunghill. In July, take houseflies, and flies that grow in anthills; the codworm and maggots until Michaelmas. And if the water is clear, you will catch fish when others take none. And from that time forth, do as you do for the roach, for usually in their biting and their baits they are alike.

The bleak is but a feeble fish, yet he is wholesome. His baits from March to Michaelmas are the same as I have written before for the roach and dace, except that, all the summer season, as far as possible, you should angle for him with a housefly; and, in the winter season, with bacon and other bait made as you will know hereafter.

The ruff is a right wholesome fish, and you must angle for him with the same baits in all seasons of the year and in the same way as I have told you for the perch; for they are alike in fishing and feeding except that the ruff is smaller. And therefore he must have the smaller bait.

The flounder is a wholesome fish and a noble one, and a subtle biter in his own way. For usually, when he sucks his food, he feeds at the bottom; and therefore you must angle for him with a lying ground-line. And he has but one kind of bait, and that is an earthworm, which is the best bait for all kinds of fish.

The gudgeon is a good fish for his size, and he bites well at the bottom. And his baits for all the year are these: the earthworm, the codworm, and maggots. And you must angle for him with a float, and let your bait be near the bottom or else on the bottom.

The minnow, when he shines in the water, then he is better.[109] And though his body is little, yet he is a ravenous biter and an eager one. And you must angle for him with the same baits as you do for gudgeon, except that they must be small.

The eel is an indigestible fish, a glutton, and a devourer of the young fry of fish. And because the pike also is a devourer of fish, I put them both behind all others for angling. For this eel, you must find a hole in the bottom of the water, and it is blue-blackish. There put in your hook till it be a foot within the hole, and your bait should be a big angle-twitch[110] or a minnow.

The pike is a good fish, but because he devours so many of his own kind

---

108. Neuter pronoun. Fish are generally masculine in this treatise.
109. *Byttyre*, "bitter," makes poor sense here, and the author often confused *e* with *i* (or *y*). The "better" minnows may be those with bright streaks or spots on the bellies or sides.
110. An earthworm, angleworm.

as well as of others, I love him the less.[111] And to catch him, you must do thus. Take a small cod hook, and take a roach or a fresh herring, and a wire with a hole in the end. And put the wire in at the mouth and out at the tail, down along the back of the fresh herring. Then put the line of your hook in after it, and draw the hook into the cheek of the fresh herring. Then put a sinker on your line a yard away from your hook, and a float midway between; and cast it in a hole which the pike frequents. And this is the best and surest device for catching the pike. There is another way of catching him. Take a frog and put it on your hook at the back side of the neck between the skin and the body, and put on a float a yard distant, and cast it where the pike haunts, and you will have him. Another way: take the same bait and put it in asafetida and cast it in the water with a cord and a cork, and you will not fail to get him. And if you care to have good sport, then tie the cord to the foot of a goose, and you will see a good tug-of-war[112] to decide whether the goose or the pike will have the better of it.

Now you know with what baits and how you must angle for every kind of fish. Now I will tell you how you must keep and feed your live baits. You must feed and keep them all together, but each kind by itself and with such things as those in and on which they live. And as long as they are alive and fresh, they are excellent. But when they are sloughing their skin or else dead, they are no good. Out of these are excepted three kinds, that is, to wit: hornets, bumblebees, and wasps. These you must bake in bread, and afterward dip their heads in blood and let them dry. Also except maggots, which, when they are grown large with their natural feeding, you must feed further with mutton fat and with a cake made of flour and honey; then they will become larger. And when you have cleansed them with sand in a bag of blanket,[113] kept hot under your gown or other warm thing for two or three hours, then they are best and ready to angle with. And cut off the leg of the frog at the knee, the legs and wings of the grasshopper at the body.

The following are baits made to last all the year. The first are flour and lean meat from the hips of a rabbit or a cat, virgin wax, and sheep's fat. Bray them in a mortar, and then mix it at the fire with a little purified honey; and so make it up into little balls, and bait your hooks with it according to their size. And this is a good bait for all kinds of freshwater fish.

Another: take the suet of a sheep and cheese in equal amounts, and bray them together a long time in a mortar. And then take flour and mix it therewith, and after that mingle it with honey and make balls of it. And that is especially for the barbel.

111. The sentiment against cannibal fish has been a lasting but not always consistent one among anglers.
112. *Haling*, "hauling, pulling."
113. A kind of heavy woolen cloth.

Another, for dace and roach and bleak: Take wheat and seethe it well and then put it in blood a whole day and a night, and it will be a good bait.

For baits for great fish, keep this rule especially: When you have taken a great fish, open up the belly, and whatever you find in it, make that your bait, for it is best.

These are the twelve flies with which you must angle for the trout and grayling; and dub them just as you will now hear me tell.[114]

March

The Dun Fly: The body of dun wool and the wings of the partridge.
Another Dun Fly: the body of black wool; the wings of the blackest drake;[115] and the jay under the wing and under the tail.[116]

April

The Stone Fly: the body of black wool, and yellow under the wing and under the tail; and the wings, of the drake. In the beginning of May, a good fly: the body of reddened[117] wool and lapped about with black silk; the wings, of the drake and of the red capon's hackle.

May

The Yellow Fly: the body of yellow wool; the wings of the red cock's hackle and of the drake dyed yellow. The Black Leaper: the body of black wool and lapped about with the herl[118] of the peacock's tail; and the wings of the red capon with a blue head.

June

The Dun Cut: the body of black wool, and a yellow stripe along either side; the wings, of the buzzard,[119] bound on with hemp that has been treated with tanbark. The Maure Fly: the body of dusky[120] wool; the wings

---

114. Owing to the fact that we discuss the interpretation of these fly dressings in detail in Chapter 11, our text here is calculated to avoid as much as possible the resolution of issues discussed there. Identification of the natural prototypes of these artificial flies is also attempted in that chapter.
115. Feather material, probably from a mallard.
116. The European jay (*Garrulus glandarius*).
117. *Roddyd;* cf. *rud,* "to make red."
118. Fibers from the shaft of a tail feather.
119. The European buzzard, of the hawk family.
120. Printed *dolke;* error for *doske,* "dusky." The tall variety of fifteenth-century *S* often resembles an *l.*

of the blackest breast feathers of the wild drake. The Tandy Fly at St. William's[121] Day: the body of tandy[122] wool; and the wings the opposite, either against the other,[123] of the whitest breast feathers of the wild drake.

July

The Wasp Fly: the body of black and lapped about with yellow thread; the wings, of the buzzard. The Shell Fly at St. Thomas' Day:[124] the body of green wool and lapped about with the herl of the peacock's tail; wings, of the buzzard.

August

The Drake Fly: the body of black wool and lapped about with black silk; wings of the breast feathers of the black drake with a black head.

These pictures are put here as examples of your hooks:[125]

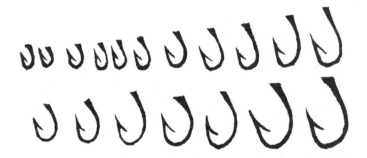

Here follows the order[126] made to all those who shall have the understanding of this aforesaid treatise and use it for their pleasures.

You that can angle and catch fish for your pleasure, as the above treatise teaches and shows you: I charge and require you in the name of all noble men that you do not fish in any poor man's private water (such as his pond, or tank, or other things necessary for keeping fish in) without his permission and good will. And that you be not in the habit of breaking any men's

121. The festival of St. William of York (William Fitzherbert Archbishop of York, twelfth century) was celebrated June 8.
122. Possibly "tawny."
123. With the sections of drake breast feathers set back to back.
124. Thomas à Becket. This is not the day of his martyrdom (December 29), but the day of his translation, i.e., when his bones were enshrined, July 7.
125. Not, as we should expect, of the flies. The latter may have been too difficult for the printer to reproduce. We illustrate our conception of the flies in Chapter 11.
126. Possibly by a different author; or perhaps an editor worked this section over. There is a slight change of style.

fish traps lying in their weirs and in other places belonging to them, nor of taking the fish away that is caught in them. For after a fish is caught in a man's trap, if the trap is laid in the public waters, or else in such waters as he rents, it is his own personal property. And if you take it away, you are robbing him, which is a right shameful deed for any noble man to do, a thing that thieves and robbers do, who are punished for their evil deeds by the neck and otherwise when they can be discovered and captured. And also if you do in the same manner as this treatise shows you, you will have no need to take other men's fish, while you will have enough of your own catching, if you care to work for them. It will be a true pleasure to see the fair, bright, shining-scaled fishes outwitted by your crafty means and drawn out on the land. Also, I charge you, that you break no man's hedges in going about your sports, nor open any man's gates without shutting them again. Also, you must not use this aforesaid artful sport for covetousness, merely for the increasing or saving of your money, but mainly for your enjoyment and to procure the health of your body and, more especially, of your soul. For when you intend to go to your amusements in fishing, you will not want very many persons with you, who might hinder you in your pastime. And then you can serve God devoutly by earnestly saying your customary prayers. And in so doing, you will eschew and avoid many vices, such as idleness, which is the principal cause inciting a man to many other vices, as is right well known. Also, you must not be too greedy in catching your said game,[127] as in taking too much at one time, a thing which can easily happen if you do in every point as this present treatise shows you. That could easily be the occasion of destroying your own sport and other men's also. When you have a sufficient mess, you should covet no more at that time. Also you should busy yourself to nourish the game in everything that you can, and to destroy all such things as are devourers of it. And all those that do according to this rule will have the blessing of God and St. Peter. That blessing, may He grant who bought us with his precious blood!

127. The quarry, i.e., the fish. The writer of the treatise proper does not use *game* in this sense.

Chapter 14

THE FIRST KNOWN ESSAY ON FLY-FISHING
PART II OF
THE COMPLEAT ANGLER
BY CHARLES COTTON

Thanks, it appears, to deadlines, Charles Cotton, poet, cavalier, and angler of the seventeenth century, wrote the first specialized essay on fly-fishing. Izaak Walton had never been able to make The Compleat Angler *complete in his first four editions, owing to his lack of knowledge of fly-fishing. In his scanty treatment of the subject, he had merely recorded from indirect sources the twelve flies that came down from* The Treatise of Fishing with an Angle. *For his fifth edition he asked his young friend and fellow Royalist, Cotton, to fill the gap, and Cotton, it appears, gave his promise. As many writers do, he put it off until the time was upon him, and then wrote it in white heat. "I was surprised," he said, "with the sudden news of a sudden new edition of your Compleat Angler; so that, having but a little more than ten days time to turn me in, and rub up my memory (for in truth I have not in all this long time, though I have often thought on't, and almost as often resolved to go presently about it) I was forced upon the instant to scribble what I here present you: which I have also endeavored to accommodate to your own Method."*

Walton's method to which he accommodated was the prose dialogue between Master (Piscator) and Pupil (Viator), imaginary characters out of Walton's first edition. In Cotton's hands, the pastoral sentiments and displays of the courtesies of the gentry, which were uppermost in the Waltonian style, only slightly veiled the first basic and original treatise on fly-fishing.

Although Cotton set down many angling charms, among them the most celebrated instruction in the sport—"fish fine, and far off"—his treatise is seldom read any longer by anglers, owing, I believe, to its archaic overlay. To bring him back into the mainstream of active angling literature, I have therefore performed an unprecedented—and for some Waltonians, perhaps unforgivable—piece of editing. I have extracted from Cotton's Part II of The Compleat Angler *the essentials of fly-fishing, eliminating all "extraneous" material. The result is a text that may be read as a direct treatise on the art by one who says straight out, and correctly, "I think myself a master in this." If I am therefore Cotton's most drastic editor, I think I am also in another aspect his most faithful. For in the text I have extracted, I have been more sparing than other Walton-Cotton editors in editing his original text (provided by the Beinecke Rare Book and Manuscript Library of Yale University), making only alterations that seemed imperative, such as corrections of obvious printer's errors and occasional changes in punctuation.*

One of the peculiar charms of fly-fishing is that although it changes, even from day to day, it is accompanied by a literature that at its best is always fresh and informative about nature and the angler—a quality it doubtless derives from the experience of what is everlasting in our ties to the natural earth. Among the delectable items to be found in Cotton are descriptions of sixty-five trout flies—the first extended list of flies on record—and a recipe for cooking trout.

TREATISE ON FLY-FISHING
by Charles Cotton (Edited by John McDonald)

From Part II of the fifth edition of Izaak Walton's *The Compleat Angler*, 1676.

To begin methodically, as a master in any art should do (and I will not deny, but that I think myself a master in this) I shall divide angling for trout or grayling into these three ways: at the top, at the bottom, and in the middle. Which three ways, though they are all of them . . . in some sort common to both those kinds of fish; yet are they not so generally and absolutely so, but that they will necessarily require a distinction, which in due place I will also give you.

That which we call angling at the top, is with a fly; at the bottom with a ground-bait; in the middle with a minnow, or ground-bait.

Angling at the top is of two sorts, with a quick [natural] fly, or with an artificial fly.

That we call angling at the bottom is also of two sorts, by hand, or with a cork, or float.

That we call angling in the middle is also of two sorts, with a minnow for a trout, or with a ground bait for a grayling. . . .

I must now come to the second way of angling at the top, which is with an artificial fly, which also I will show you how to make before I have done, but first shall acquaint you, that with this you are to angle with a line longer by a yard and a half, or sometimes two yards than your rod and with both this, and the other in a still day in the streams, in a breeze, that curls the water in the still deeps, where (excepting in May and June, that the best trouts will lie in shallow streams to watch for prey, and even then too) you are like to hit the best fish.

For the length of your rod you are always to be governed by the breadth of the river you shall choose to angle at; and for a trout river, one of five or six yards long is commonly enough, and longer (though never so neatly and artificially made) it ought not to be, if you intend to fish at ease, and if otherwise, where lies the sport?

Of these, the best that ever I saw are made in Yorkshire, which are all of one piece; that is to say, of several, six, eight, ten or twelve pieces, so neatly pieced, and tied together with fine thread below, and silk above, as to make it taper, like a switch, and to ply with a true bent to your hand; and these too are light, being made of fir wood, for two or three lengths, nearest to the hand, and of other wood nearer to the top, that a man might very easily manage the longest of them that ever I saw, with one hand; and these when you have given over angling for a season, being taken to pieces, and laid up in some dry place, may afterwards be set together again in their former postures, and will be as straight, sound, and good as the first hour they were made, and being laid in oil and color, according to your master Walton's direction, will last many years.

The length of your line, to a man that knows how to handle his rod, and to cast it, is no manner of encumbrance, excepting in woody places, and in landing of a fish, which every one that can afford to angle for pleasure, has somebody to do for him, and the length of line is a mighty advantage to the fishing at distance; and to fish *fine, and far off*, is the first and principal rule for trout angling.

Your line in this case should never be less, nor ever exceed, two hairs next to the hook, for one (though some, I know, will pretend to more art, than their fellows) is indeed, too few, the least accident, with the finest hand being sufficient to break it: but he that cannot kill a trout of twenty inches long with two, in a river clear of wood and weeds, and this [the Dove] and some others of ours are, deserves not the name of an angler.

Now to have your whole line as it ought to be, two of the first lengths, nearest the hook, should be of two hairs apiece, the next three lengths above them of three, the next three above them of four, and so of five, and six, and seven, to the very top: by which means your rod and tackle will in a manner be taper from your very hand to your hook; your line will fall much better and straighter, and cast your fly to any certain place to which the hand and eye shall direct it, with less weight and violence, that would otherwise circle the water, and fright away the fish.

In casting your line, do it always before you, and so that your fly may first fall upon the water, and as little of your line with it as possible, though if the wind be stiff, you will then of necessity be compelled to drown a good part of your line to keep your fly in the water: and in casting your fly, you must aim at the further, or nearer bank, as the wind serves your turn, which also will be with, and against you on the same side several times in an hour, as the river winds in its course, and you will be forced to angle up and down by turns accordingly; but are to endeavor, as much as you can, to have the wind evermore on your back, and always be sure to stand as far off the bank as your length will give you leave when you throw to the contrary side, though when the wind will not permit you so to do, and that you are constrained to angle on the same side whereon you stand, you must then stand on the very brink of the river, and cast your fly at the utmost length of your rod and line, up or down the river, as the gale serves. . . .

[I cut a paragraph here on Cotton's hair leader, or snell, which is obsolete —Ed.]

I am next to teach you how to make a fly; and afterwards of what dubbing you are to make the several flies I shall hereafter name to you.

In making a fly then (which is not a hackle or palmer fly for of those, and their several kinds we shall have occasion to speak every month in the year) you are first to hold your hook fast betwixt the forefinger and thumb of your left hand, with the back of the shank upwards, and the point towards your finger's end; and then take a strong small silk of the color of the fly you intend to make, wax it well with wax of the same color too (to which end you are always, by the way, to have wax of all colors about you), and draw it betwixt your finger and thumb, to the head of the shank, and then whip it twice or thrice about the bare hook, which, you must know, is done, both to prevent slipping, and also that the shank of the hook may not cut the hairs of your towght [section of the hairline] which sometimes it will otherwise do; which being done, take your line, and draw it likewise betwixt your finger and thumb, holding the hook so fast, as only to suffer it to pass by, until you have the knot of your towght almost to the middle of the shank of your hook, on the inside of it, then whip your silk twice or thrice about both hook and line, as hard as the strength of the silk will permit, which being done, strip the feather for the wings proportionable to the bigness of your fly, placing that side downwards, which grew uppermost before, upon the back of the hook, leaving so much only as to serve for the length of the wing of the point of the plume, lying reversed from the end of the shank upwards, then whip your silk twice, or thrice about the root end of the feather, hook, and towght, which being done clip off the root end of the feather close by the arming, and then whip the silk fast and firm about the hook, and towght until you come to the bend of the hook: but not further (as you do at London; and so make a very unhandsome, and, in plain English, a very unnatural and shapeless fly) which being done, cut away the end of your towght, and fasten it, and then take your dubbing which is to make the body of your fly, as much as you think convenient, and holding it lightly, with your hook, betwixt the finger, and thumb of your left hand, take your silk with the right, and twisting it betwixt the finger and thumb of that hand, the dubbing will spin itself about the silk, which when it has done, whip it about the armed hook backward, till you come to the setting on of the wings; and then take the feather for the wings, and divide it equally into two parts, and turn them back towards the bend of the hook, the one on the one side, and the other on the other of the shank, holding them fast in that posture betwixt the forefinger and thumb of your left hand, which done, warp them so down, as to stand, and slope towards the bend of the hook, and having warped up to the end of the shank, hold the fly fast betwixt the finger and thumb of your left hand, and then take the silk betwixt the finger, and thumb of your right hand, and where the warping ends, pinch or nip it with your thumb nail against your finger, and strip away the remainder of your dubbing from the silk, and then with the bare silk whip it once or twice about, make the wings to stand in due order, fasten, and cut it off; after which, with the point of a needle raise up the dubbing gently from the warp, twitch off the superfluous hairs of your dubbing, leaving the wings of an equal length (your fly will never else swim true) and the work is done. And this way of making a fly (which is certainly the best of all other) was taught me by a kinsman of mine, one Captain Henry Jackson, a near neighbor, an admirable fly-angler, by many degrees the best fly maker that ever I yet met with. . . .

[Cotton then describes himself tying a fly.] You see first how I hold my hook, and thus I begin. Look you, here are my first two or three whips about the bare hook, thus I join hook and line, thus I put on my wings, thus I twirl and lap on my dubbing, thus I work it up towards the head, thus I part my wings, thus I nip my superfluous dubbing from my silk, thus fasten, thus trim and adjust my fly, and there's a fly made. . . .

[He comments on the fact that the dubbing he used that day looks "very black" to the casual eye.]

It appears so in hand; but step to the door and hold it up betwixt your eye and the sun, and it will appear a shining red; let me tell you, never a man in England can discern the true color of a dubbing any way but that, and therefore choose always to make your flies on . . . a bright sunshine day . . . which also you may the better do, because it is worth nothing to fish in . . . and be sure to make the body of your fly as slender as you can. . . .

To begin then where I left off: my father Walton tells us but of 12

177

artificial flies only,[1] to angle with at the top, and gives their names, of which some are common with us here; and I think I guess at most of them by his description, and I believe they all breed and are taken in our rivers, though we do not make them either of the same dubbing, or fashion. And it may be in the rivers about London, which I presume he has most frequented, and where it is likely he has done most execution, there is not much notice taken of many more: but we are acquainted with several others here (though perhaps I may reckon some of his by other names too) but if I do, I shall make you amends by an addition to his catalog. And although the forenamed great master in the art of angling (for so in truth he is) tells you that no man should in honesty catch a trout till the middle of March, yet I hope he will give a man leave sooner to take a grayling, which . . . is in the dead months in his best season; and do assure you (which I remember by a very remarkable token) I did once take upon the sixth day of December one, and only one, of the biggest graylings, and the best in season, that ever I yet saw, or tasted; and do usually take trouts too, and with a fly, not only before the middle of this month, but almost every year in February, unless it be a very ill spring, indeed; and have sometimes in January, so early as New-year's-tide, and in frost and snow, taken grayling in a warm sunshine day for an hour or two about noon; and to fish for him with a grub it is then the best time of all.

I shall therefore begin my fly fishing with that month (though I confess very few begin so soon, and that such as are so fond of the sport as to embrace all opportunities, can rarely in that month find a day fit for their purpose) and tell you, that upon my knowledge these flies in a warm sun, for an hour or two in the day, are certainly taken.

January

1. A Red Brown, with wings of the male of a mallard almost white: the dubbing of the tail of a black long-coated cur, such as they commonly make muffs of; for the hair on the tail of such a dog dyes and turns to a red brown, but the hair of a smooth-coated dog of the same color will not do, because it will not dye, but retains its natural color, and this fly is taken in a warm sun, this whole month through.

2. There is also a very little Bright Dun Gnat, as little as can possibly be made, so little as never to be fished with, with above one hair next the hook, and this is to be made of a mixed dubbing of martin's fur, and the white of a hare's scut [tail]; with a very white, and small wing; and it is no great matter how fine you fish, for nothing will rise in this month but a grayling, and of them I never at this season saw any taken with a fly, of above a foot long in my life: but of little ones about the bigness of a

1. Descended from "the XII" of *The Treatise of Fishing with an Angle*—Ed.

smelt in a warm day, and a glowing sun, you may take enough with these two flies, and they are both taken the whole month through.

February

1. Where the Red Brown of the last month ends, another almost of the same color begins with this, saving that the dubbing of this must be of something of a blacker color, and both of them warpt on with red silk; the dubbing that should make this fly, and that is the truest color, is to be got off the black spot of a hog's ear: not that a black spot in any part of the hog will not afford the same color; but that the hair in that place is by many degrees softer, and more fit for the purpose: his wing must be as the other, and this kills all this month, and is called the Lesser Red Brown.

2. This month also a Plain Hackle, or palmer fly, made with a rough black body, either of black spaniel's fur, or the whirl of an ostrich feather, and the red hackle of a capon over all, will kill, and if the weather be right, make very good sport.

3. Also a Lesser Hackle with a black body also, silver twist over that, and a red feather over all, will fill your pannier [basket], if the month be open, and not bound up in ice, and snow, with very good fish; but in case of a frost and snow, you are to angle only with the smallest gnats, browns and duns you can make, and with those are only to expect graylings no bigger than sprats.

4. In this month, upon a whirling round water, we have a Great Hackle, the body black, and wrapped with a red feather of a capon untrimmed; that is, the whole length of the hackle staring out (for we sometimes barb the hackle-feather short all over, sometimes barb it only a little and sometimes barb it close underneath), leaving the whole length of the feather on the top, or back of the fly, which makes it swim better, and as occasion serves kills very great fish.

5. We make use also in this month of another Great Hackle, the body black, and ribbed over with gold twist, and a red feather over all, which also does great execution.

6. Also a Great Dun, made with dun bear's hair, and the wings of the grey feather of a mallard near unto his tail, which is absolutely the best fly can be thrown upon a river this month, and with which an angler shall have admirable sport.

7. We have also this month the Great Blue Dun, the dubbing of the bottom of bear's hair next to the roots, mixed with a little blue camlet, the wings of the dark grey feather of a mallard.

8. We have also this month a Dark Brown, the dubbing of the brown hair of the flank of a brended [burnt, or branded] cow, and the wings of the grey drake's feather.

179

And note, that these several hackles, or palmer flies, are some for one water, and one sky, and some for another, and according to the change of those, we alter their size, and color, and note also, that both in this, and all other months of the year, when you do not certainly know what fly is taken; or cannot see any fish to rise, you are then to put on a small hackle, if the water be clear, or a bigger if something dark, until you have taken one, and then thrusting your finger through his gills, to pull out his gorge, which being opened with your knife, you will then discover what fly is taken, and may fit yourself accordingly.

For the making of a hackle, or palmer fly, my father Walton has already given you sufficient direction.

March

For this month you are to use all the same hackles, and flies with the other, but you are to make them less.

1. We have besides for this month a little dun called a Whirling Dun (though it is not the Whirling Dun indeed, which is one of the best flies we have) and for this the dubbing must be of the bottom fur of a squirrel's tail and the wing of the grey feather of a drake.

2. Also a Bright Brown, the dubbing either of the brown of a spaniel, or that of a cow's flank, with a [grey wing].[2]

3. Also a Whitish Dun made of the roots of camel's hair, and the wings of the grey feather of a mallard.

4. There is also for this month a fly, called the Thorn Tree Fly, the dubbing an absolute black mixed with eight or ten hairs of Isabella-colored mohair, the body as little as can be made, and the wings of a bright mallard's feather, an admirable fly, and in great repute amongst us for a killer.

5. There is, besides this another Blue Dun, the dubbing of which it is made being thus to be got. Take a small tooth comb, and with it comb the neck of a black greyhound, and the down that sticks in the teeth will be the finest blue that ever you saw. The wings of this fly can hardly be too white, and he is taken about the tenth of this month, and lasteth till the four and twentieth.

6. From the tenth of this month also till towards the end, is taken a little Black Gnat: the dubbing either of the fur of a black water-dog, or the down of a young black water-coot, the wings of the male of a mallard as white as may be, the body as little as you can possible make it, and the wings as short as his body.

7. From the sixteenth of this month also to the end of it, we use a Bright Brown, the dubbing for which, is to be had out of a skinner's lime pits, and of the hair of an abortive calf, which the lime will turn to be so

2. Cotton's text, in apparent error, says "Grayling."

bright as to shine like gold, for the wings of this fly, the feather of a brown hen is the best; which fly is also taken till the tenth of April.

April

All the same hackles, and flies that were taken in March will be taken in this month also, with this distinction only concerning the flies, that all the browns be lapped with red silk, and the duns with yellow.

1. To these a Small Bright Brown, made of spaniel's fur, with a light grey wing; in a bright day and a clear water, is very well taken.

2. We have too a little Dark Brown, the dubbing of that color, and some violet camlet mixed, and the wing of a grey feather of a mallard.

3. From the sixth of this month to the tenth, we have also a fly called the Violet Fly, made of a dark violet stuff, with the wings of the grey feather of a mallard.

4. About the twelfth of this month comes in the fly called the Whirling Dun, which is taken every day about the mid time of day all this month through, and by fits from thence to the end of June, and is commonly made of the down of a fox-cub, which is of an ash color at the roots, next the skin, and ribbed about with yellow silk, the wings of the pale grey feather of a mallard.

5. There is also a Yellow Dun, the dubbing of camel's hair, and yellow camlet, or wool mixed, and a white-grey wing.

6. There is also, this month, another Little Brown, besides that mentioned before, made with a very slender body, the dubbing of dark brown, and violet camlet mixed, and a grey wing; which though the direction for the making be near the other, is yet another fly, and will take when the other will not, especially in a bright day, and a clear water.

7. About the twentieth of this month comes in a fly called the Horse Flesh Fly, the dubbing of which is a blue mohair, with pink-colored and red tammy mixed, a light-colored wing, and a dark brown head. This fly is taken best in an evening, and kills from two hours before sunset till twilight, and is taken the month through.

May

And now . . . that we are entering into the month of May, I think it requisite to beg not only your attention but also your best patience; for I must now be a little tedious with you, and dwell upon this month longer than ordinary; which that you may the better endure, I must tell you, this month deserves, and requires to be insisted on, forasmuch as it alone, and the next following afford more pleasure to the fly-angler, than all the rest; and here it is that you are to expect an account of the Green Drake, and

181

QUILL GORDON

Stone Fly, promised you so long ago, and some others that are peculiar to this month, and part of the month following, and that (though not so great either in bulk, or name) do yet stand in competition with the two before named; and so, that it is yet undecided amongst the anglers to which of the pretenders to the title of the May-fly, it does properly, and duly belong, neither dare I (where so many of the learned in this art of angling are got in dispute about the controversy) take upon me to determine; but I think I ought to have a vote amongst them, and according to that privilege, shall give you my free opinion, and, peradventure when I have told you all, you may incline to think me in the right. . . .

I will first begin with the flies of less esteem (though almost anything will take a trout in May) that I may afterwards insist the longer upon those of greater note, and reputation; know, therefore, that the first fly we take notice of in this month, is called

1. The Turkey Fly; the dubbing ravelled out of some blue stuff, and lapped about with yellow silk, the wings of a grey mallard's feather.

2. Next, a Great Hackle; or palmer fly, with a yellow body ribbed with gold twist, and large wings of a mallard's feather dyed yellow, with a red capon's hackle over all.

3. Then a Black Fly, the dubbing of a black spaniel's fur, and the wings of a grey mallard's feather.

4. After that a Light Brown with a slender body; the dubbing twirled upon small red silk, and raised with the point of a needle, that the ribs or rows of silk may appear through, the wings of the grey feather of a mallard.

5. Next, a Little Dun, the dubbing of a bear's dun whirled upon yellow silk, the wings of the grey feather of a mallard.

6. Then a White Gnat, with a pale wing, and a black head.

7. There is also this month a fly called the Peacock Fly, the body made of a whirl of a peacock's feather, with a red head, and wings of a mallard's feather.

8. We have then another very killing fly, known by the name of the Dun Cut, the dubbing of which is a bear's dun, with a little blue, and yellow mixed with it, a large dun wing, and two horns at the head, made of the hairs of a squirrel's tail.

9. The next is the Cow Lady, a little fly, the body of a peacock's feather, the wing of a red feather, or strips of the red hackle of a cock.

10. We have then the Cow Turd Fly;[3] the dubbing light-brown and yellow mixed, the wing the dark grey feather of a mallard. And note that besides these above-mentioned, all the same hackles and flies, the hackles only brighter, and the flies smaller, that are taken in April, will also be taken this month, as also all browns, and duns: and now I come to my Stone Fly, and Green Drake, which are the matadores for trout and grayling,

3. The Cow Dung fly in the polite usage of later centuries.

and, in their season kill more fish in our Derbyshire rivers, than all the rest past, and to come, in the whole year besides.

But first I am to tell you, that we have four several flies which contend for the title of the May-Fly, namely, the Green Drake, the Stone Fly, the Black Fly, and the Little Yellow May-Fly. And all these have their champions and advocates to dispute and plead their priority; though I do not understand why the two last named should; the first two having so manifestly the advantage, both in their beauty, and the wonderful execution they do in their season.

11. Of these, the Green Drake comes in about the twentieth of this month, or betwixt that, and the latter end (for they are sometimes sooner, and sometimes later according to the quality of the year) but never well taken till towards the end of this month, and the beginning of June. The Stone Fly comes much sooner, so early as the middle of April; but is never well taken till towards the middle of May, and continues to kill much longer than the green drake stays with us, so long as to the end almost of June; and indeed, so long as there are any of them to be seen upon the water; and sometimes in an artificial fly, and late at night, or before sunrise in a morning, longer.

Now both these flies (and I believe many others, though I think not all) are certainly and demonstratively bred in the very rivers where they are taken; our cadis or cod-bait[4] which lie under stones in the bottom of the water, most of them turning into those two flies, and being gathered in the husk, or crust, near the time of their maturity, are very easily known and distinguished, and are of all other the most remarkable, both for their size, as being of all other the biggest (the shortest of them being a full inch long, or more) and for the execution they do, the trout and grayling being much more greedy of them than of any others; and indeed the trout never feeds fat, nor comes into his perfect season, till these flies come in.

Of these, the green drake never discloses from his husk, till he be first there grown to full maturity, body, wings, and all, and then he creeps out of his cell, but with his wings so crimped, and ruffled, by being pressed together in that narrow room, that they are for some hours totally useless to him, by which means he is compelled either to creep upon the flags, sedges, and blades of grass (if his first rising from the bottom of the water be near the banks of the river) till the air, and sun, stiffen and smooth them; or if his first appearance above water happen to be in the middle, he then lies upon the surface of the water like a ship at hull (for his feet are totally useless to him there, and he cannot creep upon the water as the stone fly can) until his wings have got stiffness to fly with, if by some trout or grayling he be not taken in the interim (which ten to one he is), and then his wings stand high, and closed exact upon his back, like the butterfly,

4. Cotton's reference to "cadis or cod-bait" in this passage is obscure.

and his motion in flying is the same. His body is in some of a paler, in others of a darker yellow (for they are not all exactly of a color) ribbed with rows of green, long, slender, and growing sharp towards the tail, at the end of which he has three long small whisks of a very dark color, almost black, and his tail turns up towards his back like a mallard, from whence, questionless, he has his name of the green drake. These . . . we commonly dape or dibble with. . . .

I am now to tell you next, how to make an artificial fly, that will so perfectly resemble him, as to be taken in a rough windy day, when no flies can lie upon the water; nor are to be found about the banks and sides of the river, to a wonder, and with which you shall certainly kill the best trout and grayling in the river.

The artificial Green Drake then is made upon a large hook, the dubbing, camel's hair, bright bear's hair, the soft down that is combed from a hog's bristles, and yellow camlet well mixed together, the body long, and ribbed about with green silk, or rather yellow waxed with green wax, the whisks of the tail of the long hairs of sables, or fitchet, and the wings of the white-grey feather of a mallard, dyed yellow, which also is to be dyed thus:

Take the root of a barbary-tree, and shave it, and put to it *woody viss*, with as much alum as a walnut, and boil your feathers in it with rain-water; and they will be of a very fine yellow.

I have now done with the green drake excepting to tell you, that he is taken at all hours during his season, whilst there is any day upon the sky; and with a made fly, I once took, ten days after he was absolutely gone, in a cloudy day, after a shower, and in a whistling wind, five and thirty very great trouts and graylings betwixt five and eight of the clock in the evening, and had no less than five, or six flies with three good hairs apiece taken from me in despite of my heart, besides.

12. I should now come next to the stone fly, but there is another gentleman in my way: that must of necessity come in between, and that is the grey drake, which in all shapes and dimensions is perfectly the same with the other, but quite almost of another color, being of a paler, and more livid yellow, and green, and ribbed with black quite down his body, with black shining wings, and so diaphanous and tender, cobweb-like, that they are of no manner of use for dapping; but come in, and are taken after the green drake, and in an artificial fly kill very well, which fly is thus made: the dubbing of the down of a hog's bristles, and black spaniel's fur mixed, and ribbed down the body with black silk, the whisks of the hairs of the beard of a black cat, and the wings of the black-grey feather of a mallard.

And now I come to the stone fly. . . .

13. This same stone fly has not the patience to continue in his crust or husk till his wings be full grown; but so soon as ever they begin to put out, that he feels himself strong (at which time we call him a Jack)

squeezes himself out of prison, and crawls to the top of some stone, where if he can find a chink that will receive him, or can creep betwixt two stones, the one lying hollow upon the other (which, by the way, we also lay so purposely to find them) he there lurks till his wings be full grown, and there is your only place to find him (and from thence doubtless he derives his name) though, for want of such convenience, he will make shift with the hollow of a bank, or any other place where the wind cannot come to fetch him off. His body is long, and pretty thick, and as broad at the tail almost, as in the middle; his color a very fine brown, ribbed with yellow, and much yellower on the belly than the back, he has two or three whisks also at the tag of his tail, and two little horns upon his head, his wings, when full grown, are double, and flat down his back of the same color, but rather darker than his body, and longer than it; though he makes but little use of them, for you shall rarely see him flying, though often swimming, and paddling, with several feet he has under his belly upon the water, without stirring a wing: but the drake will mount steepleheight into the air, though he is to be found upon flags and grass too, and indeed everywhere high and low, near the river; there being so many of them in their season, as were they not a very inoffensive insect, would look like a plague; and these drakes (since I forgot to tell you before, I will tell you here) arc taken by the fish to that incredible degree, that upon a calm day you shall see the still deeps continually all over circles by the fishes rising, who will gorge themselves with those flies, till they purge again out of their gills; and the trouts are at that time so lusty and strong, that one of eight, or ten inches long, will then more struggle, and tug, and more endanger your tackle, than one twice as big in winter: but pardon this digression.

This Stone Fly . . . is to be made thus: The dubbing of bear's dun with a little brown and yellow camlet very well mixed; but so placed, that your fly may be more yellow on the belly and towards the tail underneath than in any other part, and you are to place two or three hairs of a black cat's beard on the top of the hook in your arming, so as to be turned up, when you warp on your dubbing, and to stand almost upright, and staring one from another, and note that your fly is to be ribbed with yellow silk, and the wings long, and very large, of the dark grey feather of a mallard.

14. The next May-fly is the Black Fly, made with a black body of the whirl of an ostrich feather, ribbed with silver twist, and the black hackle of a cock over all; and is a killing fly, but not to be named with either of the other.

15. The last May-fly (that is, of the four pretenders) is the Little Yellow May-Fly, in shape exactly the same with the Green Drake, but a very little one, and of as bright a yellow as can be seen; which is made of a bright yellow camlet, and the wings of a white-grey feather dyed yellow.

16. The last fly for this month (and which continues all June, though

it comes in in the middle of May) is the fly called the Camlet Fly, in shape like a moth, with fine diapered, or water wings, and with which . . . I sometimes used to dibble; and grayling will rise mightily at it. But the artificial fly (which is only in use amongst our anglers) is made of a dark brown shining camlet, ribbed over with a very small light green silk, the wings of the double grey feather of a mallard; and 'tis a killing fly for small fish, and so much for May.

June

From the first to the four and twentieth, the Green Drake and Stone Fly are taken (as I told you before).

1. From the twelfth to the four and twentieth late at night is taken a fly called the Owl Fly; the dubbing of a white weasel's tail, and a white-grey wing.

2. We have then another dun, called the Barm Fly, from its yeasty color, the dubbing of the fur of a yellow dun cat, and a grey wing of a mallard's feather.

3. We have also a Hackle with a purple body, whipped about with a red capon's feather.

4. As also a Gold Twist Hackle with a purple body, whipped about with a red capon's feather.

5. To these we have this month a Flesh Fly, the dubbing of a black spaniel's fur, and blue wool mixed, and a grey wing.

6. Also another Little Flesh Fly,[5] the body made of the whirl of a peacock's feather, and the wings of the grey feather of a drake.

7. We have then the Peacock Fly, the body and wing both made of the feather of that bird.

8. There is also the flying ant, or Ant Fly, the dubbing of brown and red camlet mixed, with a light grey wing.

9. We have likewise a Brown Gnat, with a very slender body of brown and violet camlet well mixed, and a light grey wing.

10. And another little Black Gnat, the dubbing of black mohair, and a white-grey wing.

11. As also a Green Grasshopper, the dubbing of green and yellow wool mixed, ribbed over with green silk, and a red capon's feather over all.

12. And lastly, a Little Dun Grasshopper, the body slender made of a dun camlet, and a dun hackle at the top.

July

First, all the small flies that were taken in June, are also taken in this month.

5. Whether a different *little* one, or a *second* little one is not clear.

1. We have then the Orange Fly, the dubbing of orange wool, and the wing of a black feather.

2. Also a little White Dun, the body made of white mohair, and the wings blue of a heron's feather.

3. We have likewise this month a Wasp Fly, made either of a dark brown dubbing, or else the fur of a black cat's tail, ribbed about with yellow silk, and the wing of the grey feather of a mallard.

4. Another fly taken this month is a Black Hackle, the body made of the whirl of a peacock's feather, and a black hackle feather on the top.

5. We have also another made of a peacock's whirl without wings.

6. Another fly also is taken this month called the Shell Fly, the dubbing of yellow-green Jersey wool, and a little white hog's hair mixed, which I call the Palm Fly, and do believe it is taken for a palm, that drops off the willows into the water; for this fly I have seen trouts take little pieces of moss, as they have swam down the river, by which I conclude that the best way to hit the right color is to compare your dubbing with the moss, and mix the colors as near as you can.

7. There is also taken this month a Black Blue Dun, the dubbing of the fur of a black rabbit mixed with a little yellow, the wings of the feather of a blue pigeon's wing.

August

The same flies with July.

1. Then another Ant Fly, the dubbing of the black brown hair of a cow, some red warped in for the tag of his tail, and a dark wing, a killing fly.

2. Next a fly called the Fern Fly, the dubbing of the fur of a hare's neck, that is, of the color of fern, or bracken, with a darkish grey wing of a mallard's feather, a killer too.

3. Besides these we have a White Hackle, the body of white mohair, and wrapped about with a white hackle feather, and this is assuredly taken for thistle down.

4. We have also this month a Harry Long Legs, the body made of bear's dun, and blue wool mixed, and a brown hackle feather over all.

Lastly in this month all the same browns and duns are taken, that were taken in May.

September

This month the same flies are taken, that are taken in April.

1. To which I shall only add a Camel Brown Fly, the dubbing pulled out of the lime of a wall whipped about with red silk, and a darkish grey mallard's feather for the wing.

2. And one other for which we have no name; but it is made of the black hair of a badger's skin mixed with the yellow softest down of a sanded hog.

October

The same flies are taken this month, that were taken in March.

November

The same flies that were taken in February, are taken this month also.

December

Few men angle with the fly this month, no more than they do in January: but yet if the weather be warm (as I have known it sometimes in my life to be, even in this cold country, where it is least expected) then a brown that looks red in the hand, and yellowish betwixt your eye and the sun; will both raise and kill in a clear water, and free from snow broth: but at the best 'tis hardly worth a man's labor.

And now . . . I have done with fly fishing, or angling at the top, excepting once more to tell you, that of all these (and I have named you a great many very killing flies) none are fit to be compared with the Drake and Stone Fly, both for many and very great fish; and yet there are some days, that are by no means proper for the sport, and in a calm you shall not have near so much sport even with daping, as in a whistling gale of wind, for two reasons, both because you are not then so easily discovered by the fish, and also because there are then but few flies can lie upon the water; for where they have so much choice, you may easily imagine they will not be so eager and forward to rise at a bait, that both the shadow of your body, and that of your rod, nay of your very line, in a hot calm day will, in spite of your best caution, render suspected to them: but even then, in swift streams, or by sitting down patiently behind a willow bush, you shall do more execution than at almost any other time of the year with any other fly, though one may sometimes hit of a day, when he shall come home very well satisfied with sport with several other flies: but with these two, the Green Drake and the Stone Fly, I do verily believe I could some days in my life, had I not been weary of slaughter, have loaden a lusty boy, and have sometimes, I do honestly assure you, given over upon the mere account of satiety of sport; which will be no hard matter to believe, when I likewise assure you, that with this very fly, I have in this very river that runs by us in three or four hours taken thirty, five and thirty, and forty of the best trouts in the river. What shame and pity is it then, that such a river should be destroyed by the basest sort of people, by those unlawful ways of fire and netting in the night, and of damming, groping, spearing, hanging and hooking by day, which are now grown so common, that, though we have very good laws to punish such offenders, every rascal does it, for aught I see, impune.

To conclude, I cannot now in honesty but frankly tell you, that many of these flies I have named, at least so made as we made them here, will peradventure do you no great service in your southern rivers, and will not conceal from you, but that I have sent flies to several friends in London, that for aught I could ever hear, never did any great feats with them, and therefore if you intend to profit by my instructions, you must come to angle with me here in the Peak.

CHARLES COTTON'S RECIPE FOR COOKING TROUT

Take your trout, wash, and dry him with a clean napkin; then open him, and having taken out his guts, and all the blood, wipe him very clean within, but wash him not, and give him three scotches with a knife to the bone on one side only. After which take a clean kettle, and put in as much hard stale beer (but it must not be dead) vinegar, and a little white wine, and water, as will cover the fish you intend to boil; then throw into the liquor a good quantity of salt, the rind of a lemon, a handful of sliced horse-radish root, with a handsome little fagot of rosemary, thyme, and winter-savory. Then set your kettle upon a quick fire of wood, and let your liquor boil up to the height before you put in your fish, and then, if there be many, put them in one by one, that they may not so cool the liquor, as to make it fall; and whilst your fish is boiling, beat up the butter for your sauce with a ladleful or two of the liquor it is boiling in, and being boiled enough, immediately pour the liquor from the fish, and being laid in a dish, pour your butter upon it, and strewing it plentifully over with shaved horse-radish, and a little pounded ginger, garnish your sides of your dish, and the fish itself with a sliced lemon, or two, and serve it up.

A grayling is also to be dressed exactly after the same manner, saving that he is to be scaled, which a trout never is: and that must be done either with one's nails, or very lightly and carefully with a knife for [fear of] bruising the fish. And note, that these kinds of fish, a trout especially, if he is not eaten within four, or five hours after he be taken, is worth nothing.

Chapter 15

AN EARLY ESSAY ON AMERICAN FLY-FISHING:
BY GEORGE WASHINGTON BETHUNE

George Washington Bethune is distinguished in fly-fishing for having edited the earliest edition of Walton's The Compleat Angler *in the United States (1847), and for having collected the first great library of fishing books in this country. In his edition of Walton he buried a long footnote on fly-fishing in his time, which seems to have been overlooked in discussions of early American commentary on the sport. It constitutes an essay on the subject, the earliest, I believe, of its kind.*

Not much is known in detail about American fly-fishing before the Civil War. The first comprehensive work by an American was Thaddeus Norris's classic The American Angler's Book *in 1864, which guided many angling writers, including Theodore Gordon, during the rest of that century. The late Charles Eliot Goodspeed (*Angling in America, *1939), a great bibliophile, introduced us to the evidences of American angling before Norris, but most of what we know about early American fly-fishing is drawn from three important books, all of them published in the 1840's:* The American Angler's Guide *(1845), compiled by John J. Brown, a New York tackle dealer; Bethune's edition of Walton; and Frank Forester's* Fish and Fishing *(London, 1849; New York, 1850).*

Brown tells us that fly-fishing "finds but little favor in this country." Flies, he says, were "made to order or procured from England." But he adds a significant observation: If no satisfactory fly was available, it was the practice to "examine the waters and shake the boughs of the trees, to procure the latest insect . . . and imitate nature's handiwork on the spot."

Bethune's essay gives the argument of anglers of that time, with a few

190

indigenous fly dressings. His language for natural and artificial flies is largely descriptive; he does not often give his flies artificial titles. One should keep in mind that Bethune, like all anglers of the period, was limited to fishing for Brook trout with the wet fly.

AMERICAN FLY-FISHING IN 1847[1]
by George Washington Bethune

As had been before stated, the anglers of our day are divided into two schools, which may be conveniently distinguished as the routine and the non-imitation. The former hold that the trout should be angled for only with a nice imitation of the natural flies in season at the time, and that, therefore, the flies seen on the water, or found in the belly of the fish, are to be carefully imitated. To this school belong the older writers, from Venables down, and Taylor, Blaine, Hansard, South, Shipley, and Fitzgibbon, etc., etc. The non-imitation school (which reckons among its adherents Rennie, Professor Wilson, Fisher, of the *Angler's Souvenir*, etc. etc.), hold that no fly can be made so as to imitate nature well enough to warrant us in believing that the fish takes it for the natural fly; and, therefore, little reference is to be had to the fly upon which the trout are feeding at the time. "The fish," says Professor Rennie (*Alphabet of Angling*), "appear to seize upon an artifical fly, because, when drawn along the water, it has the appearance of being a living insect, whose species is quite unimportant, as all insects are equally welcome. The aim of the angler, accordingly, ought to be to have his artificial fly calculated, by its form and colors, to attract the notice of the fish, in which case he has a much greater chance of success than by making the greatest efforts to imitate any particular species of fly." Fisher (*Angler's Souvenir*) remarks, in the same strain:

> Wherever fly-fishing is practised—in England, Scotland, Ireland, Wales, France, Germany, and America—it has been ascertained, from experience, that the best flies are those which are not shaped professedly in imitation of any particular living insect. Red, black, and brown hackles, and flies of the bittern's, mallard's, partridge's, woodcock's, grouse's, bald-coot's, martin's, or blue hen's feathers, with dubbing of brown, yellow, or orange, occasionally blended, and hackles, red, brown, or black, under the wings, are the most useful flies that an angler can use in daylight, on any stream, all the year through.

1. From the notes of George Washington Bethune in his edition—the first in the United States—of Walton's *The Compleat Angler,* New York, 1847, pp. 79–85.

191

For night-fishing in lakes, or long still ponds, no fly is better than a white hackle. The directions given in books to beat the bushes by the side of the stream, to see what kind of fly is in the water, and to open a fish's stomach to see what kind of fly the fish has been feeding on, are not deserving the least attention. The angler must be guided in his selection of flies by the state of the water—whether clear or dull, smooth or ruffled by a breeze; and also by the state of the weather, as it may be cloudy or bright. When the water is clear, and the day rather bright, small flies and hackles of a dark shade are most likely to prove successful, if used with a fine line and thrown by a delicate hand; but then it is only before eight in the morning and after six in the evening, from June to August, that the fish may be expected to rise. When the water, in such weather, is ruffled by a fresh breeze, larger hackles and flies of the same color may be used. When the water is clearing after rain, a red hackle, and a fly with a body of orange-colored mohair, dappled wings of a mallard or pea-fowl's feather, with a reddish brown hackle under them, are likely to tempt trout, at any time of day, from March to October. The old doctrine of a different assortment of flies for each month in the year is now deservedly exploded, for it is well known to practical anglers, who never read a book on the subject, and whose judgment is not biased by groundless theories, that the same flies with which they catch most fish in April will generally do them good service throughout the season. The names given to artificial flies are for the most part arbitrary, and afford no guide (with one or two exceptions) for distinguishing the fly meant. Where the materials for dressing a dozen of flies are so much alike, that when they are finished there is so little difference in appearance, that one angler will give them one name and another another, it is absurd to affix to each an individual appellation.

On the other side it is contended, that the non-imitation writers themselves admit, as experience compels them to do, that there must be an adaptation of colors in the fly, and also that certain flies will not be taken at some seasons which are freely taken at others. Nay, that though, when the fish are wantonly playful and hungry, they may rush at almost anything like an insect, when the water is clear, the day bright, and the fish coy, the angler who best imitates the natural fly of the time, and casts it with skill, "stands," to use the words of Mr. Blaine, "proudly conspicuous among his fellows."

For my own part (in common with most American anglers), I lean to the non-imitation theory, but would not carry it so far as to reject all the notions of the doctrinaires. The trout in our upland streams are more plentiful, and, clearly, less sophisticated than those with whom our transatlantic brethren are conversant. In a virgin stream (such an one as an artificial fly has never been cast upon, which the American fly-fisher sometimes meets with), the trout, if fairly on the feed, will take anything that is offered to them. I have, from mere wantonness of experiment, caught dozens from a still pool, at noon-day, with a white miller; and have rarely known a hackle, adapted to the water, and weather, and time of day, to fail. Hackles, in their several varieties, are the mainstays of the American angler, though not to the exclusion of winged flies. Thus, in the Long Island ponds and sea fed streams, hackles are almost exclusively used early in the season, followed, not supplanted by the far-famed Professor, the Green Drake, the Grey Drake, and the camlets. Indeed, a skilful angler, well acquainted with those waters, and disposed to give me information, persisted in answering to all my questions about flies in their seasons, "hackle, hackle, hackle." IIe says: "I have found the plain, black hackle, the black and blue-bodied hackle, the dark red hackle, the bright red hackle, the yellow hackle, and the partridge and woodcock hackles, decidedly the most killing flies in all American waters at all seasons, keeping this in mind, that the later the season, the brighter and gaudier-bodied fly may be used successfully. I am not an admirer of fancy flies, nor have I seen them take many or large fish on Long Island. On the lakes in the interior of New York, I have been informed that this is not the case, but that peacock's eyes, drake wings, and even gaudy macaws kill well; but were I fishing for a wager, I would stick to the various hackles, unless it were for salmon or sea trout, in taking which I believe the fancy flies preferable."

Another skilful brother of the rod says, that (the present year) about the first of April, the trout on Long Island would take freely only the grey drake, made large for the tail and smaller for the drop; though he killed several with a gnat fly of brown body and black wings.

Yet another, and a friend on whose judgment much reliance is to be placed, writes his experience of the inland streams:

When I began to fish, I bought flies according to the season in which the seller said they were good, as did some of the books; but I soon found that nothing could be ascertained in this way, and that I could judge of a fly only by actual trial, as the trout are very capricious in their taste. By observing what fly was on the water, or by putting on three or four of different colors, I could decide what fly was to their taste, and keeping that fly so far as the wings were concerned, I could change the body of the fly according to circumstances. For my part, I believe that book knowledge will help an angler in this country very little, for the obvious reason that the seasons vary so much in different places. Our fly-fishing season includes May, June, July, and August; and as a general rule for May and June, I would use—1. Drab bodies, with light or cream-colored wings. 2. Yellow bodies, with light or brown wings. 3. Red bodies, with light or brown wings. For July and August, red and brown flies.

This is, of course, not to the exclusion of the palmers or wingless hackles.

My own experience on the inland streams is not much earlier than the end of April, and my practice is to observe the fly on the waters for my tail fly, and experiment with hackles on the drop. My favorite early flies are the March Brown, Stone, Blue Dun, and the Cow Dung; to be followed, as the season advances, by the Green and Grey Drake, and later, the claret and red bodies, with light brown, sometimes more showy wings. For the hackles, the red hackle is the queen,—but a large coarse black or furnace hackle, silver ribbed, kills early: afterwards, the sorrel gold ribbed; in the summer, red and black hackles, small and very buzz. As a general rule, my flies grow smaller as the summer advances, for then the waters are lower and clearer, while the sky is brighter.

From all these opinions, the reader will see that the routine system is neither to be contemptuously rejected nor slavishly followed. There are flies that kill all the season; but the Stone Fly will not tell in August, nor the claret body in April. Still, it cannot be doubted, that the trout, like men, have their caprices of appetite, and, except in the first few days of the May-fly, they may be as glad of a chance at a fly out of season, as an epicure would be of early green peas.

In this country, fly-fishing for trout is out of question before March, and, except on Long Island, before the middle of April, that is, after the chill of the snow freshets is gone, and when the streams, though full, are clear. After the first of September, a true-hearted angler will not wet a line in a trout stream. It will therefore be readily seen, as had been observed, that directions serviceable in Great Britain and Ireland, must be greatly modified to be of use among us, from the varieties of our climate, the character of our waters, and the habits of our aquatic insects. I shall, therefore, conclude the notes on this part of our subject by a list of flies furnished by an excellent brother of our gentle art, who relieves the labors of a life most zealously devoted to the best interests of his fellow-men, by occasionally fishing the head waters of the Susquehannah and Delaware, all the tributaries to which abound in trout. His particular haunts are the streams of Pike, Wayne, and Susquehannah counties in Pennsylvania, and of Sullivan and Broome in New York. To great skill at the stream side, he unites equal aptness in making his own flies from the means within his reach. If, from the directions given, the reader should acquire a due proportion of my friend's art in making and using the flies recommended, he will have nothing to wish for but a heart equally at peace with God and man—and, when he goes a fishing,

> A day with not too bright a beam,
> And a south-west wind to curl the stream.

It must not be supposed that these flies are all that may be used, but with those others, too well known to need description, a book well supplied according to the list, is all that the fly-fisher necessarily needs. The experienced angler will recognise some old and highly valued acquaintances.

No. 1. A tail, end, or stretcher fly, on a No. 4 (Limerick) hook. Body, light slate drab, wound with the smallest gold cord and a red hackle. Wings, the brown under feather of the peacock's wing. Its tail has a tuft of red worsted (or mohair); and its head is wound round with gold cord. This is so excellent a fly as to be known in some places as The Fly. It is good as a general fly throughout the season. Made on a No. 8 hook, it may be used as a drop-fly with much execution.

No. 2. For a tail-fly on No. 5, for a drop on No. 8. Body, first wound with yellow floss silk, then a thread of crimson, then in an opposite direction a thread of gold, with a slight yellow or red hackle at the head for legs. Wings, rather full of the brown wing feathers of the peacock, or the lightest brown wing of the turkey-cock. (This fly is my friend's own invention, and he pronounces it very good. It resembles the Cow Dung, except in the body, which is gayer.)

No. 3. A dropper on a No. 6 hook. Having attached the hook to the snell, take two pieces of stiff gut about ½ to ¾ of an inch long, and, having soaked some pieces of fine gut, wind them round the stiff gut to make a tail, winding in three black hairs at the end, then bind this on the hook. The body is of peacock's herl; red hackle for legs; wings of a mottled wild duck's feather. An early fly.

No. 4. A dropper on a No. 9 hook. The body, of bright yellow floss silk, wound with gold and a red hackle. Wings, of the bright feathers on the breast of a wild pigeon, cut rather short, and dropping a little below the line of the hook. A most effective fly for May and June, indeed for the whole season. It may be varied in the color of the body by dubbing with red, etc.

No. 5. On a No. 8 hook. Resembles No. 2, with the wings of No. 4.

No. 6. A tail palmer, on a No. 4 hook. Body, black mohair, with a little orange towards the head; wound with silver, and a strong black hackle from the tail of a Poland cock. A very killing fly, though it has a coarse look, and will tell effectively through the season, especially after a flood or windy days.

(N.B. The palmers, as is well known, may be varied. When the gold or silver thread is used, the black should be wound with silver, the red with gold or silver. The angler should be provided with a plentiful assortment, both as to color and size, to suit the weather, time of day, and color of the waters. A red hackle wound with gold and silver on a dark brown dubbing, or without the tinsel, is the most killing of all the palmers. A short, thick, black hackle, wound lightly with silver over black, will kill in a bright sun at midsummer, on a fresh current or shaded pool, when nothing else will raise a fish.)

No. 7. A drop on a No. 8 or 9 hook. Body, black mohair, wound with silver, a small black hackle for legs; wings of a black cock's feather; tail tufted with two hairs.

This fly may be greatly varied.

No. 8. A dropper on a No. 9 hook. Body, red floss silk, wound with gold; the head with a small black hackle; wings, brown wing of the peacock, or the domestic cock, or the dun wing of the pigeon, or the breast-feather of the cock pigeon; varying the complexion of the fly many ways.

[Flies Nos. 9, 10, and 11 are missing in the original text.]

No. 12. A dropper on a No. 9 hook. Body and wings like No. 13, with dark red hackles, round the head, for wings. Latter end of May, June, and beginning of July.

No. 13. A dropper on No. 8 hook. Body, a brownish, greenish, or yellowish brown, wound with a small red hackle about the head; wings, brown wing-feathers of a wild pigeon; tail, tufted with two hairs.

A beautiful and effective fly for May and June.

No. 14. A dropper on a No. 8 hook. Body thin, of brown floss silk, wound with gold, pale red hackle wound about the head; wings, a cock's reddish brown wing-feather. Good the whole season, but better in July and August.

No. 15. A tail-fly on a No. 2 hook. Body of crimson, wound with gold, and a red hackle; wings of a cock's blackish grey wing-feather.

It is an English prejudice to consider night fishing ungentlemanly, because resembling poaching; but as in this country there are no game laws, we may enjoy our delightful sport by moonlight, without such scruples. Old Barker used three palmers at night: a light fly (white palmer) for darkness; a red palmer in medio; and a dark (black) palmer for lightness. The best flies for moonlight fishing are the white, and brown, and cream-colored moths. The white are made: Body, white ostrich herl, and a white cock's hackle over it; the wings from the feather of the white owl. The brown: Body, dark bear's hair and a brown cock's hackle over it; wings from the wing-feather of the brown owl. Cream-colored moth: Body, fine cream-colored fur, with pale yellow hackles; wings feather of the yellow owl of the deepest cream-color. To these add a black fly: Body, black ostrich herl, thickly wound with large black hackle; wings, the darkest wild goose wing-feather. The stone-fly also kills well at night. What fish are taken at night will generally be found to be large; and, therefore, the tackle should, as it may, be stouter than by day. . . .

INDEX

INDEX

INDEX

INDEX

INDEX